QA 66.5 LEC/886

Lecture Notes in Artificia

Subseries of Lecture Notes in Compu

Edited by J. G. Carbonell and J. Siekmann

D1759001

Lecture Notes in Computer Science

Edited by G. Goos, J. Hartmanis and J. van Leeuwen

DATE DUE FOR RETURN

NEW ACCESSION

CANCELLED

WITHDRAWN
FROM STOCK
QMUL LIBRARY

WITHDRAWN
FROM STOCK
QMUL LIBRARY

Manuela M. Veloso

Planning and Learning by Analogical Reasoning

Springer-Verlag

Berlin Heidelberg NewYork
London Paris Tokyo
Hong Kong Barcelona
Budapest

Series Editors

Jaime G. Carbonell
School of Computer Science
Carnegie Mellon University
Pittsburgh, PA 15213-3891, USA

Jörg Siekmann
University of Saarland
German Research Center for Artificial Intelligence (DFKI)
Stuhlsatzenhausweg 3, D-66123 Saarbrücken, Germany

Author

Manuela M. Veloso
Department of Computer Science
Carnegie Mellon University
Pittsburgh, PA 15213-3891, USA
veloso@cs.cmu.edu

QUEEN MARY & WESTFIELD
COLLEGE LIBRARY
(MILE END)

CR Subject Classification (1991): I.2.6, I.2.8, I.2.3

ISBN 3-540-58811-6 Springer-Verlag Berlin Heidelberg New York

CIP data applied for

This work is subject to copyright. All rights are reserved, whether the whole or part of
the material is concerned, specifically the rights of translation, reprinting, re-use of
illustrations, recitation, broadcasting, reproduction on microfilms or in any other way,
and storage in data banks. Duplication of this publication or parts thereof is permitted
only under the provisions of the German Copyright Law of September 9, 1965, in its
current version, and permission for use must always be obtained from Springer-Verlag.
Violations are liable for prosecution under the German Copyright Law.

© Springer-Verlag Berlin Heidelberg 1994
Printed in Germany

Typesetting: Camera ready by author
SPIN: 10479112   45/3140-543210 - Printed on acid-free paper

To Manel, André, and Pedro

Preface

This book describes the integration of analogical reasoning into general problem solving as a method of learning at the strategy level to solve problems more effectively. The method, based on derivational analogy, has been fully implemented in PRODIGY/ANALOGY and proven empirically to be amenable to scaling up both in terms of domain and problem complexity.

Reasoning by analogy involves a set of challenging problems, namely: how to accumulate episodic problem solving experience, how to define and decide when two problem solving situations are similar, how to organize large amounts of episodic knowledge so that it may be efficiently retrieved, and finally the ultimate problem of how to successfully transfer chains of reasoning from past experience to new problem solving situations when only a partial match exists among the corresponding problems.

In this work, the strategy-level learning process is cast for the first time as the automation of the complete cycle of constructing, storing, retrieving, and flexibly reusing problem solving experience. This book presents the interconnected algorithms designed for the generation, storage, retrieval and replay of derivational traces of problem solving episodes. The integrated learning system reduces the problem solving search effort incrementally as more episodic experience is compiled into the library of accumulated learned knowledge.

A primary goal of this work was to demonstrate an integrated view of the flexible learning and problem solving methods in large and complex domains. Scaling up the system proved to be very demanding. The current system has thus far been demonstrated in multiple domains, including a complex logistics transportation domain where it generated a library of 1000 cases. In addition to the analogical reasoning method, the book presents empirical results showing how PRODIGY/ANALOGY improved the problem-solving performance many-fold, actually increased the quality of the solutions generated, and pushed the solvability envelope to increasingly more complex classes of nonlinear planning problems.

Acknowledgements

This book is based on my PhD thesis done at Carnegie Mellon University (CMU). Special thanks are due to my adviser, Jaime Carbonell, with whom this work was done in close collaboration. Jaime shared with me many of his ideas and helped me solve many problems I faced along this work. He gave me extremely insightful advice.

I would like to thank my other thesis committee members, Tom Mitchell, Paul Rosenbloom, and Herb Simon, for all the helpful suggestions and comments on my research. Herb Simon and Tom Mitchell followed my work very closely. Herb Simon was always interested on the detailed progress of my work. He encouraged me to reach a full implementation of the system, so I could scale it up to tasks of realistic size. Thanks to Herb Simon, I have a much broader view of this research. With him I learned to appreciate many of the early research efforts in Artificial Intelligence especially in learning. In our several meetings, Tom Mitchell helped me keeping focused on my thesis goals, at the same time that he opened my interests to other related issues in machine learning. He raised challenging questions while listening carefully to my ideas and discussing his own with me. Through several email conversations, Paul Rosenbloom provided me very useful feedback on my work. He helped me clarify some of my claims of this work.

Allen Newell was not in my thesis committee. Still he shaped my thinking. We had several long meetings where we discussed my work. Allen Newell was always there pointing out the interesting points, forcing me to clarify my ideas, making sure I myself would understand well the concepts, the algorithms, the implementation. From Allen Newell I learned every day more and more what research is. Through him I understood how to work dynamically towards my research goals. He was a real mentor and friend.

I gratefully acknowledge also all the members of the PRODIGY project, in particular Craig Knoblock, Alicia Pérez, Daniel Borrajo, Steve Minton, Yolanda Gil, Oren Etzioni, Robert Joseph, Jim Blythe, Xuemei Wang, and Eugene Fink, for their helpful comments and suggestions on the work and on the dissertation. I thank all my friends at CMU for their support. In a very special way, I thank Puneet Kumar. I benefited tremendously from his ceaseless help with system changes and enhancements.

The School of Computer Science at CMU is a very special place. I acknowledge Nico Habermann for having consistently promoted a community spirit among the members of this large research group. I thank Sharon Burks for her constant willingness to make more pleasant and facilitate our students' lives.

Last, but most importantly, I would like to thank all my family for their loving support. Back in Lisbon, my parents, my parents-in-law, and all my family courageously supported and encouraged this work, in spite of the inevitable long separation. I thank them all for this. I am grateful to my parents and parents-in-law for making our returns home on vacation so wonderful, full of the little things they know we miss so much. Thank you for all their letters, their telephone calls, their visits, thank you for their love that really carried me through these years. I am very thankful also for their help taking care of my sons, André and Pedro, who love so much going to Portugal.

I thank my husband Manel, and my sons, André and Pedro, for having lived with me through the thesis work. They were always here to love me, encourage me, and make me feel that it was all worth the effort. In particular I want to thank Pedro and André for the many weekends that we spent together at CMU. They were always cheerful and packed their books and toys happily for the CMU journeys without any complaint. Also I would like to thank André and Pedro for the after-school afternoons that I could not spend with them. I waited eagerly for André's daily phone call when he got home from school, ready and responsible to stay home alone during the afternoon. It would have been very hard to complete this thesis without Manel's support. I thank him also in particular for his surprise on the day of my defense.

The work reported in this book was supported by the Avionics Laboratory, Wright Research and Development Center, Aeronautical Systems Division (AFSC), U.S. Air Force, Wright-Patterson AFB, Ohio 45433-6543 under Contract F33615-90-C-1465, ARPA Order No. 7597. The views and conclusions contained in this document are those of the author and should not be interpreted as representing the official policies, either expressed or implied, of the Defense Advanced Research Projects Agency or of the U.S. Government.

Contents

1 Introduction   **1**
 1.1 Machine learning and problem solving   2
 1.2 Analogy within PRODIGY   5
 1.3 The thesis of this book   8
 1.4 Reader's guide   11

2 Overview   **15**
 2.1 Case generation   15
   2.1.1 Defining a problem   15
   2.1.2 Problem solving search   16
   2.1.3 Justification structure   19
 2.2 Case storage   20
   2.2.1 Foot-printing the initial state   21
   2.2.2 Multiple-goal problems   23
 2.3 Automatic case retrieval   27
 2.4 Case replay   28
 2.5 Summary   30

3 The Problem Solver   **33**
 3.1 Motivation   33
   3.1.1 Linear problem solving   34
   3.1.2 Nonlinear problem solving   37
 3.2 NoLimit - The planning algorithm   39
 3.3 Formal problem solving procedure   41
   3.3.1 Failing and backtracking   44
   3.3.2 Control knowledge   46
 3.4 An example: a *one-way-rocket* problem   47
 3.5 Summary   51

4 Generation of Problem Solving Cases   **53**
 4.1 Annotating the search path   53
   4.1.1 The decision points at problem solving   54
   4.1.2 Justification structures at decision nodes   56
   4.1.3 The language   57
 4.2 The annotation procedure   58
   4.2.1 Annotating the subgoaling structure   59
   4.2.2 Annotating the failures   60
 4.3 An example in the extended-STRIPS domain   61
 4.4 Summary   65

5 Case Storage: Automated Indexing   **67**
    5.1 Identifying independent case subparts 68
        5.1.1 Transforming a total order into a partial order 69
        5.1.2 Goal indices 71
    5.2 Identifying the relevant initial state 74
        5.2.1 Disambiguating the notion of "relevant" 74
        5.2.2 Foot-printing the initial state 77
    5.3 Organization of the case library 79
    5.4 The complete storage algorithm 86
    5.5 Summary 90

6 Efficient Case Retrieval   **91**
    6.1 The ground for the retrieval procedure 91
        6.1.1 What are similar problem solving situations? 93
        6.1.2 How can retrieval be efficient in a large case library? . . 93
    6.2 Defining a similarity metric 95
        6.2.1 A direct similarity metric 96
        6.2.2 Global foot-printing similarity metric 96
        6.2.3 Interacting foot-printing similarity metric 97
    6.3 The retrieval procedure 98
        6.3.1 Indexing data structures 100
        6.3.2 Illustrative example 101
    6.4 Trading off retrieval and search costs 107
    6.5 Summary 110

7 Analogical Replay   **111**
    7.1 Replaying past problem solving episodes 111
        7.1.1 Outline of the replay procedure 112
        7.1.2 Advantages of replaying 113
        7.1.3 Feedback to memory 116
    7.2 The replay algorithm 117
        7.2.1 Generation of new search directions 118
        7.2.2 Pursuing the search 123
        7.2.3 Advancing the cases 129
    7.3 Examples 131
    7.4 Feedback: problem solver to memory 136
        7.4.1 The method explored 136
        7.4.2 Illustrative example 137
    7.5 Summary 138

8   Empirical Results   **141**

8.1   Diversity of tasks 142

    8.1.1   The *one-way-rocket* domain 143

    8.1.2   The extended-STRIPS and machine-shop domains 144

8.2   Scale up: A logistics transportation domain 146

    8.2.1   Generation of problems 146

    8.2.2   Set up of experiments 147

    8.2.3   The solvability horizon 149

    8.2.4   Cumulative running times 153

    8.2.5   Solution length 154

    8.2.6   Retrieval and replay times 156

    8.2.7   Retrieval time against the size of the case library 159

    8.2.8   Search nodes explored 160

8.3   Summary 161

9   Related Work   **163**

9.1   Generation and contents of cases 163

9.2   Storage and retrieval of cases 164

9.3   Utilization of learned knowledge 166

9.4   Summary 168

10 Conclusion   **169**

11 Bibliography   **173**

Chapter 1

Introduction

The ultimate goal of the field of Artificial Intelligence (AI) is to understand the nature of intelligence and how it can be captured by computational algorithms [Newell and Simon, 1956]. One of the more complex human intelligent processes is the ability to solve wide varieties of problems. Newell and Simon discovered how to model the human problem solving paradigm as an heuristic search in a state space [Newell and Simon, 1972]. The approach consists of interpreting each problem solving situation in terms of an initial state configuration, a set of possible actions to transform the state, and a desired goal state. The problem solving algorithm searches for a particular sequence of actions that transforms the given initial state into the desired final state. Over the years, different algorithms have been developed to perform this search.

However, AI researchers have found that these classical AI techniques for problem solving involve large amounts of search even for moderately complex problems. In particular, planning for complex problems with multiple inter-acting goals and multiple alternative plan choices is a well-recognized difficult problem due to the exponential growth of the search space as a function of with the problem complexity. In contrast, planning for simple problems is a rather tractable task. The interesting question that has held the attention of many AI researchers, present author included, is: How can a planning system solve efficiently complex problems given the fact that it can solve efficiently simple problems? To answer this question, several subareas within AI tried to develop methods for encapsulating more knowledge to reduce problem solving search. These methods range from expert system approaches, where all the knowledge is laboriously handcoded at the outset, to machine learning approaches that aim at automating the process of compiling problem solving experience into reusable knowledge. This work falls within the latter category, as it automates the acquisition of planning expertise by analogical reasoning. This book presents a novel method to automate the process of acquiring, storing, retrieving and reusing problem solving experience.

The method based on derivational analogy [Carbonell, 1986] has been fully implemented in PRODIGY/ANALOGY within the planning and learning architecture, PRODIGY [Carbonell *et al.*, 1990]. It was proven empirically to be amenable to scaling up both in terms of domain and problem complexity.

Reasoning by analogy involves a set of challenging problems, namely: how to accumulate episodic problem solving experience, how to define and decide when two problem solving situations are similar, how to organize large amounts of knowledge so that it may be efficiently retrieved, and finally the ultimate problem of how to successfully transfer chains of reasoning from past experience to new problem solving situations when only a partial match exists among corresponding problems.

In this work the strategy-level learning process is cast for the first time as the automation of the complete cycle of constructing, storing, retrieving, and flexibly reusing problem solving experience. The integrated learning system reduces the problem solving search effort incrementally as more episodic experience is compiled into the library of accumulated learned knowledge.

This introductory chapter is divided into four sections. The first section situates our approach within other machine learning methods applied to problem solving. Section 2 describes the motivation for this work within the PRODIGY architecture. Section 3 introduces the thesis of the work and its scientific contributions. Finally Section 4 presents a comprehensive reader's guide for the book.

1.1   Machine learning and problem solving

The machine learning approaches to acquiring strategic knowledge typically start with a general problem solving engine and accumulate experience in the process of solving problems the hard way (via extensive search), or via demonstrations of viable solutions by an external (human) teacher. The knowledge acquired can take many forms:

- Macro-operators composed of sequences of domain-level operators which, if applicable, take "large steps" in the problem space and thereby reduce search [Anderson, 1983, Cheng and Carbonell, 1986, Fikes and Nilsson, 1971, Korf, 1985, Minton, 1985]. In essence, intermediate decisions corresponding to steps internal to each macro-operator are bypassed via the construction of a parameterized fragment of the proven solution path into a macro-operator.

- Reformulated left-hand sides of operators and inference rules, where the new left-hand sides are stated in terms of "operational" or initial-state conditions so as to facilitate their selection and application. This is one typical output of explanation-based learning systems [DeJong and Mooney, 1986, Mitchell *et al.*, 1983, Mitchell *et al.*, 1986, Neves, 1980].

- Explicit control rules (or meta rules) that guide the selection of domain-level subgoals, operators or inference rules in the planning process. These may also be generated by the explanation-based learning process when the basic architecture of the problem solver itself is axiomatized and available to the learning module, along with the domain theory [Minton, 1988a].

- Generalized "chunking" of all decisions taken by the problem solver, including goal selection, operator selection and other impasse-driven decisions that required search. The output of these internal decisions are at once compiled into new chunks by a background reflex process and become immediately available to the problem solver's recognition process [Laird *et al.*, 1986, Newell, 1980].

- Memorized actual instance solutions annotated with intermediate problem solving states (such as subgoal trees, causes of intermediate planning failure, justifications for each selected planning step, etc.). These are used in analogical reasoning [Carbonell, 1983, Carbonell, 1986] and case-based reasoning (CBR) [Hammond, 1986, Kolodner, 1980, Schank, 1982] to reduce search by using the solutions of similar past problems to guide the planner in constructing the solution to the new problem.

All of these methods seek to compile existing domain knowledge into more effective form by combining it with search control knowledge acquired through incremental practice. In essence, the idea is to transform book knowledge into practical knowledge that can be applied much more readily, occasionally compromising generality for efficiency of application, but retaining the initial knowledge as a safety net.

The problem solving methods developed so far in AI can be organized in a problem solving reasoning continuum ranging from *search-intensive* to *knowledge-intensive* methods, as shown in Figure 1.1.[1]

Pure search-intensive methods search exhaustively for a solution from first principles, i.e., individual steps that model atomic actions in the task domain and may be chained to form a solution to a problem. Pure knowledge-intensive methods for problem solving presuppose the existence of a collection of instance or generalized solutions from where the problem solver may retrieve and eventually instantiate the adequate solution. Variations from these two extreme approaches extend the search-intensive paradigm to searching guided by local control knowledge, while the knowledge-intensive extreme extends to case-based reasoning approaches in which the retrieved solution may be adapted after being retrieved and instantiated.

There is however a big gap between these two problem solving directions, namely searching from first principles and retrieving and adapting complete solutions. Derivational analogy was proposed by Carbonell ([Carbonell, 1986]) to fill in this gap as a method that would draw nearer the search- and the knowledge-intensive paradigms. Derivational analogy is a problem solving method that replays and modifies past problem solving traces in new similar situations. Therefore the problem solver in addition to its domain principles is able to use past experience in the form of complete problem solving episodes.

---

[1] This picture was drawn by Jaime Carbonell in one of our discussions.

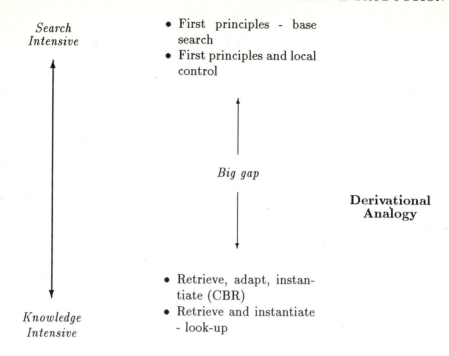

Figure 1.1: Problem solving reasoning continuum.

There have been several research efforts following the derivational analogy framework, including [Mostow, 1989, Kambhampati and Hendler, 1992, Blumenthal, 1990, Bhansali and Harandi, 1993] with which I compare in detail this work in Chapter 9. This work draws also upon the original derivational analogy strategy, but goes largely beyond it. First, I refine and extend the initial derivational analogy to replay the rich episodic memory structures in the non-linear problem solver of PRODIGY. I essentially design and implement a flexible case-based reconstructive reasoning process that can be guided by multiple similar relevant cases. Second, the work achieves seamless integration of derivational analogy with basic means-ends problem solving where past experience provides guidance for chains of successful decisions and knowledge about failures to avoid. Third, the system organizes the accumulated episodes in a case memory and incorporates an efficient procedure for retrieval of similar situations. Fourth, this work includes a complete implementation, providing comparative empirical evidence to evaluate the utility of recycling and organizing past experience in the derivational analogy framework.

In a nutshell, this work is novel in the automation of the complete analogical cycle, namely the generation (annotation), storage, retrieval, and replay of episodic knowledge. It follows a domain-independent approach and it is demonstrated in particular in a case library of several orders of magnitude greater than most of the other case-based reasoning (or knowledge-intensive) systems, in terms of the size of the case library and the granularity of the individual cases.

In Artificial Intelligence, it is particularly challenging and important to validate the algorithmitic solutions designed, as most of the approaches proposed may look equally plausible. Although there are situations where analytical validation may be possible, empirical experimentation is generally the only appropriate method to demonstrate the power of a designed hypothesis. The results from our extensive empirical tests demonstrate that the algorithms we designed support largely our hypothesis that learning by analogical reasoning greatly improves the performance of a problem solving system in large and complex domains.

Finally, analogical reasoning in PRODIGY/ANALOGY learns from multiple problem solving examples, differing from other inductive techniques applied to problem solving [Zelle and Mooney, 1993, Quinlan, 1990] in that it learns complete sequences of decisions as opposed to individual rules. Under this perspective, analogical reasoning shares characteristics with learning macro-operators. However problem solving cases may be partially reused, in that intermediate decisions corresponding to choices internal to each case can be bypassed or adapted, if their justifications do not longer hold. Furthermore, cases guide but do not dictate the reconstruction process as opposed to introducing new operators at individual decisions. The boundary between macro-operators and problem solving cases as defined in this work becomes less well defined in situations where there is partial reuse of macro-operators [Yang and Fisher, 1992]. We are currently researching in understanding the conditions under which the different granularities of control knowledge [Allen *et al.*, 1992], i.e., rules, macros, or flexible cases, should be used especially in complex and scaled up domains.

1.2   Analogy within PRODIGY

PRODIGY is an integrated intelligent architecture that explores different learning strategies to support efficient general purpose planning [Carbonell *et al.*, 1990]. Learning methods acquire domain and problem specific control knowledge in the form of factual and strategic knowledge. All of PRODIGY's learning modules share the same general problem solver and the same domain representation language (see Figure 1.2).

The operator-based problem solver produces a complete search tree, encapsulating all decisions – right ones and wrong ones – as well as the final solution. This information is used by each learning component in different ways: to extract search control rules via explanation-based learning (EBL) [Minton, 1988b], to build derivational traces (cases) by the derivational analogy [Veloso, 1992] (and as presented in this book), to analyze key decisions by a knowledge acquisition interface [Joseph, 1989], or to formulate focused experiments [Carbonell and Gil, 1990]. The axiomatized domain knowledge is also used to learn a hierarchy of abstraction layers (ALPINE) [Knoblock, 1994], and generate control rules by static partial evaluation (STATIC) [Etzioni, 1993]. Because both EBL and this work on learning by analogy acquire control knowledge from examples, we now

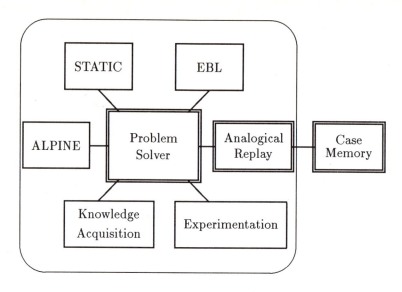

Figure 1.2: The PRODIGY architecture.

briefly relate the motivation to explore this technique by contrasting it with the EBL approach.

PRODIGY/EBL uses a strong learning method by which the domain theory is interpreted under the bias of each particular problem solving example. The domain theory is reformulated into a more operational description that enables the problem solver to search more efficiently for solutions to problems. The results produced by this learning technique are very significant [Minton, 1988b].

The EBL learner performs an eager effort of explaining and generalizing correctly the local and individual decisions of the problem solving episode. The method requires a complete domain theory to ground the generalization of the failures and successes encountered as a unique example is analyzed. Figure 1.3 summarizes the characteristics of the mechanism that contrast most directly to the research goals of this work. PRODIGY/EBL applies its learned knowledge only when the new decision making situation exactly (or fully) matches the learned operationalized control knowledge, i.e., the complete set of applicability conditions of the learned knowledge need to unify with a new situation.

PRODIGY/EBL:

- Produces generalized **provably correct** control knowledge.
- Requires **complete** domain theory.
- Performs **eager** learning.
- Learns from **local** decisions.
- Reuses **exactly** matched learned knowledge.

Figure 1.3: Some characteristics of the PRODIGY/EBL learner.

PRODIGY/ANALOGY can be seen as a major relaxation of the restrictions inherent in the EBL paradigm. Figure 1.4 summarizes the characteristics of the analogical reasoner designed and developed in this work.

Instead of investing substantial effort deriving general local rules of behavior from each example as PRODIGY/EBL does, PRODIGY/ANALOGY automatically generates and stores annotated traces of solved problems (cases) that are elaborated further when needed to guide similar problems. Compiled experience is then stored with little post processing. The complete problem solving episode is interpreted as a global decision-making experience where independent subparts can be reused as a whole. Furthermore, the domain theory does not need to be completely specified as the problem solving episodes are loosely interpreted and not fully generalized. The explanation effort is done incrementally on an "if-needed" basis at storage, retrieval and adaptation time when new similar situations occur. Finally, maybe the most clearly recognized characteristic of the analogical reasoner is its ability to reuse partially matched learned experience.

PRODIGY/ANALOGY:

- Produces control knowledge empirically from **justified episodic** traces. (A justification can be weaker than a strict proof.)
- Performs **lazy** learning (on an "if-needed" basis).
- Does **not** require a **complete** domain theory.
- Learns from local and **global** decisions chains.
- Reuses **partially** matched learned experience.

Figure 1.4: Characteristics of PRODIGY/ANALOGY as opposed to PRODIGY/EBL.

The immediate support for the utility of the analogical approach is that, on one hand, some domains may be incompletely specified for which EBL is not able to generate deductive proofs [Duval, 1991, Tadepalli, 1989]. On the other hand, in complex domains, EBL can become very inefficient with long deductive chains producing complex rules for situations that may seldom, if ever, be exactly repeated. Finally, the localized character of the learned knowledge in EBL is a source for an increase of the control knowledge available to match and select from at decision making time.

While the discussion above provides direct motivation for the exploration of the analogical reasoning framework in PRODIGY, we believe that the two learning methods are complementary, rather than orthogonal, in their learning abilities. It is one of our current research directions to thoroughly investigate on the integration of these two learning paradigms. This book reports on the validity of the analogical learning paradigm as an efficient learning technique in particular for large and complex problem solving tasks. Though the focus of the empirical experiments ran was primarily to compare the analogical reasoner with the base-level PRODIGY's planner, we subsequently draw a brief comparison between the two learning paradigms from the empirical results obtained.

1.3   The thesis of this book

Reasoning by analogy involves a set of challenging problems, namely how to accumulate episodic problem solving experience; how to define and decide when two problem solving situations are similar; how to organize large amounts of knowledge so that it may be retrieved efficiently; and finally the ultimate problem of how to successfully transfer chains of reasoning from previously solved problems to new ones when only a partial match exists among them (see Figure 1.5).

- How to accumulate episodic problem solving experience? *What to preserve from the search tree?*

- How to organize a large case library? *What are the appropriate indices?*

- How to retrieve past experience efficiently? *What are similar problem solving situations?*

- How to reuse a set of previously solved analogous problems? *What to transfer from partial matches?*

Figure 1.5: Challenges of analogical reasoning.

This work addresses all these challenges and provides methods implemented successfully for large and complex planning problems in a diversity of domains. This achievement is due mostly to the design of a fully and strongly integrated problem solving engine and case library memory manager. This novel integration allows the system to generate, store, retrieve, and replay past cases, i.e., derivational traces of past problem solving episodes automatically and efficiently. Learning occurs by accumulation and reuse of cases, and by tuning the indexing structure of the memory model to retrieve progressively more appropriate cases. On one hand search is reduced at the problem solving level by replaying past similar cases. On the other hand the system learns the relative relevance of the memory indices incrementally by interpreting the behavior of the problem solver replaying retrieved cases.

The problem solver and the case library manager communicate as shown in Figure 1.6, where W_i is the initial world, G is the goal to be achieved, W_f is the final world, *Sol* is the solution found, *Analogs* are the retrieved candidate similar cases, and *Feedback* represents both the new solved problem and information about the utility of the candidate analogs in reaching a solution.

In a nutshell, in the integrated system designed and developed in this book, the problem solver has the ability (and mandate):

1. to ask the memory manager for advice on how to solve a problem, (i.e., guidance based on past experience, stored as annotated derivational traces),

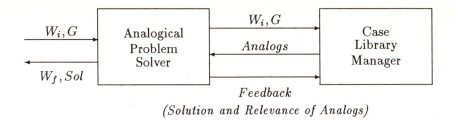

Figure 1.6: Synergy: problem solver and memory.

2. to replay the past solutions received as analogs and create an annotated solution for the new problem based both on the guidance received from the memory manager, and on the domain theory available, and

3. to return to the memory manager both, information about the utility of the guidance received for creating the solution (i.e., the relevance of the retrieved cases), and the new justified case (a new annotated derivational trace).

Memory organization is in a closely coupled dynamic relationship with the problem solving engine. The memory manager has the ability (and mandate):

1. to search efficiently its case library for a set of cases solved in the past that adequately relate to the new problem presented by the problem solver,

2. to reorganize the memory indexing links, as a function of the feedback received from the problem solver on the utility, in solving the new problem, of the guidance provided by the retrieved cases.

The methodology followed in this work can be divided into two phases: *(i)* to develop the overall integrated system by designing one by one each of its constituents functional modules, and *(ii)* to validate empirically the implemented system in complex domains.

In the first phase we initially created a complete nonlinear problem solver that searches for the solution to a problem by performing means-ends analysis using the domain theory. We extended this base-level problem solver into an analogical reasoner with the capabilities to generate episodic justified derivational traces from its search experience, and to replay past similar problem solving episodes. We completed the analogical reasoning cycle by developing the algorithms for the organization and access to the case library. Clearly this incremental building methodology is a closed loop process where the development of each functional aspect may affect the other modules and contribute to their refinement.

In the second phase the goal is to validate the algorithms developed through extensive experiments in a diversity of domains including a complex one from the problem solving viewpoint. We explored the scaling up properties of the designed integrated learner and problem solver by generating and testing the system performance in a case library of more than 1000 cases.

Scientific Contributions

This book reports contributions in the three areas of machine learning, case-based reasoning, and planning.

Contributions to Machine Learning

Utility of partial match:

- *Learning from similar experience:* We successfully demonstrate the utility of transferring problem solving experience in partially matched new situations.

- *Multi-case replay - from simple to complex problems:* We construct a solution to a new problem by merging multiple similar past cases. This method enables the learner to solve complex problems after being trained by simple problems.

- *Self-tuning memory organization:* We propose an incremental method to learn the relevance of the indexing features of the compiled experience. The memory would be dynamically reorganized based on feedback from the problem solver on the utility of the guidance provided.

Extending the power of time-bounded problem solving:

- *Speed-up factor (2× - 40×):* The problem solver is able to solve many problems more efficiently by analogy than by base search. The empirical results we obtained show cumulative speed-ups of up to a factor of 5.3 and individual speeds-up approaching a factor of 40.

- *Pushing the solvability horizon:* An additional contribution to the speed-up experienced is the fact that many of the problems that remain unsolved by the basic problem solver are solved by the analogical reasoner, and none for which the opposite is true.

Contributions to Case-Based Reasoning

Spanning the gamut from CBR to general planning: Previous CBR research efforts concentrated on developing efficient techniques for indexing, retrieving, and adapting problem solving episodes in special purpose environments. The book extends the gamut of CBR from special purpose memory managing techniques to wide general purpose problem solving and planning.

Automatic identification of relevant memory indices: The *foot-printing* algorithm designed and implemented in this work contributes to disambiguate the identification of which features of a world configuration are relevant to solving a given problem. These features are identified uniquely from the derivational trace of the particular problem solving search episode.

Unifying multiple cases into replay mechanism: We elaborate a sophisticated replay and reconstruction algorithm that merges multiple similar past cases guided by their individual annotated justification structures.

Multiple indexing of cases: A problem solving episode may be a collection of independent subparts that can be reused separately. The book presents an algorithm that efficiently partially orders a totally ordered problem solving episode by using the dependency structure of the plan produced by the problem solver. The connected components of the resulting partially ordered graph identify the independent subparts of the complete case and the corresponding sets of interacting goals which are used to multiply index the case into its independently reusable fragments.

Scale up in the size of the case library: The book provides empirical validation of the algorithms developed for the memory organization and analogical problem solving within a large case library of more than 1,000 elaborated cases in a complex domain.

Full automation throughout: The book consists of a fully automated framework for the complete cycle of analogical problem solving, namely for case generation, storage, retrieval, and replay.

Contributions to Planning

Nonlinear planner generates cases as derivational traces: This work includes the design and implementation of a nonlinear problem solver that reasons about totally ordered plans and is complete as it can interleave goals and subgoals at any search depth. This problem solver generates derivational traces, i.e., cases to be stored, annotating successes and failures from its episodic search experience.

Mutually recursive analogical replay and base-level planner: The analogical problem solver can recursively plan by adapting a set of similar plans, and plan by searching from the domain theory.

Generality of planner: The analogical planner is domain independent and hence is a general purpose problem solver. It runs in multiple domains, and of realistic size.

1.4   Reader's guide

This book is organized in ten chapters. Chapter 2 illustrates the complete analogical reasoning cycle with a simple example overviewing the full system. The example also serves as illustration for the algorithms described in the following chapters. Chapter 3 presents the base-level nonlinear problem solver. Chapter 4 describes how a case is generated from a problem solving search episode. It introduces the complete justification structures annotated at the decision nodes.

Chapter 5 introduces the storage mechanism. It defines how to index the cases and how to organize the case library. Chapter 6 discusses the retrieval method. It presents the algorithms and discusses the efficiency of the strategy. Chapter 7 presents the replay algorithm to construct a solution to the new problem by following and merging multiple guiding cases. Chapter 8 shows empirical results on the problem solving performance obtained when scaling up the system in the complex logistics transportation domain building a case library of more than 1000 cases. Finally Chapter 9 draws bridges between this work and other research efforts, and Chapter 10 presents conclusions and discusses some future research directions. Figure 1.7 provides a comprehensive picture to guide the reader.

It is worth adding a simple explanation for the order of the chapters. Although the retrieval and analogical replay are at the beginning of the analogical reasoning cycle, as shown in Figure 1.7, for the sake of clarity of contents, their presentation is preceded by the description of how a case is generated and what are the contents of a case (Chapter 4), and how a case is indexed (Chapter 5) in memory. The order of the chapters represents therefore the evolution of the system starting with an empty case library.

A note on the terminology   The terms "base-level nonlinear problem solver," "problem solver without analogy," "NoLimit," and "NoLimit without analogy" are used interchangeably and refer to the nonlinear problem solver [Veloso, 1989].

Similarly, we use interchangeably the terms "analogical reasoner," "analogical problem solver," "NoLimit with analogy," and "PRODIGY/ANALOGY". They refer to the developed problem solver that uses derivational analogy for generating, storing, retrieving, and replaying the accumulated cases. This analogical problem solver is an extension of the base-level nonlinear problem solver.

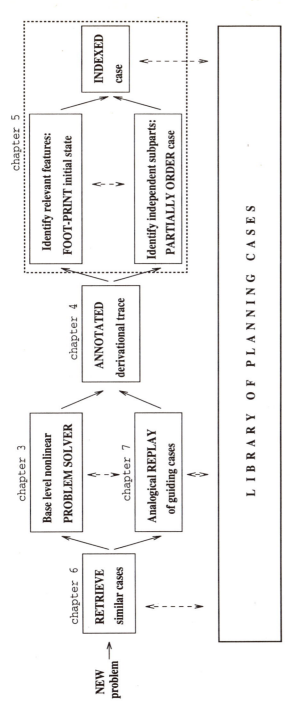

Figure 1.7: A reader's guide to the book: The complete analogical reasoning planning cycle in PRODIGY/ANALOGY. When a new problem is presented to be solved, PRODIGY/ANALOGY retrieves from its library of planning cases, one or more, if needed, past problem solving cases that are jointly found similar to the new problem. A solution is constructed by replaying the decision making process of the past cases in the new situation. PRODIGY/ANALOGY uses its past episodic experience and may also resort to its domain theory to plan for the divergences among the past and new situations. PRODIGY/ANALOGY accumulates a new case from the derivational trace of the problem solving episodes. The new cases are stored in the library indexed by the relevant features of the initial state and the sets of goals that interacted among each other in the solution generated.

Chapter 2

Overview

This chapter illustrates the complete analogical cycle through a simple example showing how the individual components presented in the later chapters are integrated together by a unique coherent idea. The exemplary problems are taken from a logistics transportation domain. In this domain, packages are to be moved among different cities. Packages are carried within the same city in trucks and between cities in airplanes. At each city there are several locations, e.g., post offices and airports. Trucks and airplanes may not be available on demand, and each can carry multiple packages. The problems used in this example are simple for the sake of a clear illustration of the overall reasoning process, but PRODIGY/ANALOGY was tested with problems involving up to 20 goals, over 100 literals in the initial state, and over 200 decision-long solutions.

The example starts with an empty case library. The initial problems are solved by the base-level problem solver using the available domain theory and stored in the case library as indexed annotated cases. After some problems are stored in the case library, the example shows a new problem solved by analogy with previous similar ones. Two analogous problems are retrieved from memory and replayed to produce a solution to the new problem.

2.1 Case generation

This section shows how a problem is defined, how the base problem solver searches for a solution and generates a case from the derivational trace of the problem solving search episode.

2.1.1 Defining a problem

Consider a problem where an object is at a post office and the goal is to have it inside a truck located in the same city as the object. The truck is initially at the city's airport. The solution to this problem is to drive the truck from the airport to the post office and then load the object into the truck. This section shows how the planner searches for a solution to this simple problem, presenting the

alternatives it encounters and the final solution. The system generates a case
to store in memory the derivational trace of the corresponding problem solving
episode.

Figure 2.1 shows an illustration of the problem with a description of the initial
state and goal statement as they are specified to the problem solver. The specific
instances of the world configuration are organized in classes in a type hierarchy.
Figure 2.1 (a) shows that there are two objects (or packages), **ob4** and **ob7**, one
truck **tr9**, and one airplane **pl1**. There is one city **c3** where there is a post
office **p3** and an airport **a3**. Figure 2.1 (b) describes the initial state where **ob4**
is at the post office **p3**, **ob7** is at the airport **a3**, at which there are also both
carriers, **tr9** and **pl1**. The goal, as shown in Figure 2.1 (c), is to have object **ob4**
inside the truck **tr9**.

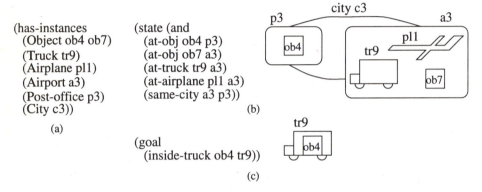

<pre>
(has-instances   (state (and
   (Object ob4 ob7)   (at-obj ob4 p3)
   (Truck tr9)   (at-obj ob7 a3)
   (Airplane pl1)   (at-truck tr9 a3)
   (Airport a3)   (at-airplane pl1 a3)
   (Post-office p3)   (same-city a3 p3))
   (City c3))   (b)
          (a)

                    (goal
                       (inside-truck ob4 tr9))
                                              (c)
</pre>

Figure 2.1: Example **ex1**: (a) class distribution of instances, (b) initial state, (c)
goal statement.

For illustration purposes, Figure 2.2 introduces two operators of this logistics
transportation domain that are relevant to solving the given problem.[1] Operators are defined as a list of preconditions necessary to be true in the state before
the operator can be applied, and a list of changes to be performed to the state
when the operator is applied. The operator **LOAD-TRUCK** specifies that an object
can be loaded into a truck if the object and the truck are at the same location, and the operator **DRIVE-TRUCK** states that a truck can move freely between
locations within the same city.

2.1.2   Problem solving search

The problem solver uses a backward chaining means-ends analysis search procedure with full subgoal interleaving. Figure 2.3 shows the problem solving trace
as the sequence of decisions made during the search to try to achieve the final
goal. When different alternatives are available the problem solver chooses randomly among them which one to pursue further. The trace is a sequence of goal

---

[1] The complete set of operators can be found in [Veloso, 1992].

```
(OPERATOR LOAD-TRUCK                    (OPERATOR DRIVE-TRUCK
  (params (((<obj> OBJECT)                 (params (((<truck> TRUCK)
            (<truck> TRUCK)                          (<loc-from> LOCATION)
            (<loc> LOCATION)))                       (<loc-to> LOCATION)))
  (preconds                               (preconds
    (and                                    (and
      (at-obj <obj> <loc>)                    (at-truck <truck> <loc-from>)
      (at-truck <truck> <loc>)))              (same-city <loc-to> <loc-from>)))
  (effects                                (effects
    ((add (inside-truck <obj> <truck>))     ((add (at-truck <truck> <loc-to>))
     (del (at-obj <obj> <loc>)))))           (del (at-truck <truck> <loc-from>)))))
```

Figure 2.2: Operators LOAD-TRUCK and DRIVE-TRUCK.

choices followed by operator choices followed occasionally by applying operators to the state when their preconditions are true in that state and the decision for immediate application is made.

```
<cl> (nlrun-prob 'ex1)                   4. tn4 (load-truck ob4 tr9 a3)
****************************                 ops-left: ((load-truck ob4 tr9 p3))
Solving the problem ex1:                 5. tn5 (at-obj ob4 a3)
Initial state :                          6. tn9 (unload-truck ob4 tr9 a3)
((at-obj ob4 p3) (at-truck tr9 a3)       ***
 (same-city a3 p3))
Goal statement:                             FAILURE - goals in loop:
(inside-truck ob4 tr9)                      ((inside-truck ob4 tr9))
***************************                  ****************************
Starting a search path                      Starting a new search path

1. tn1 (done)                            1. tn1 (done)
2. tn2 (*finish*)                        2. tn2 (*finish*)
3. tn3 (inside-truck ob4 tr9)            3. tn3 (inside-truck ob4 tr9)
4. tn4 (load-truck ob4 tr9 a3)           4. tn10 (load-truck ob4 tr9 p3)
ops-left: ((load-truck ob4 tr9 p3))      ***
5. tn5 (at-obj ob4 a3)                   5. tn11 (at-truck tr9 p3)
6. tn6 (unload-airplane ob4 pl1 a3)      6. tn12 (drive-truck tr9 a3 p3)
ops-left: ((unload-truck ob4 tr9 a3))    7. TN13 (DRIVE-TRUCK TR9 A3 P3)
7. tn7 (inside-airplane ob4 pl1)         8. TN14 (LOAD-TRUCK OB4 TR9 P3)
8. tn8 (load-airplane ob4 pl1 a3)        9. TN15 (*FINISH*)

FAILURE - goals in loop:                    ****************************
((at-obj ob4 a3))                           This is the solution found:
****************************
Starting a new search path                  (DRIVE-TRUCK tr9 a3 p3)
                                            (LOAD-TRUCK ob4 tr9 p3)
1. tn1 (done)                               (*FINISH*)
2. tn2 (*finish*)                        nil
3. tn3 (inside-truck ob4 tr9)            <cl>
```

Figure 2.3: Problem solving running trace.

To differentiate between goal predicates and the names of the instantiations of the operators, we use operator names derived from verbs and goal predicates names prefixed by prepositions. Therefore (load-truck ob4 tr9 a3) refers to the operator **LOAD-TRUCK** with instantiated values **ob4** for the object variable **<obj>**, **tr9** for the truck variable **<truck>**, and **a3** for the location variable **<loc>** (see Figure 2.2). (inside-truck ob4 tr9) is a goal literal that unifies with "inside-truck" effect of the operator **LOAD-TRUCK**.

In the trace, the operators applied are written in uppercase letters. The steps are numbered for each particular search path. Each step further has a **tn** number that tells the chronological order of the search expansion of that step. When a failure is encountered, the problem solver has a simple backtracking strategy that guarantees the completeness of its search procedure. This example illustrates two instances of chronological backtracking, i.e., upon failure, the problem solver returns to its last choice point in its current search path, and pursues the search from there with another alternative (e.g., a different operator, a different variable instantiation, or a different goal ordering).

According to the domain as specified in Figure 2.2, there are two instantiated operators that are *relevant* to the given goal, i.e., (inside-truck ob4 tr9) unifies with the effect (inside-truck <obj> <truck>) of the operator **LOAD-TRUCK**, namely with instantiations (load-truck ob4 tr9 p3) and (load--truck ob4 tr9 a3). The object **ob4** can be loaded into the truck **tr9** either at the post office **p3** or at the airport **a3**. Step 4 of the trace in Figure 2.3 shows these two alternatives. Node **tn4** at that step 4 shows that initially the alternative of loading the truck at the airport **a3** is pursued.

While pursuing this alternative, the problem solver subgoals on putting the object at the airport where the truck is, as shown in node **tn5**. An object can be put at an airport either by unloading it from an airplane or from a truck, as specified in the domain knowledge. Pursuing the choice of unloading the airplane, the problem solver finds again the need to subgoal on the goal (at-obj ob4 a3) that is already chosen in the search path at node **tn5** and not achieved yet. This corresponds to a goal loop and the problem solver detects a failure. Without knowledge of the reason for the failure, the problem solver backtracks chronologically and tries again unsuccessfully to unload **ob4** at the airport from a truck, as shown in node **tn9**. The solution is finally encountered when the problem solver chooses the correct alternative of loading the truck **tr9** at the post office **p3**, where the object **ob4** is located. It first drives truck **tr9** from the airport **a3** to **p3**. Nodes **tn10** through **tn15** show this sequence of decisions.[2]

The next step consists of showing how a problem solving episode is converted into a storable *case* to be reused in future similar problem solving situations guiding the problem solver through its search space. The case captures the failures encountered as well as the successful path.

---

[2]It is worth noticing that the problem solver can use efficient methods, like dependency-directed backtracking, to significantly reduce the search effort of its means-ends analysis cycle [Blythe and Veloso, 1992]. These methods in general do not capture domain specific control knowledge such as goal interactions, and the machine learning approaches developed for problem solving automate the process of acquiring that knowledge. In principle, best performance should be obtained by a combination of these synergistic methods.

2.1.3 Justification structure

While generating a solution to a problem, the problem solver accesses a large amount of knowledge that is not explicitly present in the final plan returned, such as the subgoaling links among the different steps. The problem solving process is a largely unguided search for a solution where different alternatives are generated and explored, some failing and others succeeding.

The purpose of solving problems by analogy is to reuse past experience to guide the generation of the solution for new problems, avoiding a completely new search effort. Transformational analogy [Carbonell, 1983] and most CBR systems (as summarized in [Riesbeck and Schank, 1989]) replay past solutions by modifying (*tweaking*) the retrieved final solution plan as a function of the differences found between the past and the current new problem without consideration of subgoaling structure or other decisions processed at original problem solving time. However, when the solution is constructed during the original problem solving episode, local and global reasons for search decisions are naturally accessible. A final solution represents a sequence of operations that corresponds only to a particular successful search path.

Derivational analogy [Carbonell, 1986] compiles the justifications at each decision point and annotates these at the different steps of the successful path. When replaying a solution, PRODIGY/ANALOGY reconstructs the reasoning process underlying the past solution. Justifications are tested to determine whether modifications are needed, and when they are needed, justifications provide constraints on possible alternative search paths. In essence, PRODIGY/ANALOGY benefits from past successes, failures, and interactions.

Returning to the example, the problem solving trace of Figure 2.3 can also be represented as an or-tree as shown in Figure 2.4. The search nodes corresponding to the solution found are the solid rectangles while the dashed ones represent the other nodes explored that led to failures. The node numbering represents the order of search expansion corresponding to the trace in Figure 2.3.

Figure 2.5 shows the case generated from the problem solving episode shown in Figure 2.4. The entire search tree is not stored in the case, but only the annotated decision nodes of the final successful path. The subgoaling structure and the record of the failures are annotated at the nodes of the solution path. Each goal is a precondition of some operator and each operator is chosen and applied because it is relevant to some goal that needs to be achieved. The alternatives that are explored and failed are stored with an attached reason of failure.

As an example, node cn2 corresponds to the search tree node tn8 (see Figure 2.4). This search node has a sibling alternative tn2 which was explored and failed. The failed subtree rooted at tn2 has two failure leaves, namely at tn6 and tn7. These failure reasons that support the choice of the right step at node tn8 are annotated at the case node cn2. At replay time these justifications are retested and early pruning of alternatives, reducing therefore the future search effort.

In summary, automatic case generation occurs by extending the general problem solver with the ability to introspect into its internal decision cycle, recording

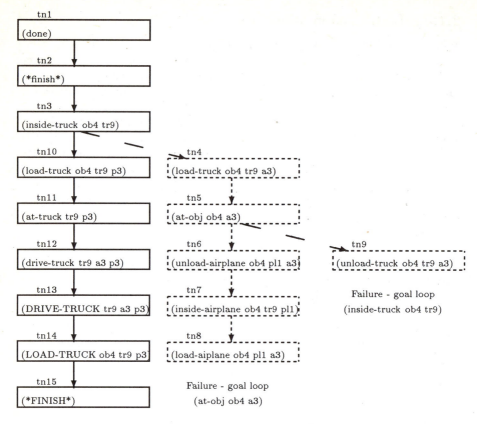

Figure 2.4: The search episode of Figure 2.3 represented as a search tree - the numbering of the nodes shows the order of expansion.

the justifications for each decision during its extensive search process. Examples of these justifications are: links between choices capturing the subgoaling structure, records of explored failed alternatives, and pointers to applied control knowledge. A case, i.e., a stored problem solving episode, consists of the solution trace augmented with these annotations.

2.2   Case storage

The episodic problem solving experience captured in a case is stored into a library of cases. One of the important issues to address in organizing the case library is the issue of identifying the appropriate features to use as indices for the cases. The immediate indices are the initial state description and the goal statement, as a problem is directly identified by these. In this section the example is pursued to show how a case corresponding to a particular solution found is indexed by its goal and by the features of the initial state that are relevant to the solution.

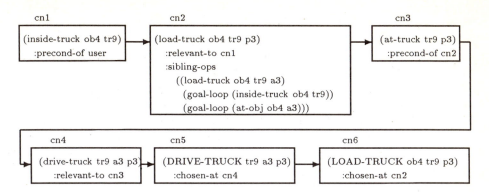

Figure 2.5: The resulting generated case corresponding to the search episode of Figure 2.4. Notice that applying an operator (represented in uppercase letters) is a distinct decision from the corresponding operator selection (represented in lowercase letters), e.g. nodes cn2 and cn6 are distinct.

2.2.1 Foot-printing the initial state

It is a well recognized difficult problem to identify the features of a world configuration that are in general *relevant* to achieve a goal state. The example shows the approach we develop to *foot-print* the initial state, identifying the set of relevant features as a function of the goal statement and of the particular solution encountered.

By following the subgoaling links in the derivational trace of the solution path, the system identifies for each goal the set of weakest preconditions necessary to achieve that goal. It creates recursively the *foot-printed* state by doing a goal regression for the goal conjuncts, i.e., projecting back each goal's weakest preconditions into the literals in the initial state. The literals in the initial state are categorized according to the goal conjunct that needed them to reach the solution. Goal regression acts as an immediate episodic explanation of the successful path.

```
(((at-obj ob4 p3) (inside-truck ob4 tr9))
 ((at-truck tr9 a3) (inside-truck ob4 tr9))
 ((same-city a3 p3) (inside-truck ob4 tr9))
 ((at-obj ob7 a3) nil)
 ((at-airplane pl1 a3) nil))
```

Figure 2.6: The foot-printed initial state for the problem **ex1** corresponding to the case shown in Figure 2.5.

Figure 2.6 shows the foot-print of the initial state for the example problem as an association between the literals in the initial state and the goals they contributed to achieve. Note that the package **ob7** and the airplane **pl1** are not in the foot-print of (**inside-truck ob4 tr9**).

Figure 2.6 shows the foot-print of the initial state for the example problem as an association between the literals in the initial state and the goals they contributed to achieve. Note that the package **ob7** and the airplane **pl1** are not in the foot-print of (**inside-truck ob4 tr9**).

The case is indexed through the parameterized goal and foot-printed initial state. Figure 2.7 sketches the contents of the memory after the case of Figure 2.5 has been stored. The indexing goals are stored in a hash table pointing to a discrimination network of the foot-printed initial state. The parameterized goal (**inside-truck <p35> <t42>**) is the top level index for the case. This goal index points to a discrimination network that contains the foot-printed initial state to index the case (the case in this example is named **case-ex1-2**). The substitution ((**<p35>.ob4**) (**<t42>.tr9**) (**<po15>.p3**) (**<ap50>.a3**)) is generated when parameterizing the problem solving situation.

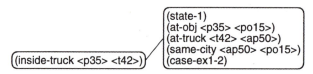

Figure 2.7: Contents of the case library after storing problem **ex1**.

To show the role of the discrimination network for the initial state, consider a sequence of three additional problems. The next problem is another simple one-goal problem and the next subsection shows two additional two-goal problems. The case generation details for these problems are skipped these problems and the contents and indices of the case library are shown after the corresponding cases are stored.

Introducing into memory another one-goal case

Consider the problem **ex2** in Figure 2.8 where an object **ob2** must be inside of an airplane **pl7**.

The object is initially at an airport **a5** ready to be loaded into the airplane. The airplane is at a different airport **a11**. As the object is already at an airport, a good solution to this problem is to fly the airplane into the airport where the object is at, namely **a5**, and then load the object into the airplane. The search space that the problem solver explores to find this solution could involve considering moving the object first to the airplane's location if there were more airplanes available. The domain theory does not restrict the problem solver from exploring this hypothesis. In fact this could be a more efficient solution to the problem in a more complex situations with more airplanes and more packages to reallocate. Figure 2.9 (a) shows the solution returned for this problem while Figure 2.9 (b) shows the foot-printed initial state.

The memory is expanded with one more case. Figure 2.10 shows the indexing of this new case. The contents of the new memory node **state-2** is the foot-printed initial state of the solution.

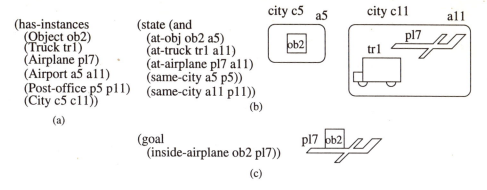

(has-instances
  (Object ob2)
  (Truck tr1)
  (Airplane pl7)
  (Airport a5 al1)
  (Post-office p5 p11)
  (City c5 cl1))

(a)

(state (and
  (at-obj ob2 a5)
  (at-truck tr1 al1)
  (at-airplane pl7 al1)
  (same-city a5 p5))
  (same-city al1 p11))

(b)

(goal
  (inside-airplane ob2 pl7))

(c)

Figure 2.8: Example problem **ex2**: (a) class distribution of instances, (b) initial state, (c) goal statement.

```
:solution '(                    :state-goal '(
  (fly-airplane pl7 al1 a5)       ((at-obj ob2 a5) (inside-airplane ob2 pl7))
  (load-airplane ob2 pl7 a5)      ((at-airplane pl7 al1) (inside-airplane ob2 pl7))
  (*finish*))                     ((same-city al1 p11) nil)
                                  ((same-city a5 p5) nil))
        (a)                                   (b)
```

Figure 2.9: Problem **ex2**: (a) solution, (b) foot-printed initial state.

(inside-airplane <p25> <a70>)

(state-2)
(at-obj <p25> <ap29>)
(at-airplane <a70> <ap2>)
(case-ex2-1)

Figure 2.10: Additional contents of the case library after problem **ex2**.

2.2.2 Multiple-goal problems

The problems below illustrate how the storage mechanism handles multiple-goal problems. (The details of the case generation are skipped once again.)

Figure 2.11 shows a two-goal problem where one object **ob10** must be taken to an airport **a5**, as represented in the goal conjunct (**at-obj ob10 a5**) and another object **ob11** must be inside of the truck **tr5**, as represented in the goal conjunct (**inside-truck ob11 tr5**).

Figure 2.12 (a) shows the solution encountered for this problem, while Figure 2.12 (b) shows the foot-printed initial state.

In order to efficiently store and reuse large complex multi-goals problems, the system identifies the independent subparts of a problem solving experience. This allows a solution to be reused for its independent subparts. I developed an algorithm that partially orders the solution by greedily analyzing the dependencies among the plan steps. The connected components of the partially ordered plan determine the set of interacting goals (see Section 5.1). Figure 2.13 shows

```
(has-instances          (state (and                (goal (and
  (OBJECT ob10 ob11)       (at-obj ob11 p6)           (inside-truck ob11 tr5)
  (TRUCK tr4 tr5 tr6)      (at-truck tr6 a6)          (at-obj ob10 a5)))
  (AIRPLANE pl30)          (at-airplane pl30 a6)            (c)
  (AIRPORT a5 a6)          (at-truck tr4 p5)
  (POST-OFFICE p5 p6)      (inside-truck ob10 tr4)
  (CITY c5 c6))            (at-truck tr5 a5)
        (a)               (same-city a6 p6)
                          (same-city a5 p5)))
                                (b)
```

Figure 2.11: Example problem **ex3**: (a) class distribution of instances, (b) initial state, (c) goal statement.

```
:solution '(                    :state-goal '(
  (drive-truck tr4 p5 a5)         ((inside-truck ob10 tr4) (at-obj ob10 a5))
  (unload-truck ob10 tr4 a5)      ((at-obj ob11 p6) (inside-truck ob11 tr5))
  (drive-truck tr6 a6 p6)         ((at-truck tr5 a5) (inside-truck ob11 tr5))
  (load-truck ob11 tr6 p6)        ((at-truck tr4 p5) (at-obj ob10 a5))
  (drive-truck tr6 p6 a6)         ((at-truck tr6 a6) (inside-truck ob11 tr5))
  (unload-truck ob11 tr6 a6)      ((same-city p5 a5) (at-obj ob10 a5))
  (load-airplane ob11 pl30 a6)    ((same-city a6 p6) (inside-truck ob11 tr5))
  (fly-airplane pl30 a6 a5)       ((at-airplane pl30 a6) (inside-truck ob11 tr5)))
  (unload-airplane ob11 pl30 a5)
  (load-truck ob11 tr5 a5)
  (*finish*))
        (a)                                      (b)
```

Figure 2.12: Problem **ex3**: (a) solution, (b) foot-printed initial state.

the resulting partial order for the solution in Figure 2.12. The nodes represent the plan steps now partially ordered with respect to each other based on precondition dependencies. The nodes labeled *s* and *f* correspond to the start and finish plan steps respectively and are not considered when determining the connected components of the graph.

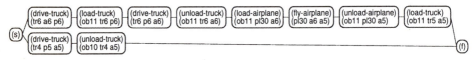

Figure 2.13: Partially ordered plan for example **ex3**.

Figure 2.13 shows that the two goals of problem **ex3** do not interact, as the plan steps required to achieve each goal individually are in different connected components of the partially ordered plan (steps *s* and *f* excluded).

In particular the object **ob10** is initially inside of the truck **tr4**. This truck is driven from the post office **p5** to the airport **a5** and **ob10** is unloaded at this airport which is the object's goal destination. The partially ordered solution shows that the two steps (**drive-truck tr4 p5 a5**) and (**unload-truck ob10 tr4 a5**) do not interact with the additional plan steps necessary to achieve the other goal conjunct (**inside-truck ob11 tr5**).

The case is stored in memory indexed by the two independent goals. Figure 2.14 shows the part of the case library that is changed after the problem **ex3** is solved and stored into memory. The case is multiply indexed by the two independent goals and their corresponding foot-printed initial state in different discrimination networks.

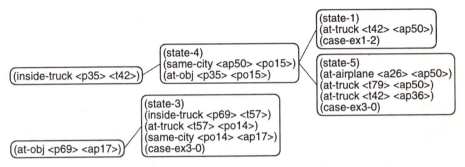

Figure 2.14: Contents of the case library related to the new stored problem **ex3**.

Note that before the problem **ex3** is incorporated into the case library, the network indexed by the goal (inside-truck <p35> <t42>) is as represented in Figure 2.7. The foot-printed initial state of problem **ex3** for the goal **inside-truck**, as shown in Figure 2.12 (b), matches part of the foot-printed initial state stored in memory. Namely it matches the subset (at-obj <p35> <po15>) (same-city <ap50> <po15>). This subset of literals is common to both problems **ex1** and **ex3** and becomes the root of the discrimination network, at node (state-4). The remaining two other nodes, namely (state-1) and (state-5) store the differences between the initial states of the two problems.

An additional two-goal problem

The following additional example illustrates the situation where again two independent conjunctive goals are solved but the memory is reorganized in a different way. Figure 2.15 shows a problem situation similar to the one in problem **ex3**, where the goals are the same but the initial location of one of the objects, **ob11** is different.

For the purpose of illustrating the memory organization and indexing ignore whether the problem is solved by the basic problem solver or by analogical reasoning and consider simply that a solution to the problem was reached. Figure 2.16 (a) shows this solution, from whose derivational trace the foot-printed initial state is derived, as shown in Figure 2.16 (b).

Each literal is annotated with the goal it contributes to achieve. In particular the literal (same-city a6 p6) is not used to achieve either of the goals. In fact the truck **tr6** is initially at the airport and does not need to drive among locations in the city. Therefore no information is used about city **c6**'s airport **a6** and post office **po6**.

```
(has-instances          (state (and                    (goal (and
  (OBJECT ob10 ob11)       (inside-truck ob11 tr6)        (at-obj ob10 a5)
  (TRUCK tr4 tr5 tr6)      (at-truck tr6 a6)              (inside-truck ob11 tr5)))
  (AIRPLANE pl30)          (inside-truck ob10 tr4)
  (AIRPORT a5 a6)          (at-truck tr4 p5)
  (POST-OFFICE p5 p6)      (at-truck tr5 a5)
  (CITY c5 c6))            (at-airplane pl30 a6)
                           (same-city a6 p6)
                           (same-city a5 p5)))
         (a)                        (b)                             (c)
```

Figure 2.15: Example problem **ex4**: (a) class distribution of instances, (b) initial state, (c) goal statement.

```
:solution '(                       :state-goal '(
  (unload-truck ob11 tr6 a6)         ((inside-truck ob10 tr4) (at-obj ob10 a5))
  (load-airplane ob11 pl30 a6)       ((inside-truck ob11 tr6) (inside-truck ob11 tr5))
  (drive-truck tr4 p5 a5)            ((at-truck tr5 a5) (inside-truck ob11 tr5))
  (unload-truck ob10 tr4 a5)         ((at-truck tr4 p5) (at-obj ob10 a5))
  (fly-airplane pl30 a6 a5)          ((at-truck tr6 a6) (inside-truck ob11 tr5))
  (unload-airplane ob11 pl30 a5)     ((same-city p5 a5) (at-obj ob10 a5))
  (load-truck ob11 tr5 a5)           ((at-airplane pl30 a6) (inside-truck ob11 tr5))
  (*finish*))                        ((same-city a6 p6) nil))
         (a)                                       (b)
```

Figure 2.16: Problem **ex4**: (a) solution, (b) foot-printed initial state.

Figure 2.17 shows the partially ordered solution found. Again, the two goals do not interact as the plan that achieves them is separated into two distinct connected components.

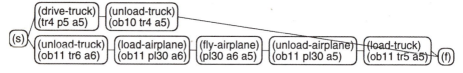

Figure 2.17: Partially ordered plan for example **ex4**.

Each discrimination network for the initial state indices is top-level indexed by the set of goals shared by all the cases indexed by it. The case **ex4** is indexed separately by the two goals. The foot-printed initial state relevant to the goal `inside-truck` is incorporated into the discrimination network that is already present in the library indexed by this goal. This time however the initial state does not match the initial states of the two previously solved and stored problems **ex1** and **ex3**. Figure 2.18 shows the resulting memory organization with the new state node, (`state-6`).

Finally note that the problem **ex3** and **ex4** match totally with respect to the other goal solved, (`at-obj <p69> <ap17>`). The system identifies the case *more interesting*, i.e., more useful for reuse purposes and stores only that one. In a nutshell, given two structurally identical cases, the case that corresponds to a shorter solution, or that explored more nodes from the search space, is

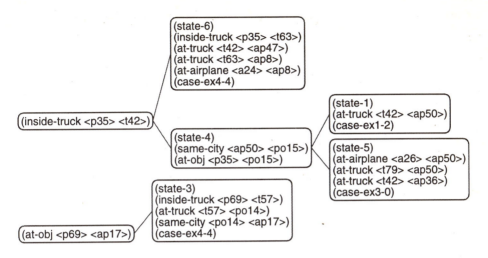

Figure 2.18: Case library after example **ex4**.

potentially more useful for the replay mechanism. In this example the problem solving episode for problem **ex4** is found more interesting and this case is indexed instead of **case-ex3-0**.

2.3 Automatic case retrieval

Consider that the case library consists now of the four problems **ex1**, **ex2**, **ex3**, and **ex4** solved and stored as shown in Figure 2.18 and Figure 2.10. The remainder of this example illustrates the retrieval and replay mechanisms. Consider the problem situation given in Figure 2.19.

```
(has-instances          (state (and                (goal (and
  (OBJECT ob2 ob4)         (at-obj ob4 p5)            (inside-airplane ob2 p17)
  (TRUCK tr9)              (at-truck tr9 p5)           (inside-truck ob4 tr9)))
  (AIRPLANE p17)          (inside-truck ob2 tr9)              (c)
  (AIRPORT a5 a11)        (at-airplane p17 a11)
  (POST-OFFICE p5 p11)    (same-city a11 p11)
  (CITY c5 c11))          (same-city a5 p5)))
       (a)                       (b)
```

Figure 2.19: Example problem **mult1**: (a) class distribution of instances, (b) initial state, (c) goal statement.

There are two goals. The retrieval procedure searches to see if the case library has any case where the two goals were found to be two interacting goals. As it does not find such a case, it returns two distinct cases, each covering one of the two goals. Figure 2.20 shows the output of the retrieval procedure for problem **mult1**. Problems **ex1** and **ex2** are returned as the two similar problem solving situations in memory to guide respectively the goal (inside-truck ob4 tr9) and (inside-airplane ob2 pl7).

```
<cl> (retrieve-analogs 'mult1)

  Analogs to prob mult1:
  (((inside-airplane ob2 pl7) case-ex2-1
    ((<p25> . ob2) (<a70> . pl7) (<ap2> . a11))
     1 0.5 2 "state-net-2")
   ((inside-truck ob4 tr9) case-ex1-2
    ((<p35> . ob4) (<t42> . tr9) (<po15> . p5))
     1 0.33333334 2 "state-net-1"))
 nil
 <cl>
```

Figure 2.20: Retrieving analogous past situations for problem mult1.

Each goal is associated with a guiding past case retrieved as similar to the present situation according to a role substitution match also shown in the figure. The three numbers that follow the case name represent the similarity value between the new and past situations. They show the match degree between the goals and the initial states. Finally the state network that points to the retrieved similar case is also returned.

The analogical reasoner requests from the case library similar past situations. The retrieval strategy is based on searching for the same interacting goals followed by incrementally searching for a substitution that satisfies a pre-established matching degree. When a case is retrieved as similar to a new situation, the partial match found between the old and new situations defines partial bindings to the variablized past case.

2.4   Case replay

Figure 2.21 sketches the reconstruction solution process for problem mult1 guided by the two past cases ex1 and ex2. The new situation is shown at the right of the figure and the two past guiding cases on its left.

The transfer occurs by merging the two guiding cases and performing any additional work needed to accomplish remaining subgoals. In this example the cases are serially merged to make this overview presentation simple. Chapter 7 discusses several other merging strategies.

The new problem to be solved consists of a two-conjunct goal, namely to load an object ob4 into a truck tr9 and to load another object ob2 into an airplane pl7. The retrieval procedure returns the two past cases ex1 and ex2 each partially matching one of the goal conjuncts. The figure shows the guiding cases already with the variables substituted by the matching bindings. The top case, namely the case to solve problem ex1, corresponds to the situation where

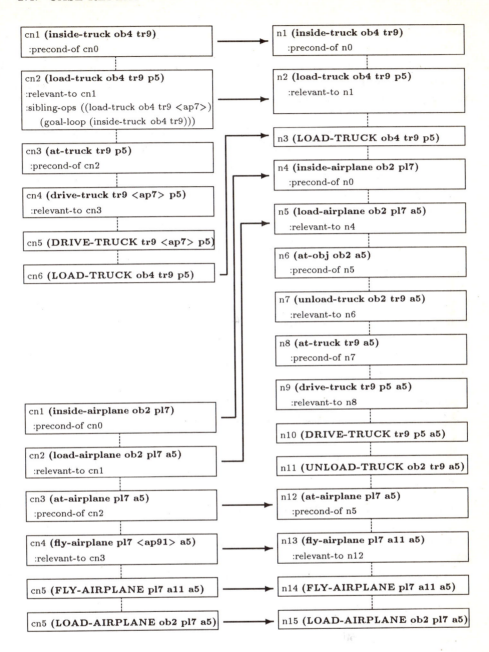

Figure 2.21: Following multiple cases – Serial merging during derivational replay.

an object was also to be loaded into a truck. However this truck was at the airport of the city and not at the post office. The bottom case, namely the case to solve problem **ex2**, corresponds to a situation where an object is to be loaded into an airplane and the object is already at the airport.

Record of past failures helps pruning alternatives ahead. In particular, the case nodes cn3 through cn5 of the top case are not reused, as there is a truck already at the post office in the new problem. On the other hand, the nodes n6 through n11 correspond to unguided additional planning work done in the new case, as the object ob2 needs to be brought to the airport a5.

Finally notice that, at node n2, the replay mechanism prunes out an alternative possible suitable operator, namely to load the truck at any airport, because of the recorded past failure at the node cn2 from the top case. The recorded reason for that failure, namely a goal-loop for the goal (inside-truck ob4 tr9), holds again in the new situation, as that goal is in the current set of open goals, at node n1.

Storing the new solved problem into memory

The storage method applies now to this new problem solved by analogy. The independent subparts of the case are identified by the algorithm that partially orders the case. Figure 2.22 shows the output of this algorithm. The graph shows only one connected component which means that the two goals interact and are not independent with respect to this particular solution constructed. This is the situation because the resources are shared, namely the truck tr9 and the airplane p17.

Figure 2.22: Partially ordered plan for example mult1.

Figure 2.23 sketches the contents of the case library after the five problems, ex1, ex2, ex3, ex4, and mult have been solved and stored. Notice that the case named case-mult1-100 corresponding to the problem mult1 is stored in a separate discrimination network indexed by the conjunction of the two interacting goals.

The process continues smoothly in the same analogical reasoning cycle. When new problems are proposed to the problem solver, the retrieval procedure searches the case library for similar past situations, the extended analogical problem solver replays the retrieved cases and generates the case to be stored from its problem solving episode. The new case is indexed by the set of interacting goals and by the relevant initial state and stored into the case library.

2.5   Summary

This example run illustrates the different phases of the analogical reasoner, to wit:

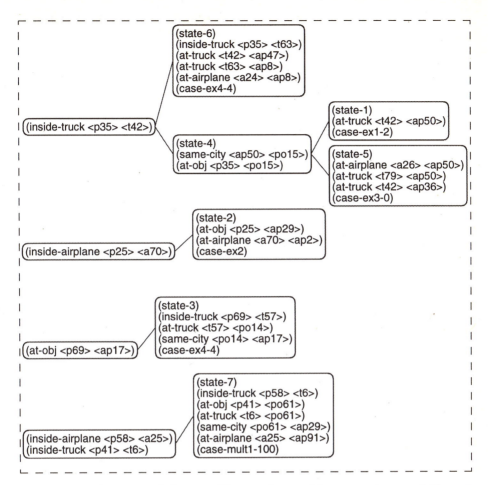

Figure 2.23: Contents of the case library after problems **ex1** (case-ex1-2), **ex2** (case-ex2-1), **ex3** (case-ex3-0), **ex4** (case-ex4-4), and **mult1** (case-mult1-100) have been solved and stored.

- A problem is given to the system to be solved. The problem solver generates a case from the problem solving experience by annotating it with the justifications for the decisions made during the search process.

- To store a generated case the system identifies the foot-printed initial state, i.e., the relevant literals of the initial state that contributed to the achievement of the different goals.

- Furthermore, by partially ordering the solutions for multiple-goal problems, the independent subparts of the cases are determined and the corresponding sets of interacting goals are used to index the case.

- When a new problem is proposed to the system the problem solver retrieves from the case library a set of analogous problem solving situations.

- The analogical problem solver replays the multiple analogous cases by merging the steps from each case, guided by the justification structures attached to each decision node.

Chapter 3

The Problem Solver

A **nonlinear** problem solver is able to explore and exploit interactions among multiple conjunctive goals, whereas a **linear** one can only address each goal in sequence, independent of all the others. Hence, nonlinear problem solving is desired when there are interactions among simultaneous goals and subgoals in the problem space. For the design of the base-level problem solver for this work, we explored a method to solve problems nonlinearly, that generates and tests different alternatives at the operator and at the goal ordering levels. Commitments are made throughout the search process, in contrast to a least-commitment strategy [Sacerdoti, 1975, Tate, 1977, Wilkins, 1989], where decisions are deferred until all possible interactions are recognized. We implemented a nonlinear problem solver, NoLimit, which follows this approach within the PRODIGY architecture. (NoLimit stands for **No**nlinear problem solver using casual com**mit**ment.)

This chapter is organized in five sections. Section 1 motivates the nonlinear problem solving approach we developed with a discussion on the issues that differentiate linear and nonlinear problem solving. Section 2 informally describes the general search procedure used by NoLimit which is formalized in Section 3. Section 4 illustrates the problem solving procedure with a complete example. Finally, Section 5 summarizes the chapter.

3.1 Motivation

Consider the following idealized planning problem: given a formal description of an initial state of the world, a set of operators that can be executed to make transitions from one world state to another, and a goal statement, find a **plan**, to *transform* the initial state into a final state in which the goal statement is true. The goal statement is a partial description of a desired state satisfiable by one or more states. Consider that the goal statement is defined as a conjunction of goals. This raises the issue of how to deal with possible interactions among the conjuncts [Chapman, 1987]. A simple approach, followed by linear planners, such as STRIPS [Fikes and Nilsson, 1971], is to solve one goal at a time. A final solution to a problem is a **sequence** of complete subsolutions to each one of the goals, and recursively to the subgoals. This approach has an underlying assumption of independence among conjunctive goals. This method can be slightly improved by allowing any permutation of the original top-level goals to be considered. Another level of improvement is obtained if the problem solver can reconsider any goal or subgoal that was achieved once and then deleted while working on a different goal. The planner reaches a solution when all the goals are true in some world state.

3.1.1   Linear problem solving

Linear planning suffers from both **non-optimality** and **incompleteness**: non-optimality in terms of finding solutions that involve doing and undoing operators unnecessarily; incompleteness in terms of missing a solution to problems when one exists. Both these problems are due to the fact, mentioned above, that linear planning works on one goal at a time. The two examples below illustrate these problems.

An example on the non-optimal character of linear planning

The problem described below is known as the *Sussman anomaly* as it was identified by Sussman in [Sussman, 1975]. Consider the blocksworld with the following operator:

- *MOVE(x,y,z)* moves block x from the top of y to the top of z. y and z can be either the table or another block. *MOVE* is applicable only if x and z are clear, and x is on y. The table always has clear space. A block is clear if it does not have any other block on top.

Figure 3.1 shows the problem. Note that the goal statement is expressed as a conjunction of two literals. It does not fully describe the final desired state. Instead it specifies only the conditions that must be met in order to consider the problem solved.

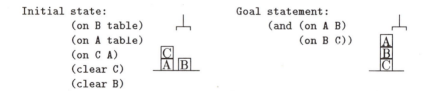

Figure 3.1: The Sussman anomaly: Find a plan to transform the initial state to achieve the goal statement.

A linear planner can generate two non-optimal plans as shown in Figure 3.2. These plans are found because the linear planner can consider different permutations of the conjunctive goals, and work on a single goal more than once, i.e., admitting that a goal might need to be reachieved. For both plans, the initial state and the goal statement are the ones shown in Figure 3.1.

Goal	Steps of the Plan	State
		C/A B
(on B C)	(MOVE B table C)	B/C/A
(on A B)	(MOVE B C table)	C/A B
	(MOVE C A table)	A C B
	(MOVE A table B)	A/C B
(on B C)	(MOVE A B table)	A C B
	(MOVE B table C)	B/A C
(on A B)	(MOVE A table B)	A/B/C

Goal	Steps of the Plan	State
		C/A B
(on A B)	(MOVE C A table)	A C B
	(MOVE A table B)	A/C B
(on B C)	(MOVE A B table)	A C B
	(MOVE B table C)	B/A C
(on A B)	(MOVE A table B)	A/B/C

Figure 3.2: Two linear plans that solve the Sussman anomaly inefficiently.

The two plans differ in the choice of the first goal considered. Both plans are non-optimal, as both have actions that are done and undone unnecessarily. For example, in the first plan, as the goal (on B C) is selected first, B is moved from the table to the top of C, and then moved back to the table to clear C, so that the goal (on A B) may be achieved. Similarly, if (on A B) is selected first, A is moved to the top of B and then back to the table, when (on B C) is considered. These inefficiencies arise because the linear planner *forgets* about the other goals while trying to achieve a particular goal in the conjunctive set. More formally, this means that, if the goal statement is the conjunction of goals $G_1, \ldots, G_k$, the linear planner does not consider any of the goals $G_j, j \neq i$, when working on goal G_i. An optimal solution to the Sussman anomaly is the three-step plan: (MOVE C A table), (MOVE B table C), (MOVE A table B).

Non-optimality is a problem that could, however, be overcome by a post-processing module that removes unnecessary steps after the planning is completed [Rich and Knight, 1991]. It is not straightforward to think of a general way to deal with arbitrary repetitions of the same goal and other suboptimal plan steps. Detecting loops in the state is not a guaranteed mechanism, as a situation could occur where an operator would always change the state but in *irrelevant* ways with respect to the goals. One can say that in this particular example of the Sussman anomaly, the linear planner is lucky to find a solution, even if non-optimal, by working repeatedly on the same goals. In general, however, linear planners may fail drastically, as discussed below.

An example on the incompleteness of linear planning

A much more serious problem occurs when a linear planner fails to solve a problem that could be solved if goal interactions were properly considered through interleaving of subgoals. In the next example the linear planner fails to produce any solution at all. Consider the set of operators given in Figure 3.3 that define the *one-way-rocket* domain. The operator MOVE-ROCKET shows that the ROCKET can move only from a specific location locA to a specific location locB. An object can be loaded into the ROCKET at any location by applying the operator LOAD-ROCKET. Similarly, an object can be unloaded from the ROCKET at any location by using the operator UNLOAD-ROCKET.

```
(LOAD-ROCKET                (UNLOAD-ROCKET               (MOVE-ROCKET
 (params                     (params                      (params nil)
  ((<obj> OBJECT)             ((<obj> OBJECT)              (preconds
   (<loc> LOCATION)))          (<loc> LOCATION)))           (at ROCKET locA))
 (preconds                   (preconds                    (effects
  (and                        (and                         ((add (at ROCKET locB))
   (at <obj> <loc>)            (inside <obj> ROCKET)         (del (at ROCKET locA)]
   (at ROCKET <loc>))          (at ROCKET <loc>)))
 (effects                    (effects
  ((add (inside <obj> ROCKET)) ((add (at <obj> <loc>))
   (del (at <obj> <loc>)]       (del (inside <obj> ROCKET)]
```

Figure 3.3: The three operators defining the *one-way-rocket* domain.

Consider the problem of moving two given objects obj1 and obj2 from the location locA to the location locB as expressed in Figure 3.4. (Although NoLimit solves much more complex and general versions of this problem, the present minimal form suffices to illustrate the need for nonlinear planning.)

```
(has-instances OBJECT obj1 obj2)
(has-instances LOCATION locA locB)

Initial State:                      Goal Statement:
        (at obj1 locA)                      (and (at obj1 locB)
        (at obj2 locA)                           (at obj2 locB))
        (at ROCKET locA)
```

Figure 3.4: A problem in the *one-way-rocket* domain.

Figure 3.5 shows the two incomplete plans that a linear planner produces before failing. The two possible permutations of the conjunctive goals are tried without success. Accomplishing either goal individually inhibits the accomplishment of the other goal as a precondition of the operator LOAD-ROCKET cannot be achieved. The ROCKET cannot be moved back to the object's initial position. An

example of a solution to this problem is the following plan: (LOAD-ROCKET obj1
locA), (LOAD-ROCKET obj2 locA), (MOVE-ROCKET), (UNLOAD-ROCKET obj1 locB),
(UNLOAD-ROCKET obj2 locB).

Goal	Plan
(at obj1 locB)	(LOAD-ROCKET obj1 locA)
	(MOVE-ROCKET)
	(UNLOAD-ROCKET obj1 locB)
(at obj2 locB)	*failure*

Goal	Plan
(at obj2 locB)	(LOAD-ROCKET obj2 locA)
	(MOVE-ROCKET)
	(UNLOAD-ROCKET obj2 locB)
(at obj1 locB)	*failure*

Figure 3.5: Two failed linear plans for the *one-way-rocket* problem. The second
conjunctive goal cannot be achieved because the ROCKET cannot return to pick
up the remaining object.

The failure presented is due to the *irreversibility* of the operator MOVE-ROCKET,
combined with the linear strategy used. An operator is **irreversible** if it transforms a world state S_{old} into a new state S_{new} and there is no sequence of operators that transforms the state S_{new} back into the state S_{old}. An operator is
reversible otherwise. Linear planners may generate non-optimal solutions in the
presence of reversible operators and may fail to find solutions in the presence
of irreversible operators. Planning with irreversible operators requires special
mechanisms to *avoid* artificial deadends.

3.1.2 Nonlinear problem solving

We claim that there has been some ambiguity in previous work in the use of the
terms **linear** and **nonlinear** planning. Linear planning has been used in the
context of planners that generate totally ordered plans. The discussion below
shows why total ordering is not specific to linear planners.

Linear planning refers to the following correlated characteristics:

- searching using a *stack* of goals, not allowing therefore interleaving
  of goals at different depths of search,
- generating solutions as sequential concatenation of complete subsolutions for conjunctive goals, and, recursively, for conjunctive subgoals.

The notion of nonlinear planning was motivated by recognizing problems like
the Sussman anomaly in a linear planner such as STRIPS [Sussman, 1975]. The
approach proposed to face this anomaly consisted of deferring making decisions
while building the plan [Sacerdoti, 1975]. The result of a planner that follows
this least-commitment strategy is a partially ordered plan as opposed to a totally

ordered one, and consequently the term *nonlinear plan* is used. However, the essence of the *nonlinearity* is not in the fact that the plan is partially ordered, but in the fact that a plan need not be a linear concatenation of complete subplans. NoLIMIT can generate *totally* ordered plans that are *nonlinear*, i.e., they cannot be decomposed into a sequence of complete subplans for the conjunctive goal set. Therefore generating totally ordered plans is not, per se, a true characteristic of a linear planner. (In fact a totally ordered plan is itself a *degenerate* partially ordered one.)[1]

Summarizing, nonlinear planning refers to the following characteristics:

- searching using a *set* of goals, allowing therefore interleaving of goals and subgoals at different depths of search,
- generating solutions that are not necessarily a sequence of complete subsolutions for the conjunctive goals.

In both linear and nonlinear planning, the final solution can be presented as a partially ordered plan, as one can be built from a totally ordered plan. Section 5.1 presents the algorithm to accomplish this transformation. To conclude this general discussion about linear and nonlinear planning, the next paragraphs discuss the complexity of using a least-commitment strategy and that of an intelligent casual-commitment one [Minton *et al.*, 1989].

Least-commitment and intelligent casual-commitment

In a least-commitment planning strategy, decisions are deferred until no further progress is possible, and then all constraints carried forward are considered in making a decision.[2] Typically what happens is that conjunctive goals are assumed to be independent and worked separately, producing unordered sets of actions to achieve the goals. From time to time, the planner fires some plan critics that check for interactions among the individual subplans. If conflicting interactions are found, the planner commits to a specific partial ordering that avoids conflicts. There may be cases for which actions stay unordered during the whole planning process, leading to a final partially ordered plan. In this strategy, it is NP-hard [Chapman, 1987] to determine if a given literal is true at a particular instant of time while planning, when actions are dependent on the state of the world, as all paths through the partial order must be verified. To avoid this combinatorial explosion, planners that follow this least-commitment strategy use *heuristics* to reduce the search space to determine the truth of a proposition.

A casual-commitment strategy corresponds to searching for a solution by generating and testing alternatives in both the ordering of goals and possible operators to apply. The planner commits to the most promising goal order and operator selection, backtracking to test other orderings and selections, if

---

[1]NoLIMIT can also return a partially ordered plan as a solution to a problem, by analyzing the dependencies among the steps in the totally ordered solution encountered for that problem.

[2]Note that the convex hull decision space of all pertinent constraints can be empty (planning failure) or contain more than one possibility (requiring search if subsequent information generates new constraints not satisfied by the chosen decision).

and only if a failure is reached. Using this approach, there is no problem in determining the truth of a proposition at a certain time, as a state of the world is updated during the search. However, in the worst case, the method involves an exponential search over the space of solutions. Like the previous approach, NoLimit uses *heuristics* to reduce this exponential search. Provably incorrect alternatives are eliminated and heuristically preferred ones are explored first [Newell *et al.*, 1963, Waterman, 1970]. The control knowledge transforms a simple casual-commitment strategy into an *intelligent* casual-commitment one, leading to an intelligent exploration of the different alternatives.

In a nutshell, least commitment corresponds to breadth-first search over the space of possible plans, and intelligent casual commitment corresponds to best-first heuristic search. The former derives some benefit from structure sharing among alternative plans (the partial order) and the latter benefits from any intelligence that can be applied at decision points - and the direct computation of the world state when necessary. Recent research efforts [Minton *et al.*, 1991, Barrett *et al.*, 1991] compare these two planning approaches and show interesting trade-offs on the efficient use of the two methods.

3.2 NoLimit - The planning algorithm

NoLimit is a nonlinear planner that follows an intelligent casual-commitment approach. As in PRODIGY's linear problem solver [Minton *et al.*, 1989], NoLimit provides a rich action representation language coupled with an expressive control language. The operators are represented by preconditions and effects. The preconditions are expressed in a typed first order predicate logic. They can contain conjunctions, disjunctions, negations, and both existential and universal quantifiers with typed variables. Variables in the operators may be constrained by arbitrary functions. In addition, the operators can contain conditional effects, which depend on the state in which the operator is applied. A class (type) hierarchy organizes the objects of the world.

The basic search procedure is, as in the linear planner [Minton *et al.*, 1989], a means-ends analysis [Ernst and Newell, 1969] backward chaining mode following a casual-commitment search method. A basic means-ends analysis module tries to apply operators that reduce the differences between the current world and the final desired goal state (a partial description of the world). Basically, in a backward chaining mode, given a goal literal not true in the current world, the planner selects one operator that adds (in case of a positive goal, or deletes, in case of a negative goal) that goal to the world. We say that this operator is *relevant* to the given goal. If the preconditions of the chosen operator are true, the operator can be *applied*. If this is not the case, then the preconditions that are not true in the *state*, become *subgoals*, i.e., new goals to be achieved. The cycle repeats until all the conjuncts from the goal expression are true in the world. NoLimit proceeds in this apparently simple way. Its nonlinear character stems from working with a **set** of goals in this cycle, as opposed to the top goal in a goal stack. Dynamic goal selection enables NoLimit to interleave plans, exploiting common subgoals and addressing issues of resource contention. Search control knowledge may be applied at all decision points: which relevant operator to apply (if there are several), which goal or subgoal to address next, whether to reduce a new subgoal or to apply a previously selected operator whose preconditions are satisfied, what objects in the state to use as bindings of the typed variables in the operators.

The next section presents formally this search algorithm including the procedure for backtracking when a failure is encountered. To precede that formal description, Figure 3.6 shows the skeleton of NoLimit's search algorithm without presenting details on the actions to take upon failure.

---

1. Check if the goal statement is true in the current state, or there is a reason to suspend the current search path.

   If yes, then either return the final plan or backtrack.

2. Compute the *set* of *pending goals* $\mathcal{G}$, and the set of possible *applicable operators* $\mathcal{A}$.

3. Choose a goal G from $\mathcal{G}$ or select an operator A from $\mathcal{A}$ that is directly applicable.

4. If G has been chosen, then

   • *expand goal* G, i.e., get the set $\mathcal{O}$ of *relevant instantiated operators* for the goal G,
   • choose an operator O from $\mathcal{O}$,
   • go to step 1.

5. If an operator A has been selected as directly applicable, then

   • *apply* A,
   • go to step 1.

Figure 3.6: A skeleton of NoLimit's search algorithm.

Step 1 of the algorithm checks whether the user given goal statement is true in the current state. If this is the case, then the system has reached a solution to the problem. NoLimit can run in *multiple-solutions* mode, where NoLimit shows each solution found and continues searching for more solutions, which it groups into *buckets* of solutions. Each *bucket* has different solutions that use the same set of plan steps (instantiated operators).

Step 2 computes the set of pending goals. A goal is *pending* iff it is a precondition of a *chosen* operator that is not true in the state. The *subgoaling* branch of the algorithm continues, by choosing, at step 3, a goal from the set of pending goals. The problem solver *expands* this goal by getting the set of *instantiated operators* that are relevant to it (step 4). NoLimit now *commits* to a relevant operator. This means that the goal just being expanded is to be achieved by applying this *chosen* operator.

Step 2 further determines the set of *applicable* operators. An operator is *applicable* iff all its preconditions are true in the state. (Note that the procedure can apply several operators in sequence by repeatedly performing step 5 in case there are multiple applicable operators. Such situations occur when, fulfilling a subgoal, satisfies the preconditions of more than one pending operator.) The *applying* branch continues by choosing to apply this operator at step 3, and applying it at step 5, by updating the state. The problem solver may choose to defer the application of an operator if the effects of the operator invalidate the achievement of other pending goals.

This schematic description shows that a search path is a sequence of decisions on goals, operators, and applied operators. A search path is therefore defined by the following regular expression: (*goal chosen-operator applied-operator**)*.

The next section formalizes the search tree, the search and the backtracking procedures. The full analogical problem solver is an extension of this basic problem solver as we will describe in the subsequent chapters of the book. The formalization below facilitates the presentation of these extensions, namely in the problem solving introspection and annotation capability (see chapter 4) and in the replay mechanism (see chapter 7).

3.3 Formal problem solving procedure

The problem solving procedure is a sequence of decisions made while searching for a solution to a given problem. Decisions correspond to *search nodes* organized in a *search tree*.

Let a **problem solving state** $\mathcal{S}$ be the pair (S, T), where:

- S is the state of the world,

- and T is the search tree already expanded.

The *search tree* T is represented as a directed acyclic graph $T = (N, E)$ [Aho *et al.*, 1974]. The set of nodes N represents the set of choices made along the search and the edges capture the sequence of decisions made. The search tree has the following properties:

- A search node $n \in N$ can be either a *goal node* $g \in G$, a *chosen operator node* $o \in O$, or an *applied operator node* $a \in A$: $N = G \cup O \cup A$, and A, G and O are mutually disjoint.

- There is only one node with no incident edges, the root, which is called the *start goal node*, $n_0 \in G$; $n_0 = $ (done).

- n_0 has only one child, called the *start operator node*, $n_1 \in O$; $n_1 = $(*finish*).

- Every node $n \in N$, except n_0 has exactly one incident edge.

- A *search path* P is a path in the tree, i.e., $P = (n_0, n_1, \ldots, n_k)$, iff $(n_i, n_j) \in E$, $i = 0, \ldots, k - 1, j = 1, \ldots, k$. P is of length $k + 1$. There is a unique search path from the root to every node in the tree.

Another set of facts follows from the problem solving cycle as presented in Figure 3.6:[3]

- A *search path* P is an ordered sequence of search nodes satisfying the following regular expression: $(g \; o \; a^*)^*$.

- A search node $n \in N$ can be either an *active, failed,* or *suspended* node. Let $\mathcal{A}_N, \mathcal{F}_N, \mathcal{S}_N$ be respectively the set of active, failed and suspended nodes of a tree. Then $N = \mathcal{A}_N \cup \mathcal{F}_N \cup \mathcal{S}_N$, and $\mathcal{A}_N, \mathcal{F}_N$, and $\mathcal{S}_N$ are mutually disjoint.

- For each search tree T, there is a unique *active leaf node, act,* i.e., $\exists^1 \; n \in N : (n \in \mathcal{A}_N) \wedge (n \text{ is a leaf})$. This such unique n is the active leaf, *act.*

- The *active search path,* $\mathcal{P}$, is the unique path from the root, n_0, to *act.*

- A node is active if it is in the active search path, i.e., $\forall n \in N : (n \in \mathcal{P}) \Rightarrow (n \in \mathcal{A}_N)$.

The problem solving procedure generates a sequence of problem solving steps. The **problem solving step** function, *step,* maps problem solving states into problem solving states, i.e., *step*: $S \times T \rightarrow S \times T$. Figure 3.7 defines the stepping procedure executed by the problem solver.

The problem solving procedure walks through the search tree in two main phases, namely **expanding** and **exploring** the search space:

Expand : Generate the children of the active leaf node *act*; These children represent the possible next steps in the search procedure (step 1).

Explore : Choose the new step from the set of possible ones; The search procedure terminates successfully (step 10) when all the goals are achieved. The active search path may be pursued (step 15), or backtracking is required in situations where the choices made lead to failures (steps 3 and 12).

Figure 3.8 describes the first of these phases, namely the procedure to generate children for the different kinds of search nodes.

According to the fact that a search path is a sequence of nodes $(g \; o \; a^*)^*$ the child of a goal node g is an operator node o. Step 4 of the procedure in Figure 3.8 calls a procedure to compute all the possible children operator nodes. **Compute_Relevant_Instantiated_Operators** (*act*, T, $\mathcal{D}$) identifies the operators (or/and inference rules) that have an effect that unifies with the goal at the active goal node, *act.* These operators are the relevant operators to the goal. This means that if when applied their effects are such that the goal

---

[3] These facts are declarative and their procedural meaning is described by the problem solving algorithms presented next.

Input : A search tree $T = (N, E)$, sets $\mathcal{A}_N, \mathcal{F}_N, \mathcal{S}_N$ of the active, failed, and suspended search tree nodes, and act, the active leaf node.;

Output : An expanded search tree $T' = (N', E')$, new sets $\mathcal{A}_{N'}, \mathcal{F}_{N'}, \mathcal{S}_{N'}$ of the new active, failed, and suspended search tree nodes, and a new active leaf node.

procedure **Problem_Solving_Step** $(N, E, \mathcal{A}_N, F_N, S_N, act)$:
1. $children\_set \leftarrow$ **Generate_Children** (T, act)
2. if $children\_set = \emptyset$
    then
3.   Return **Backtrack_Path** $(N, E, \mathcal{A}_N, \mathcal{F}_N, \mathcal{S}_N, act,$
        no-choices, $children\_set)$
    else
4. $N' = N \cup children\_set$
5. $E' = E \cup \{(act, n) : n \in children\_set\}$
6. $T' = (N', E')$
7. $termination\_reason \leftarrow$ **Check_Termination_Reason** $(\mathcal{A}_N, act)$
8.   case $termination\_reason$
9.   success
10.   Return **Success** $(N, E, \mathcal{A}_N, \mathcal{F}_N, \mathcal{S}_N, act)$
11.   failure
12.   Return **Backtrack_Path** $(N, E, \mathcal{A}_N, \mathcal{F}_N, \mathcal{S}_N \cup children\_set, act,$
        $termination\_reason, \emptyset)$
13.   otherwise
14. $S'_N = S_N \cup children\_set$
15.   Return **Pursue_Active_Search_Path** $(act, children\_set, T')$

Figure 3.7: Problem solving stepping.

is achieved, i.e., it becomes true in the new state. The implementation of this procedure involves the development of matching and unification techniques.[4]

Once again according to the sequence of nodes $(g \ o \ a^*)^*$, for each search path, the child of an operator o or of an applied operator a is either a goal node or an applied operator. Step 6 of the procedure in Figure 3.8 calls a procedure to compute the set of pending goals. In the active search path, the active operator nodes correspond to the operators that were not yet applied to the state. **Compute_Pending_Goals** (act, T) identifies all the preconditions of that set of active operator nodes that are not true in the current state. This is the new set of pending goals, i.e., the set of goals that must be achieved in order that the chosen operators may be applied. The procedure **Identify_Applicable_Operators** (act, T) at step 7 identifies the applicable operators from the set of active operator nodes. An operator is applicable iff all of its preconditions are true in

---

[4] A recent research effort in the PRODIGY group focuses on developing efficient matching algorithms [Wang, 1992].

Input : A search tree $T = (N, E)$, the active leaf node *act*.

Output : A set of the search children available.

procedure **Generate_Children** (T, act):

1. $\mathcal{D}$ ← the domain theory.
2. case *act*
3.   goal node
4.   Return **Compute_Relevant_Instantiated_Operators** $(act, T, \mathcal{D})$
5.   otherwise
6.   *pending_goals_set* ← **Compute_Pending_Goals** (act, T)
7.   *applicable_operators_set* ← **Identify_Applicable_Operators** (act, T)
8.   Return *pending_goals_set* ∪ *applicable_operators_set*

Figure 3.8: Generating the children for a problem solving search tree.

the state. The set of pending goals and applicable operators is returned as the children nodes for the problem solving active search leaf.

Figure 3.9 shows the procedure to commit to a new choice from the set of generated children. This choice is controlled by the control knowledge available. This is encapsulated in the call to the procedure **Controlled_Choice**. The extended analogical problem solver considers the guiding cases for the controlled decisions in addition to (or instead of) control rules.

The control knowledge available may reduce the set of possible choices to the empty set. In this situation backtracking is needed as the search cannot be pursued further from this point. The next section describes the failing and backtracking procedure. Section 3.3.2 discusses the controlled decision making procedure.

3.3.1 Failing and backtracking

A cause for failure is reaching a subgoal that is unachievable for lack of relevant operators, in which case the path fails and is abandoned.

In addition NoLimit considers other failures that propose abandoning a search path. The two main ones follow:

- Goal loop - If a subgoal is generated that is still pending earlier in the path, then a goal loop is recognized.

- State loop - If applying an operator generates a world state that was previously visited, then a state loop is recognized.

Figure 3.10 describes the procedure to backtrack in a particular search path. The problem solver uses a default chronological backtracking strategy that can be overwritten by specific backtracking control guidance.

. When there are no relevant operators, step 3 shows that NoLimit backtracks directly to the operator that requires the current active goal as a precondition.

Input : A search tree $T = (N, E)$, the active leaf node *act*, and the set
  of children nodes, *children_set* returned by **Generate_Children**.

Output : An expanded search tree $T' = (N', E')$, new sets $\mathcal{A}_{N'}, \mathcal{F}_{N'}, \mathcal{S}_{N'}$ of
  the new active, failed, and suspended search tree nodes, and a new
  active leaf node.

procedure **Pursue_Active_Search_Path** (*act*, *children_set*, T):
1. case *act*
2.   goal node
3.   *new_active_leaf* ← **Controlled_Choice** (**operator**, *children_set*,T)
4.   otherwise
5.   *applicable_ops* ← $\{n \in children\_set$: n is an applicable operator node$\}$
6.   *pending_goals* ← $\{n \in children\_set$: n is a goal node$\}$
7.   if *applicable_ops* $\neq \emptyset$
          then
8.   *apply_or_subgoal* ← **Controlled_Choice** (**apply_or_subgoal**,
            children_set, T)
9.   case *apply_or_subgoal*
10.   apply
11.   *new_active_leaf* ← **Controlled_Choice** (**apply**, *children_set*, T)
12.   **Apply_Operator** (*new_active_leaf*)
13.   subgoal
14.   *new_active_leaf* ← **Controlled_Choice** (**goal**, *children_set*, T)
          else
15.   *new_active_leaf* ← **Controlled_Choice** (**goal**, *children_set*, T)
16. if *new_active_leaf*
17.   then **Update_Node_Status** (*new_active_leaf*, T)
18.   else **Backtrack_Path** (T, *act*, $\emptyset$)

Figure 3.9: Committing in the active search path.

In fact the procedure **Backtrack_to_Dependent_Op** is more careful in finding
the correct backtracking point. If an applied operator node is found in the
search path that is responsible for the deletion of the current goal literal from
the state, then the algorithm considers the choices alternative to applying the
deleting operator. The default backtracking strategy otherwise is chronological
backtracking. However NoLimit has the ability to call *backtracking* control
rules – step 5 – that accept (or reject) a particular backtracking point as a good
(or bad) one, thus performing a better allocation of resources (bindings) and
permitting dependency-directed backtracking or other disciplines that override
the chronological backtracking default. When a backtracking choice point is
found, an alternative choice is considered and the search proceeds exploring this
new alternative.

Input : A search tree $T = (N, E)$, the sets $\mathcal{A}_N$, $\mathcal{F}_N$, $\mathcal{S}_N$ of the active, failed, and suspended search tree nodes, the active leaf node *act*, the *termination_reason* that caused the backtracking procedure to be invoked, and the *children_set* of *act*.

Output : An expanded search tree $T' = (N', E')$, new sets $\mathcal{A}_{N'}, \mathcal{F}_{N'}, \mathcal{S}_{N'}$ of the new active, failed, and suspended search tree nodes, and a new active leaf node.

procedure **Backtrack_Path** $(N, E, \mathcal{A}_N, \mathcal{F}_N, \mathcal{S}_N,, \; act,$
              termination_reason, children_set)

1. case *termination_reason*
2.   *no-relevant-operators*
3.   *new_active_leaf* ← **Backtrack_to_Dependent_Op** (*act, T*)
4.   otherwise
5.   *new_active_leaf* ← **Controlled_Backtrack** (*act, T*)
6. if *new_active_leaf*
   then
7. $\mathcal{A}_{N'} = \{n: n$ is in the path from the root to *new_active_leaf*\}
8. $\mathcal{F}_{N'} = \mathcal{F}_N \cup children\_set \cup (\mathcal{A}_N \setminus \mathcal{A}_{N'})$
9. $\mathcal{S}_{N'} = \mathcal{S}_N \setminus \{new\_active\_leaf\}$
   else
10.   **Exhaustive_Search_Failure**

Figure 3.10: Backtracking in a search path of a problem solving search tree.

3.3.2   Control knowledge

The search algorithm involves several choice points, namely:

- What *goal* to subgoal, choosing it from the set of pending goals – steps 14, 15, Fig. 3.9.

- What *operator* to choose in pursuit of the particular goal selected – step 3, Fig. 3.9.

- What *bindings* to choose to instantiate the selected operator – step 3, Fig. 3.9.

- Whether to *apply* an applicable operator or defer application and continue *subgoaling* on a pending goal – step 8, Fig. 3.9.

- Whether the search path being explored should be *suspended*, continued, or abandoned – step 7, Fig. 3.7.

- Upon failure, which *past choice point* to backtrack to, or which *suspended path* to reconsider for further search – steps 3 and 5, Fig. 3.10.

Decisions at all these choices are taken based on user-given or learned control knowledge to guide the casual commitment search. Control knowledge can *select, reject, prefer,* or *decide* on the choice of alternatives [Minton *et al.*, 1989, Veloso, 1989]. This knowledge guides the search process and helps to reduce the exponential explosion in the size of the search space. Previous work in the linear planner of PRODIGY uses explanation-based learning techniques [Minton, 1988a] to extract from a problem solving trace the explanation chain responsible for a success or failure and compile search control rules therefrom. We develop instead a case-based approach that consists of storing individual problems solved in the past to guide all the decision choice points when solving similar new problems. The machine learning and knowledge acquisition work supports No LIMIT's casual-commitment method, as it assumes there is *intelligent* control knowledge, exterior to its search cycle, that it can rely upon to take decisions.

3.4 An example: a *one-way-rocket* problem

The example below shows how No LIMIT searches for a solution to the *one-way-rocket* problem introduced earlier (see Figures 3.3 and 3.4) tracing the expansion of the search tree.

Figure 3.11 shows an actual trace output by No LIMIT. Operators in uppercase correspond to the applied operator nodes. The annotations "ops-left", "goals-left", and "applicable-ops-left" refer to the alternative choices still left to pursue at the corresponding search level. When several alternatives are available one was selected randomly, as no other specific control knowledge was provided.

The trace shows that three search paths are explored. The first search path (with 11 nodes, `tn1` through `tn11`) fails due to a goal loop encountered when trying to work on the operator (`load-rocket obj1 locB`). This goal loop is encountered by the procedure **Check_Termination_Reason** (see step 7 in Figure 3.7). This failure results in calling the procedure **Backtrack_Path**, which in the absence of any backtracking control knowledge, backtracks chronologically to the alternative (`load-rocket obj1 locA`) (see step 11 of the second search path). This operator has the precondition (`at rocket locA`) that becomes now a subgoal as it is no longer true in the state because the operator (`MOVE-ROCKET`) was applied at step 9. There is however no operator that adds that goal to the state which means that **Generate_Children** returns the empty set. The backtracking procedure is called again. This time, as the termination reason is known to be that there are no relevant operators for the goal, the procedure backtracks directly to the step that deleted that goal (see steps 2-3 in Figure 3.10). At step 8 of the third and last search path explored the application of the operator (`MOVE-ROCKET`) is postponed and the search terminates successfully.

To illustrate the formalization, we consider two points in the search procedure and instantiate the concepts introduced.

```
<cl> (nlrun-prob 'rocket-2objs)              11. tn12 (load-rocket obj1 locA)
****************************                      ***
Solving the problem rocket-2objs:            12. tn13 (at rocket locA)
 Initial state :                                     goals-left: ((inside obj2 rocket))
  ((at obj1 locA) (at obj2 locA)              ***
   (at rocket locA))
Goal statement:                              FAILURE - no relevant operators
 (and (at obj1 locB) (at obj2 locB))         ****************************
****************************                  Starting a new search path
Starting a search path
                                              1. tn1 (done)
 1. tn1 (done)                                2. tn2 (*finish*)
 2. tn2 (*finish*)                            3. tn3 (at obj1 locB)
 3. tn3 (at obj1 locB)                            goals-left: ((at obj2 locB))
     goals-left: ((at obj2 locB))             4. tn4 (unload-rocket obj1 locB)
 4. tn4 (unload-rocket obj1 locB)             5. tn5 (at obj2 locB)
 5. tn5 (at obj2 locB)                            goals-left: ((at rocket locB))
     goals-left: ((at rocket locB))           6. tn6 (unload-rocket obj2 locB)
 6. tn6 (unload-rocket obj2 locB)             7. tn7 (at rocket locB)
 7. tn7 (at rocket locB)                          goals-left: ((inside obj1 rocket)
     goals-left: ((inside obj1 rocket)                       (inside obj2 rocket))
                  (inside obj2 rocket))       8. tn8 (move-rocket)
 8. tn8 (move-rocket)                         ***
 9. tn9 (MOVE-ROCKET)                         9. tn14 (inside obj1 rocket)
     goals-left: ((inside obj1 rocket)            goals-left: ((inside obj2 rocket))
                  (inside obj2 rocket))      10. tn15 (load-rocket obj1 locA)
10. tn10 (inside obj1 rocket)                     ops-left: ((load-rocket obj1 locB))
     goals-left: ((inside obj2 rocket))      11. tn16 (LOAD-ROCKET obj1 locA)
11. tn11 (load-rocket obj1 locB)                  goals-left: ((inside obj2 rocket))
     ops-left: ((load-rocket obj1 locA))          applicable-ops-left: (move-rocket)
***                                          12. tn17 (inside obj2 rocket)
                                                  applicable-ops-left: (move-rocket)
                                             13. tn18 (load-rocket obj2 locA)
FAILURE - goals in loop:                          ops-left: ((load-rocket obj2 locB))
        ((at obj1 locB))                     14. tn19 (LOAD-ROCKET obj2 locA)
****************************                       applicable-ops-left: (move-rocket)
Starting a new search path                   15. tn20 (MOVE-ROCKET)
                                             16. tn21 (UNLOAD-ROCKET obj2 locB)
 1. tn1 (done)                               17. tn22 (UNLOAD-ROCKET obj1 locB)
 2. tn2 (*finish*)                           18. tn23 (*FINISH*)
 3. tn3 (at obj1 locB)
     goals-left: ((at obj2 locB))
 4. tn4 (unload-rocket obj1 locB)                ****************************
 5. tn5 (at obj2 locB)                           This is the solution found:
     goals-left: ((at rocket locB))
 6. tn6 (unload-rocket obj2 locB)                    (LOAD-ROCKET obj1 locA)
 7. tn7 (at rocket locB)                             (LOAD-ROCKET obj2 locA)
     goals-left: ((inside obj1 rocket)              (MOVE-ROCKET)
                  (inside obj2 rocket))              (UNLOAD-ROCKET obj2 locB)
 8. tn8 (move-rocket)                                (UNLOAD-ROCKET obj1 locB)
 9. tn9 (MOVE-ROCKET)                                (*FINISH*)
     goals-left: ((inside obj1 rocket)     nil
                  (inside obj2 rocket))     <cl>
10. tn10 (inside obj1 rocket)
     goals-left: ((inside obj2 rocket))
```

Figure 3.11: Tracing NoLimit solving the *one-way-rocket* problem.

Step 8 of the first search path:

- The problem solving state $\mathcal{S}_8$ is the pair (S_8, T_8), where S_8 is the state of the world, and T_8 is the expanded search tree

  $S_8 = \{(\texttt{at obj1 locA}), (\texttt{at obj2 locA}), (\texttt{at rocket locA})\}$, and

  $T_8 = (N_8, E_8)$, where

  > $N_8 = \{\texttt{tn1, tn2, tn3, tn4, tn5, tn6, tn7, tn8}\} \cup \{\texttt{tn3}_1, \texttt{tn5}_1,$
  > $\texttt{tn7}_1, \texttt{tn7}_2\}$, where $\texttt{tni}_j$ are the unexplored alternatives at the
  > nodes $\texttt{tni}$, respectively, e.g., $\texttt{tn5}_1 = (\texttt{at rocket locB})$.
  > $E_8 = \{(\texttt{tni},\texttt{tnj}), \text{i}= 1,\ldots,7, \text{j}= 2,\ldots,8\}$

- G_8, O_8, A_8 are the sets of goal, chosen operator, and applied operator nodes:

  $G_8 = \{\texttt{tn1, tn3, tn5, tn7}, \texttt{tn3}_1, \texttt{tn5}_1, \texttt{tn7}_1, \texttt{tn7}_2\}$

  $O_8 = \{\texttt{tn2, tn4, tn6, tn8}\}$

  $A_8 = \emptyset$

- $\mathcal{A}_{N_8}, \mathcal{F}_{N_8}, \mathcal{S}_{N_8}$ are the sets of active, failed, and suspended search nodes respectively, in the search tree T_8:

  $\mathcal{A}_{N_8} = \{\texttt{tn1, tn2, tn3, tn4, tn5, tn6, tn7, tn8}\}$

  $\mathcal{F}_{N_8} = \emptyset$

  $\mathcal{S}_{N_8} = \{\texttt{tn3}_1, \texttt{tn5}_1, \texttt{tn7}_1, \texttt{tn7}_2\}$

- $act = \texttt{tn8}$, the active leaf.

Given this particular problem solving state, the following sequence of procedure calls takes place, according to the **Problem_Solving_Step** procedure in Figure 3.7:

> **Generate_Children**(T_8,tn8) returns $\{\texttt{tn9},\texttt{tn9}_1, \texttt{tn9}_2\}$, with $\texttt{tn9} = $ (MOVE-ROCKET), $\texttt{tn9}_1 = $ (inside obj1 rocket), $\texttt{tn9}_2 = $ (inside obj2 rocket).

> **Pursue_Active_Search_Path**(tn8,$\{\texttt{tn9},\texttt{tn9}_1, \texttt{tn9}_2\}$,$T_8'$) returns the new active leaf **tn9** corresponding to the choice of applying the operator (MOVE-ROCKET) instead of continuing subgoaling on one of the alternative pending goals $\texttt{tn9}_1$, or $\texttt{tn9}_2$.

After the operator (MOVE-ROCKET) is applied at step 9, the problem solving state changes accordingly and the search tree parameters of the new search tree follow.

Step 9 of the first search path:

- The problem solving state $\mathcal{S}_9$ is the pair S_9, T_9, where S_9 is the state of the world, and T_9 is the expanded search tree

  $S_9 = \{$(at obj1 locA), (at obj2 locA), (at rocket locB)$\}$, and
  $T_9 = (N_9, E_9)$, where

      $N_9 = \{$tn1, tn2, tn3, tn4, tn5, tn6, tn7, tn8, tn9$\} \cup \{$tn3$_1$, tn5$_1$, tn7$_1$, tn7$_2$, tn9$_1$, tn9$_2\}$
      $E_9 = \{$(tni,tnj), i$= 1,\ldots,8$, j$= 2,\ldots,9\}$

- G_9, O_9, A_9 are the sets of goal, chosen operator, and applied operator nodes:

  $G_9 = \{$tn1, tn3, tn5, tn7, tn3$_1$, tn5$_1$, tn7$_1$, tn7$_2$, tn9$_1$, tn9$_2\}$
  $O_9 = \{$tn2, tn4, tn6, tn8$\}$
  $A_9 = \{$tn9$\}$

- $A_{N_9}, \mathcal{F}_{N_9}, \mathcal{S}_{N_9}$ are the sets of active, failed, and suspended search nodes respectively, in the search tree T_9:

  $A_{N_9} = \{$tn1, tn2, tn3, tn4, tn5, tn6, tn9$\}$
  $\mathcal{F}_{N_9} = \emptyset$
  $\mathcal{S}_{N_9} = \{$tn3$_1$, tn5$_1$, tn7$_1$, tn7$_2$ tn9$_1$, tn9$_2\}$

- $act = $ tn9, the active leaf.

The state changes and the nodes **tn7** and **tn8** are no longer active as the operator (**MOVE-ROCKET**) (chosen at **tn8**) is applied at **tn9**, achieving the goal (at rocket locB) at the node **tn7**. The computation of the new set of pending goals does not consider the operator **tn8** any longer as an active node. Similarly the check for a goal loop does not consider the goal **tn7** being therefore viable to subgoal more than once on the same goal in the same search path.

Figure 3.12 shows the same problem solving episode of Figure 3.11 as a search tree. It shows only the children nodes explored that succeed and fail. The children left untried are not shown in this figure, but can be seen in the trace of Figure 3.11. Note that NoLimit solves this problem, where linear planners fail (but where of course other nonlinear planners also succeed), because it switches attention among goals in the goal set. An example of this is when at step 5 NoLimit switches attention to the conjunctive goal (at obj2 locB) before completing the first conjunct (at obj1 locB). The final solution shows that the complete subplans for the each of the two given conjunctive goals are interleaved and cannot be organized in strict linear sequence. NoLimit explores the space of possible attention foci and only after backtracking does it find the correct goal interleaving. The machine learning research in PRODIGY explores methods to automatically learn from the problem solving experience and reduce search dramatically, converting automatically the problem solver into an expert one.

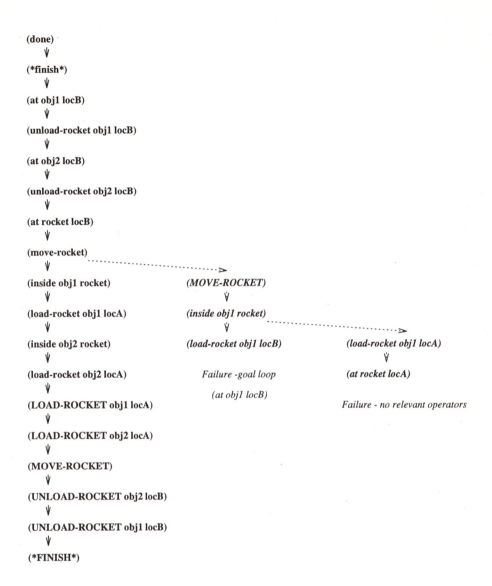

Figure 3.12: The search episode of Figure 3.11 represented as a search tree.

3.5   Summary

NoLimit is a completely implemented nonlinear planner that uses an intelligent casual-commitment strategy to guide its search process. The casual-commitment method used to achieve its nonlinear character is in contrast to the least-commitment strategy used in other nonlinear planners. NoLimit has the ability to call user-given or automatically acquired control knowledge in the form of control rules or guiding cases at all its choice points. The subsequent chapters of this book describe the extensions of NoLimit into an analogical problem solver that replays past problem solving episodes.

Chapter 4

Generation of Problem Solving Cases

In general, problem solvers and planners perform search for a solution to a problem situation, generating and exploring a large space of alternatives. The choices made and the reasons why they succeed or fail are the learning opportunities to any problem solver, in particular also to NoLimit, the nonlinear problem solver we developed for the PRODIGY architecture [Veloso, 1989]. Derivational analogy captures the rationale and dependency structure underlying the solution found. The reasoning links among the search steps are remembered and reused in addition to the final solution.

This chapter describes how the nonlinear problem solving algorithm is augmented to generate problem solving *cases* to be stored and reused from the derivational traces of the problem solving search experience. Section 1 discusses the question of what to remember and save from a problem solving episode. Section 2 presents formally the procedure to annotate the search nodes while searching for a solution. Section 3 illustrates the generation of a case with an example from the extended-STRIPS domain. Finally Section 4 draws a summary of the chapter.

4.1 Annotating the search path

While searching for a solution to a problem situation, the problem solver explores a very large search space where different alternatives are generated, some failing and others succeeding. The crucial question is what to preserve from the problem solving search episode in order to reconstruct (parts of) the solution in future similar situations. The two extreme options are to remember only the final solution or the complete search tree. While the latter option is too expensive to be pursued, there are several approaches that follow the former one. Transformational analogy [Carbonell, 1983] and most case-based reasoning systems (as summarized in [Riesbeck and Schank, 1989]) replay past solutions by modifying directly a solution to a similar past problem. The adaptation is based on the differences recognized between the past and the current new problem. However a final solution represents a sequence of operators that correspond only to a particular successful search path. A more general approach involving partial replay and multiple-solution merging requires additional structure pertaining to dependencies among the steps in the solution. Derivational analogy aims at capturing the rationale and dependency structure underlying the solution encountered. This implies that the reasoning links among the search steps are remembered in addition to the final solution. As the analogical paradigm involves reusing the past problem solving experience to guide new problem solving episodes by reducing the level of search needed, the following two main concerns determine what is preserved from the search tree:

1. The search information retained must respond to what is needed to know at replay time in order to reduce search: At replay time the problem solver needs guidance for making choices.

2. The cost of capturing the rationale must be low, i.e., no complex computation such as proof-based eager explanation efforts are needed. Retain therefore what is *naturally* known at search time.

To comply with these concerns, the problem solver must:

- Identify the decision points in the search procedure where guidance may prove useful to provide memory of the justifications for the choices made. (All decisions in the "glass-box" PRODIGY architecture.)

- Use a clear "language" to capture these justifications at search time and associate a meaning so that they can be used at replay time.

- Explain the underlying rationale following a minimal effort approach. No costly attempt is made to infer generalized behavior from a unique problem solving trace.

The problem solver is hence extended with the ability to identify and to record the reasons for the decisions taken at the different choice points encountered while searching for a solution. The justifications compiled at each decision point are annotated at the different steps of the successful path. When replaying a solution, the derivational analogy engine can then reconstruct the reasoning process underlying the past solution. Justifications are tested to determine whether modifications are needed, and when they are needed, justifications provide constraints on possible alternatives search paths (see Chapter 7).

4.1.1 The decision points at problem solving

Each search node in the problem solving search tree, as introduced in Chapter 3, is a decision node. The choice at each node is the result of answering the choice points identified in Section 3.3.2.

Given a goal search node, the questions on the reasons why this goal is pursued are:

- Who needs this goal, i.e., this goal is a *precondition* of which operator(s)?

- Why is this particular goal chosen out of the set of other *sibling* or alternative choices available, if any?

- Why subgoal on this goal, instead of applying an available applicable operator (in pursuit of some different goal), if any are applicable?

- Were any of the alternative choices tried in the search that later failed? Why did the problem solver abandon those paths? What were the reasons for the eventual failures?

Similarly for a chosen operator node, the questions on the reasons why a particular operator is chosen are:

- Who needs this operator? Which goal is this operator relevant to, i.e., if this operator is applied, which of its effects matched a pending goal?

- Why choosing this particular operator out of the set of other *sibling* or alternative operators available, if any?

- Were any of the alternative choices tried in the search? Why did the problem solver abandon those paths? What were the reasons for the eventual failures?

Finally for a particular applied operator node, the questions on the reasons why this operator is applied are:

- Why applying this particular operator out of the set of other *sibling* or alternative choices available (other applicable operators, or other goals to pursue), if any?

- Why apply this operator, instead of subgoaling in other pending goals, if any?

- Were any of the alternative choices tried in the search? Why did the problem solver abandon those paths? What were the reasons for the eventual failures?

The problem solver is extended with the ability to capture the answers to these questions, i.e., the justifications on why the choices are made. Justifications at these choice points may point to user-given guidance, to preprogrammed control knowledge, to automatically-learned control rules responsible for decisions taken, to past cases used as guidance, or simply to search tree topology (e.g., only choice, arbitrary choice, last choice left, etc). They also represent links within the different choices and their related generators, in particular capturing the subgoaling structure. At choice points, the system records the failed alternatives and the cause of their failure by enumerating the reasons for abandoning the leaves of the subtrees rooted at the failed alternative. The next section shows the augmented structure of the decision nodes that allows the problem solver to annotate the justifications.

4.1.2   Justification structures at decision nodes

Figure 4.1 shows the skeleton of the different decision nodes. The different justification slots capture the context in which the decision is taken and the reasons that support the choice.

```
Goal Node                    Chosen Op Node               Applied Op Node
 :choice                      :choice                      :choice
 :sibling-goals               :sibling-relevant-ops         :sibling-goals
 :sibling-applicable-ops      :why-this-operator           :sibling-applicable-ops
 :why-subgoal                 :relevant-to                 :why-apply
 :why-this-goal                                            :why-this-operator
 :precond-of                                               :chosen-at
                                                           :preconds
                                                           :adds
                                                           :dels
```

| (a) Goal Decision Node | (b) Chosen Operator Decision Node | (c) Applied Operator Decision Node |

Figure 4.1: Justification record structure, to be instantiated at decision points during problem solving.

The language for the justification slots and their values enables the recording of the reasons supporting the choices made and also allows the flexibility to annotate any additional external information. The *choice* slots point to the selection made, namely the selected goal or operator. The *sibling-* slots enumerate the alternatives to the choice made. At a goal node and applied operator node (see Figure 4.1 (a) and (c)), the goals left in the current set of goals still to be achieved constitute the sibling-goals annotation. For completeness the problem solver may postpone applying an operator whose preconditions are satisfied and continue subgoaling on a still unachieved goal. These possible applicable operators are the contents of the alternative *sibling-applicable-ops* slot. At a chosen operator node, the sibling operators are the possible other different instantiated operators that are also relevant to the goal being expanded, i.e., the operators that, if applied, will achieve that goal. NoLIMIT annotates the reason why these alternatives were not pursued further according to its search experience (either not tried, or abandoned due to a failure). The *why-* slots present the reasons (if any) the particular decision was made. These reasons range from arbitrary choices to specific control knowledge that dictated the selection. These reasons are tested at replay time and are interpretable by the analogical problem solver.

The subgoaling structure is captured by the slot *precond-of* at a goal node, and the slot *relevant-to* at a chosen operator node. At reconstruction time, these slots play an important role in providing information that has practically no matching cost, on one hand on the set of relevant operators for a given goal, and on the other hand, on the set of instantiated preconditions of an operator.

Finally at the applied operator node, the slots *preconds, adds* and *dels* refer respectively to the instantiated preconditions of the operator, and the literals added and deleted to the state when the operator is applied. (All variables of the applied operators are assigned specific objects in the state.) This information is useful to preserve because it may be expensive to recompute it due to the powerful expressive operator language which permits quantification on the list of preconditions and conditional effects in the list of effects. The *chosen-at* slot points to the decision node where the applied operator was initially chosen.

The problem and the generated annotated solution become a *case* in memory. The case corresponds to the search tree compacted into the successful path as a sequence of annotated decision nodes as presented in Figure 4.1. When replaying a solution, the derivational analogy engine can reconstruct the reasoning process underlying the past solution. Justifications are tested to determine whether modifications are needed, and when they are needed, justifications provide constraints on possible alternatives search paths.

4.1.3   The language

Within the fixed set of slots introduced in Figure 4.1, we designed a language to fill those slots, capturing the reasons known to the problem solver and also allowing the flexibility to annotate any additional external information. Chapter 7 discusses how this language is interpreted at replay time.

The choice slot   The value of the choice slot is either a literal representing a goal or an instantiated operator name.

Example:
```
:choice (at obj2 locB)        :choice (load-rocket obj1 locA)
```

The sibling slots   The value of these slots is a list of alternatives (either goals or operators) each one attached to a list of the failures encountered and the size of their rooted subtrees, or the annotation that they were **not-tried**. The failures refer to the situations presented in Section 3.3.1. They take values from the set {*no-relevant-ops, goal-loop,* and *state-loop*} with the corresponding goal arguments.

Example:
```
:sibling-goals (((inside obj1 rocket) not-tried 0))
:sibling-applicable-ops ((MOVE-ROCKET)
                          (:no-relevant-ops (at rocket locA))
                          (:goal-loop (at obj1 locB)) 5)
```

The subgoaling slots   The goal node slot *precond-of* is a list of pointers to the operator nodes for which this goal is one of their preconditions. The operator node slot *relevant-to* points to the goal that needs this operator to be applied in order for the goal to be achieved. (An operator may later prove to be relevant to more than one goal. However the operator is chosen as relevant to a unique

goal. The possible other goals that are achieved when the operator is applied
are seen as felicitous side effects.)

Example:

```
:precond-of (cn10 cn2)
:relevant-to cn3
```

The why slots   The values for these slots, *why-subgoal, why-this-goal, why-
apply*, and *why-this-operator* can be:

select followed by a select control rule name,

prefer followed by a prefer control rule name and the alternatives it was
    preferred over,

reject followed by a reject control rule name and the alternative that
    was rejected in favor of this one,

case followed by the case step name that suggested the selection of the
    step,

function followed by the function call and its arguments which are usu-
    ally the bindings of an instantiated operator,

why-user followed by a function given by a user that may be tested at
    replay time.

It is the *why-user* value that allows a user to dictate selections and attach
reasons for their selection.

Example:

```
:why-this-operator
  ((select operator pick-up-for-holding)
   (function (adjacent room1 room2)))
:why-this-goal (case case-test-22-3)
:why-apply (why-user (prefer-apply-p))
             (defun prefer-apply-p ()
               (if (applicable-ops-p)
                   (select decision apply)
                   (select decision subgoal)))
```

4.2   The annotation procedure

Consider that the search nodes have the structure presented in Figure 4.1. The
base level problem solver is extended with the ability to assign values to the slots
of the decision nodes schemas. The annotations are done at search time when
the justifications are available and the annotation procedures correspond only
to additional bookkeeping. There is therefore a negligible effective time cost in
extending the search procedures with that capability.

4.2.1   Annotating the subgoaling structure

Figure 4.2 extends the base level procedure **Pursue_Active_Search_Path** as introduced in Figure 3.9.

Input :   A search tree $T = (N, E)$, the active leaf node act, and the set of children nodes, $children\_set$ returned by **Generate_Children**.

Output :   A new active leaf node. As a side effect it annotates the pertinent search nodes with the reasons for the choice.

procedure **Pursue_Active_Search_Path** (act, $children\_set$, T'):
1.case act
2. goal node
3. $new\_active\_leaf \leftarrow$ **Controlled_Choice** (operator, $children\_set, T'$)

> 3a. **sibling-relevant-ops** (new_active_leaf) $\leftarrow children\_set \setminus \{ new\_active\_leaf \}$
> 3b. **why-this-operator** (new_active_leaf) $\leftarrow$ used-control *(operator, bindings)*
> 3c. **relevant-to** (new_active_leaf) $\leftarrow act$

4. otherwise
5. $applicable\_ops \leftarrow \{n \in children\_set$: n is an applicable operator $\}$
6. $pending\_goals \leftarrow \{n \in children\_set$: n is a goal $\}$
7.   if $applicable\_ops \neq \emptyset$
8. $apply\_or\_subgoal \leftarrow$ **Controlled_Choice** (apply_or_subgoal, $children\_set$, T)
9.   case $apply\_or\_subgoal$
10.   apply
11. $new\_active\_leaf \leftarrow$ **Controlled_Choice** (apply, $children\_set$, T')
12.   **Apply_Operator** (new_active_leaf)

> 12a.   **sibling-goals** (new_active_leaf) $\leftarrow pending\_goals$
> 12b.   **sibling-applicable-ops** (new_active_leaf) $\leftarrow$
> $applicable\_ops \setminus \{new\_active\_leaf\}$
> 12c.   **why-apply** (new_active_leaf) $\leftarrow$ used-control *(apply-or-subgoal)*
> 12d.   **why-this-operator** (new_active_leaf) $\leftarrow$ used-control *(applied-operator)*
> 12e.   **preconds** (new_active_leaf) $\leftarrow$ get-preconds-slot
> 12f.   **adds** (new_active_leaf) $\leftarrow$ new-state $\setminus$ old-state
> 12g.   **dels** (new_active_leaf) $\leftarrow$ old-state $\setminus$ new-state

13.   subgoal
14. $new\_active\_leaf \leftarrow$ **Controlled_Choice** (goal, $children\_set$, T')
15.   else $new\_active\_leaf \leftarrow$ **Controlled_Choice** (goal, $children\_set$, T')

> 15a. if is-a new_active_leaf goal node
> 15b. then **sibling-goals** (new_active_leaf) $\leftarrow pending\_goals \setminus \{new\_active\_leaf\}$
> 15c.   **sibling-applicable-ops** (new_active_leaf) $\leftarrow applicable\_ops$
> 15d.   **why-subgoal** (new_active_leaf) $\leftarrow$ used-control *(apply-or-subgoal)*
> 15e.   **why-this-goal** (new_active_leaf) $\leftarrow$ used-control *(goal)*
> 15f.   **relevant-to** (new_active_leaf) $\leftarrow$ needing-active-operators (new_active_leaf)

16.if new_active_leaf
17.   then **Update_Node_Status** (new_active_leaf, T')
18.   else **Backtrack_Path** (T', act,$\emptyset$)

Figure 4.2: Annotating the justifications at the search decision nodes.

As presented in Section 3.3, this procedure is responsible for committing to a new active search node selected from a set of possible children nodes. This procedure has access at search time to the reasons why decisions are made and particular search directions are pursued. The boxed steps as shown in Figure 4.2 correspond to the extension to the base-level algorithm. The annotations to the goal, chosen operator, and applied operator nodes are done respectively, after steps 3, 12, and 15. Steps 3a-3c, steps 12a-12g, and steps 15a-15f annotate the justifications at the chosen operator decision nodes, the applied operator nodes, and the goal decision nodes, respectively. Steps 3a, 12a-b, and 15b-c store the alternative choices; steps 3b, 12c-d, and 15d-e record the reasons why the choices are made; steps 3c, and 15f annotate the subgoaling links between the goals and operators; and steps 12e-g keep the instantiated preconditions and effects of the applied operators.

4.2.2   Annotating the failures

The backtracking procedure introduced in Figure 3.10 is called when a failure or other termination reason is encountered for some search path.

Input : A search tree $T = (N, E)$, the sets $\mathcal{A}_N$, $\mathcal{F}_N$, $\mathcal{S}_N$ of the active, failed, and suspended search tree nodes, the active leaf node *act*, the *termination_reason* that caused the backtracking procedure to be invoked, and the *children_set* of *act*.

Output : An expanded search tree $T' = (N', E')$, new sets $\mathcal{A}_{N'}, \mathcal{F}_{N'}, \mathcal{S}_{N'}$ of the new active, failed, and suspended search tree nodes, and a new active leaf node.

procedure **Backtrack_Path** $(N, E, \mathcal{A}_N, \mathcal{F}_N, \mathcal{S}_N,,$ *act,*
            termination_reason, children_set)
1. case *termination_reason*
2.   *no-relevant-operators*
3.   *new_active_leaf* ← **Backtrack_to_Dependent_Op** (*act, T*)
4.   otherwise
5.   *new_active_leaf* ← **Controlled_Backtrack** (*act, T*)
6. if *new_active_leaf*
7. then $\mathcal{A}_{N'} = \{$n: n is in the path from the root to *new_active_leaf*$\}$
8. $\mathcal{F}_{N'} = \mathcal{F}_N \cup children\_set \cup (\mathcal{A}_N \setminus \mathcal{A}_{N'})$
9. $\mathcal{S}_{N'} = \mathcal{S}_N \setminus \{new\_active\_leaf\}$

9a.   *abandoned_sibling* ← **Get_Abandoned_Sibling** (*new_active_leaf*)
9b.   *corresponding*-**sibling**-*slot* (*new_active_leaf*) ← *substitute in slot*
      (abandoned_sibling, termination_reason, size_of_failed_subtree)
      for abandoned_sibling

10.else **Exhaustive_Search_Failure**

Figure 4.3: Backtracking in a search path of a problem solving search tree with annotation of the failure reasons at the search decision nodes.

The procedure **Backtrack_Path** is extended with additional bookkeeping

to record the failure information as shown in the steps boxed after step 9 in Figure 4.3. Backtracking sets the planner's attention at a previous search node where there are other alternatives not yet explored which satisfy the constraints imposed by the backtracking control knowledge. The procedure **Get-**
_Abandoned_Sibling returns the sibling alternative corresponding to the path of the search that was just active and is now being abandoned. The termination reason is recorded in conjunction with the abandoned sibling alternative. The extended analogical problem solver also records the size of the abandoned subtree as a rough measure of the relevance of the failure.

4.3 An example in the extended-STRIPS domain

This section presents an example to illustrate some of the points of the automatic generation of an annotated case. The extended-STRIPS domain [Minton, 1988a] consists of a set of rooms connected through doors. A robot can move around between the rooms carrying or pushing objects along. Doors can be locked or unlocked. Keys to the doors lay in rooms and can be picked up by the robot.[1] Figure 4.4 shows some simplified operators used in the example to be presented. As usual, variables are in brackets and types are written in upper case.

```
(OPERATOR GO-THRU
  (params (<roomx> ROOM)
    (<roomy> (and ROOM
      (adjacent <roomx> <roomy>)))
    (<door> (and DOOR
    (connects <door> <roomx> <roomy>)]
  (preconds (and (dr-open <door>)
              (inroom robot <roomx>)]
  (effects ((del (inroom robot <roomx>))
            (add (inroom robot <roomy>))
    (if ((<obj> OBJECT)) (holding <obj>)
      ((del (inroom <obj> <roomx>))
      (add (inroom <obj> <roomy>)]
```

```
(OPERATOR GOTO-BOX
  (params ((<obj> BOX)
          (<room> ROOM)]
  (preconds (and (inroom <obj> <room>)
                (inroom robot <room>)]
  (effects ((add (next-to robot <obj>))
    (if ((<something> (or OBJECT DOOR)))
      (next-to robot <something>)
      ((del (next-to robot <something>)]
```

```
(OPERATOR OPEN-DOOR
  (params ((<room> ROOM)
          (<door> (and DOOR
          (door-to-room <door> <room>)]
  (preconds (and (inroom robot <room>)
              (door-closed <door>)
              (~ (door-locked <door>)]
  (effects ((del (door-closed <door>))
            (add (door-open <door>)]
```

```
(OPERATOR CLOSE-DOOR
  (params ((<room> ROOM)
          (<door> (and DOOR
          (door-to-room <door> <room>)]
  (preconds (and (inroom robot <room>)
              (door-open <door>)]
  (effects ((del (door-open <door>))
            (add (door-closed <door>)]
```

Figure 4.4: Some operators from the extended-STRIPS domain.

---

[1] The complete set of operators and inference rules for this domain is shown in [Carbonell *et al.*, 1992].

The operator GO-THRU moves the robot through a doorway, and the operator GOTO-OBJ puts the robot next to an object when the robot and the object are in the same room. The operators OPEN-DOOR and CLOSE-DOOR open and close a door, respectively. A door may only be open if it is unlocked.

Figure 4.5 (a) shows the initial state and (b) the goal statement of an example problem from the extended-STRIPS domain, say problem *strips2-5*. The rooms are numbered at their corners and the doors are named according to the rooms they connect. Doors may be open, closed, or locked. In particular, door24 connects the rooms 2 and 4 and is locked. The door door34 is closed and, for example, door12 is open. The number of the boxes can be inferred by the attached description of the initial state. Note that box3 is in room4. The problem solver must find a plan to reach a state where door34, connecting room3 and room4, is closed, and the robot is next to box3. The problem is simple to illustrate the complete generation of a case corresponding to a problem solving search episode.

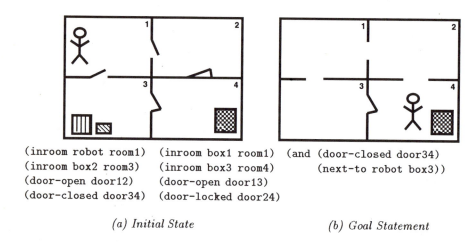

(inroom robot room1)	(inroom box1 room1) (and (door-closed door34)
(inroom box2 room3)	(inroom box3 room4) (next-to robot box3))
(door-open door12)	(door-open door13)
(door-closed door34)	(door-locked door24)

(a) Initial State   *(b) Goal Statement*

Figure 4.5: Example problem definition in the extended-STRIPS domain; The goal statement is a partial specification of the final desired state: the location of other objects and the status of other doors remains unspecified.

Without any analogical guidance (or other form of control knowledge) the problem solver searches for a solution by applying its primitive means-ends analysis procedure. Figure 4.6 shows a search tree episode to solve the problem. According to the problem solving stepping procedure discussed in Chapter 3, the search path is a sequence of goals, and operators chosen and applied. For example, node cn2 is one of the user-given goal conjuncts, namely (next-to robot box3). From the set of operators shown in Figure 4.4 the problem solver identifies and instantiates the operator (goto-box box3) as a relevant one to that goal, as shown at node cn3. This operator cannot be applied immediately as one of its preconditions is not true, namely (inroom robot room4). This precondition becomes a new goal to achieve and is chosen at node **cn4**. The search proceeds until a solution is found. The final plan is the sequence of the applied nodes of the successful search path, namely the nodes **cn8, cn11, cn12, cn15, cn16, cn17**, corresponding to the solution (GO-THRU door13), (OPEN-DOOR door34), (GO-THRU door34), (CLOSE-DOOR door34), (GOTO-BOX box3), (*FINISH*).

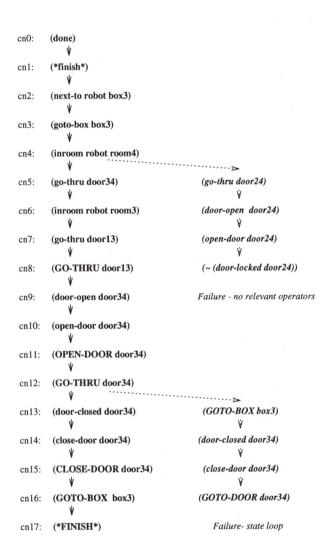

Figure 4.6: A search episode to solve the problem in Figure 4.5 represented as a search tree.

Figure 4.7 shows schematically the complete successful solution path represented in a table. For simplicity of representation, the decision nodes are annotated only with their subgoaling links.

Node type	Node number	:choice	:precond of	:relevant to
goal	cn0	(done)		
chosen-op	cn1	(*finish*)		cn0
goal	cn2	(next-to robot box3)	cn1	
chosen-op	cn3	(goto-box box3)		cn2
goal	cn4	(inroom robot room4)	cn3	
chosen-op	cn5	(go-thru door34)		cn4
goal	cn6	(inroom robot room3)	cn5	
chosen-op	cn7	(go-thru door13)		cn6
applied-op	cn8	(GO-THRU door13)		
goal	cn9	(door-open door34)	cn5	
chosen-op	cn10	(open-door door34)		cn9
applied-op	cn11	(OPEN-DOOR door34)		
applied-op	cn12	(GO-THRU door34)		
goal	cn13	(door-closed door34)	cn1	
chosen-op	cn14	(close-door door34)		cn13
applied-op	cn15	(CLOSE-DOOR door34)		
applied-op	cn16	(GOTO-BOX box3)		
applied-op	cn17	(*FINISH*)		

Figure 4.7: A simplified case corresponding to a solution to the problem in Figure 4.5; A case is an annotated successful problem solving episode.

As described above, NoLimit starts working on the goal (next-to robot box3) at node cn2, as the door34 is closed in the initial state. At node cn4, it subgoals on getting the robot into room4. Now note that both room2 and room3 are adjacent to room4. By backward chaining, NoLimit finds these two alternatives as relevant operators to the goal (inroom robot room4), namely the operators (go-thru door34), shown as node cn5, or (go-thru door24). The latter fails as shown in Figure 4.6 in the failed subtree rooted at node cn4. Figure 4.8 (a) shows the complete annotated decision node cn5 considering that NoLimit searched the alternative (go-thru door24) before pursuing the successful operator (go-thru door34). Note that door24 is locked and there is no key for it in the initial state. In the search episode this failure corresponds to a subtree off of the finally successful node cn4. The analogical reasoner creates a case by annotating the successful path with its sibling failed alternatives. It attributes the reason of a failure to the last failed leaf of the searched subtree, and also other failed leaves whose termination reasons are meaningful in the final active search path.

After this failure, NoLimit pursues its search at node cn5 as shown in Figure 4.6 and Figure 4.7. It alternates choosing the relevant operator for each goal, and applying it if all its preconditions are true in the state, or continuing subgoaling on a goal of the new goal set.

Node cn13 is also worth remarking and Figure 4.8 (b) shows its expansion. At that search point NoLimit has the alternative of immediately applying the operator (goto-box box3), as it becomes applicable as soon as robot enters

```
Chosen-operator decision node cn5          Goal decision node cn13
  :choice (go-thru door34)                   :choice (door-closed door34)
  :sibling-relevant-ops                      :sibling-goals nil
    (((go-thru door24)                       :sibling-applicable-ops
       (:no-relevant-ops                       (((GOTO-BOX box3)
         (~ (door-locked door24)))))              (:state-loop)))
  :why-this-operator                         :why-subgoal nil
    ((function (adjacent room3 room4))       :why-this-goal nil
     (function (connects door34 room3 room4)))  :precond-of cn1
  :relevant-to cn4
                                                    (b) Goal node cn13
        (a) Chosen operator node cn5
```

Figure 4.8: Zoom of some justified decision nodes.

room4 at node cn12, or subgoaling in the goal (door-closed door34) which became a goal when door34 was open at node cn11. Because NoLimit is a nonlinear planner with the ability to fully interleave all the decisions at any search depth [Veloso, 1989, Rosenbloom *et al.*, 1990], it successfully finds the optimal plan to solve this problem. Figure 4.8 (b) represents this problem solving search situation where NoLimit explores first the eager choice of applying any applicable operator, namely the sibling-applicable-op (GOTO-BOX box3). This ordering however leads to a failure, as when returning back to close door34, after achieving (next-to robot box3), NoLimit encounters a state loop. It recognizes that it was in the same state before, and backtracks to the correct ordering, postponing the application of the operator (GOTO-BOX box3), at node cn16, to after accomplishing the goal (door-closed door34).

Without guidance NoLimit explores the space of all possible attention foci and orderings of alternatives, and only after backtracking does it find the correct goal interleaving. The idea of compiling problem solving episodes is to learn from its earlier exploration and reduce search significantly by replaying the same reasoning process in similar situations.

4.4 Summary

The annotation procedure involves:

- The elaboration of the derivational analogy model in terms of the appropriate data structures for the justifications underlying the decision making process in the problem solving episodes.

- The extension of the base-level problem solver to compile justifications under a lazy evaluation approach. There is a negligible bookkeeping cost in the extension of the problem solver with the annotation capabilities.

- The specification of a flexible and precise language to express the justifications at the decision nodes.

- The generation of a case as a search tree compacted into the decision nodes in the successful solution path. These nodes are annotated with the justifications that resulted in the sequence of correct and failed decisions that lead to a solution to the problem.

Chapter 5

Case Storage: Automated Indexing

The previous chapter presented how the problem solver generates cases from the derivational trace of its problem solving search experience. A case is the final successful search path annotated with the justifications of the reasons the choices were made and a record of the failures encountered. This chapter introduces the next logical phase in the analogical reasoning process, namely how to store the episodic knowledge generated.

We introduce how the episodic knowledge generated is stored efficiently. The processes for knowledge storage and retrieval can greatly affect the utility of a learning system due to the apparent tradeoff between the benefits of increasing the size of the knowledge base and the costs of retrieving its contents [Minton, 1988b]. In fact, in many speedup learning systems, storage seems to be simply a matter of adding the new knowledge to the beginning or end of a list, and retrieval a matter of iterating over the items in the list. In this work we consider the organization of the new constructed knowledge as an essential part of the overall learning process. We developed indexing and retrieval techniques that proved to be absolutely mandatory when we scaled up the system to a large case library of learned problem solving episodes. We experienced that the organization of stored knowledge greatly affects retrieval and reuse costs. Recent work [Doorenbos *et al.*, 1992] has also used efficient matching or locating methods to avoid the utility problem.

We present the algorithms we developed for identifying a set of appropriate case indices of problem solving episodes. The goal statement and the initial state of a problem situation define the problem and should be used as indices for the solution case generated. A naïve approach may consider the goal statement and the complete initial state directly as indices.[1] This approach is suited for simple one-goal problems where the initial state is specified with a reduced set

---

[1] In Chapter 8, we show empirical results that compare this simple approach with the more elaborate indexing technique to be presented in this chapter.

of features. However, for complex problem solving situations with multiple goals and a very large number of literals in the initial state, the indexing mechanism must be more selective for the sake of the utility of the indices at retrieval time.

The chapter is organized in five sections. A complete case may be a concatenation of several independent subparts that can potentially be reused separately. The first section presents the algorithm to transform a totally ordered plan into a partially ordered one by analyzing the dependencies among the solution steps. The connected subgraphs of the resulting partially ordered graph correspond to the different sets of interacting goals. These sets are used as the goal indices for the case. Section 2 shows how to identify an additional set of indices from the initial state. The algorithm determines the relevant features of the initial state with respect to the solution recorded in the case. Section 3 describes the resulting organization of the case library and illustrates it with an example. Section 4 summarizes formally the overall storage procedure. Finally Section 5 concludes the chapter with a review of the main points of the storage mechanism.

5.1   Identifying independent case subparts

NoLimit produces a solution to a problem as an apparently totally ordered sequence of operators and therefore of decisions made. This is an apparent total order, because each decision is not necessarily completely dependent on every of its precedents. We designed an algorithm that identifies the independent sub-solutions by extracting the partially ordered graph from the totally ordered plan returned [Veloso *et al.*, 1990]. The algorithm identifies a partially ordered instantiated solution, as opposed to using the episodic solution to generate the minimal set of generalized ordering constraints [Mooney, 1988]. The algorithm runs in polynomial time in the number of steps in the solution in contrast with the exponential run time of the search algorithm.

Consider a partial order as a directed graph (V, E), where V, the set of vertices, is the set of steps (instantiated operators) of the plan, and E is the set of edges (ordering constraints) in the partial order. Let $V = \{op_0, op_2, \ldots, op_{n+1}\}$. A square matrix $\mathcal{P}$ represents the graph, where $\mathcal{P}[i, j] = 1$, if there is an edge from op_i to op_j. There is an edge from op_i to op_j, if op_i must *precede* op_j, i.e., $op_i \prec op_j$. The inverse of this statement does not necessarily hold, i.e., there may be the case where $op_i \prec op_j$ and there is not an edge from op_i to op_j. The relation $\prec$ is the *transitive closure* of the relation represented in the graph for the partial order. Without loss of generality, consider operators op_0 and op_{n+1} of any plan to be the additional operators named *start* and *finish* (see Chapter 3), represented in the figures below as s and f.

Figure 5.1 shows a simple example of a partial order. Legal orderings are, for example, $(s, op_1, op_2, op_3, op_4, op_5, op_6, f)$, or $(s, op_1, op_5, op_2, op_6, op_3, op_4, f)$, or $(s, op_1, op_5, op_3, op_2, op_6, op_4, f)$. The ordering $(s, op_5, op_6, op_3, op_2, op_4, op_1, f)$ is not legal as op_1 must precede op_2, op_3, and op_4.

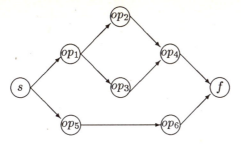

Figure 5.1: An example of a partially ordered plan.

5.1.1 Transforming a total order into a partial order

A plan step op_i necessarily precedes another plan step op_j if and only if op_i adds a precondition of op_j, or op_j deletes a precondition of op_i. For each problem, the start operator s adds all the literals in the initial state. The preconditions of the finish operator f are set to the user-given goal statement. Let the totally ordered plan T be the sequence $op_1, \ldots, op_n$ returned by NoLimit as the solution to a problem. Figure 5.2 shows the algorithm to generate the partially ordered plan, P, from this totally ordered one, T.

Step 1 loops through the plan steps in the *reverse* of the execution order. Steps 2-4 loop through each of the preconditions of the operator, i.e., plan step. The procedure **Last_Op_Responsible_For_Precond** (one possible implementation is shown in Figure 5.7) takes a precondition as argument and searches from the operator op_i, back to, at most the operator s, for the first operator (*supporting_operator*) that has the effect of adding that precondition. Note that one such operator must be found as the given T is a solution to the problem (in particular the initial state is added by the operator s). All the *supporting_operators* of an operator op_i must precede it. The algorithm sets therefore a directed edge from each of the former into the latter. Step 5 checks if the operator being processed is the finish operator (op_{n+1}). It that is the case, step 6 labels the edges in the graph from the *supporting_operators* to the preconditions of the operator op_{n+1}. The procedure **Label_Goal_Edge** labels these edges with the added precondition, i.e., the user defined goal conjunct. This explicitly marks the operators directly responsible for achieving the goal statement.[2]

Steps 7-10 loop through each of the delete effects of the operator. The procedure **All_Ops_Needing_Effect** searches for all the operators applied earlier in the solution, which need, i.e., have as a precondition, each delete effect of the operator. These are the *supported_operators*. Steps 9-10 capture the precedence relationships by adding directed edges from each *supported_operator* to the operator that deletes some of their preconditions.

Steps 11-14 guarantee that the primary adds of this operator are preserved in the partially ordered plan. An add effect is primary if it in the subgoaling chain of a user given goal conjunct. The procedure **Ops_Deleting_Primary_Add**

---

[2] This information is used to directly identify the goals corresponding to parts of the graph (see Section 5.1.2).

Input :   A totally ordered plan $\mathcal{T} = op_1, op_2, \ldots, op_n$, the start operator
     s (op_0) with add effects set to the initial state, and the finish
     operator f (op_{n+1}) with preconditions set to the user given goal
     statement.

Output :   A partially ordered plan represented as a directed graph $\mathcal{P}$.

procedure **Build_Partial_Order**($\mathcal{T}$, s, f):
1. for $i \leftarrow (n+1)$ down-to 1 do
2.   for each *precond* in **Preconditions_of**(op_i) do
3.   *supporting_operator* ← **Last_Op_Responsible_For_Precond**
                              ($precond, s, i$)
4.   **Add_Directed_Edge** (*supporting_operator*,op_i,$\mathcal{P}$)
5.   if $i = n+1$
6.   then **Label_Goal_Edge** (*supporting_operator*,f,$\mathcal{P}$,*precond*)
7.   for each *del* in **Delete_Effects**(op_i) do
8.   *supported_operators* ← **All_Ops_Needing_Effect** (del, i)
9.   for each *supported_operator* do
10.   **Add_Directed_Edge** (*supported_operator*,op_i,$\mathcal{P}$)
11.   for each *add* in **Primary_Adds** (op_i) do
12.   *adversary_operators* ← **Ops_Deleting_Primary_Add** (add, i)
13.   for each *adversary_operator* do
14.   **Add_Directed_Edge** (*adversary_operator*,op_i,$\mathcal{P}$)
15. $\mathcal{P}$ ← **Remove_Transitive_Edges**($\mathcal{P}$)
16. Return $\mathcal{P}$

Figure 5.2: Building a partial order from a total order.

identifies the *adversary_operators* that, earlier in the plan, delete a primary add.
Any such operator cannot be performed after the current operator. Hence step 14
sets a directed edge from each *adversary_operator* to the operator under consideration.

Finally, step 15 removes all the transitive edges of the resulting graph to
produce the partial order. Every directed edge e connecting operator op_i to
op_j is removed, if there is another path that connects the two vertices. The
procedure **Remove_Transitive_Edges** tentatively removes e from the graph
and then checks to see whether vertex op_j is reachable from op_i. If this is the
case, then e is removed definitively, otherwise e is set back in the graph. Step 16
returns the partial order generated.

If n is the number of operators in the plan, p is the average number of
preconditions, d is the average number of delete effects, and a is the average number of add effects of an operator, then steps 1-14 of the algorithm
Build_Partial_Order run in $O((p + d + a)n^2)$. Note that the algorithm takes
advantage of the given total ordering of the plan, by visiting, at each step, only
earlier plan steps. The final procedure **Remove_Transitive_Edges** runs in
$O(e)$, for a resulting graph with e edges [Aho *et al.*, 1974]. Empirical experi-

ence with test problems shows that the algorithm **Build_Partial_Order** runs in meaningless time compared to the search time to generate the input totally ordered plan.

An example

We now illustrate the algorithm running in the simple *ONE-WAY* rocket problem introduced in Section 3.1.1. NoLimit returns the totally ordered plan $T = $ (LOAD-ROCKET obj1 locA), (LOAD-ROCKET obj2 locA), (MOVE-ROCKET), (UNLOAD-ROCKET obj1 locB), (UNLOAD-ROCKET obj2 locB). Let op_i be the ith operator in T. Figure 5.3 shows the partial order generated by the algorithm, before removing the transitive edges. As previously seen, the goal of the problem is the conjunction (and (at obj1 locB) (at obj2 locB)). These two predicates are added by the UNLOAD steps, namely op_4 and op_5. The edges labeled "g" show the precedence requirement between op_4 and op_5, and the finish operator f. The numbers at the other edges in Figure 5.3 represent the order by which the algorithm introduces them into the graph.

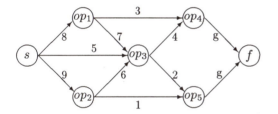

op1: (LOAD-ROCKET obj1 locA)
op2: (LOAD-ROCKET obj2 locA)
op3: (MOVE-ROCKET)
op4: (UNLOAD-ROCKET obj1 locB)
op5: (UNLOAD-ROCKET obj2 locB)

Figure 5.3: Partial order with transitive edges.

As an example of some of the steps of the algorithm, note that while processing op_5, namely (UNLOAD-ROCKET obj2 locB), step 3 sets the edges 1 and 2, as the preconditions of op_5, namely (inside obj1 ROCKET) and (at ROCKET locB) (see Figure 3.3), are added by op_2 and op_3 respectively. When processing op_3, (MOVE-ROCKET), edge 5 is set because op_3's precondition, (at ROCKET locA), is in the initial state. The edges 6 and 7 are further set by step 10, because op_3 deletes (at ROCKET locA) that is needed (as a precondition) by the earlier steps op_1 and op_2. Step 15 removes the transitive edges, namely edges 1, 3, and 5. The resulting graph is returned as the final partial order.

5.1.2 Goal indices

The partially ordered graph as generated by the algorithm of Figure 5.2 is a graph with one unique connected component as all the vertices are connected through the start and finish vertices. These nodes are introduced however for uniformity purposes for the algorithm and are not directly part of the final solution. Consider that the remaining operators of the plan are named the *effective* operators.

The independent subparts of the solution are the different connected subgraphs of the partially ordered graph of the effective operators. Each subpart achieves a subset of the conjuncts of the initial goal statement. The goals in each subset *interact* with respect to the particular plan encountered as stated in Definition 1.

Definition 1 Interacting goals with respect to a particular plan:
Given
- *the conjunctive goal* $\mathcal{G} = G_1, G_2, \ldots, G_n$,
- *the set of connected subgraphs* $\mathcal{P}^c = \{(V_k^c, E_k^c)\}$ *of the partially ordered plan* $\mathcal{P}$, *where each* V_k^c *is a set of operators in* $\mathcal{P}$ *connected through dependencies* E_k^c,

let op_{G_i} *be the operator in some* V_c^k *that is responsible for achieving the goal* G_i.

Two goals G_i, G_j **interact** *with respect to the solution* $\mathcal{P}$, *iff the operators* op_{G_i} *and* op_{G_j} *are in the same connected subgraph, i.e.,* $\exists k : (op_{G_i} \in V_c^k) \wedge (op_{G_j} \in V_c^k)$.

A particular problem may have many different solutions. These solutions may differ in the set of operators in the plan. Definition 1 captures goal dependencies of a particular solution found. If the ordering constraints between achieving two goals are domain dependent, then all the solutions to a particular problem will have the two goals interacting. On the other hand the dependencies may be the result of a particular problem solving path explored. In this case for some solutions the goals may interact and for some others they may not.

To illustrate this difference, we discuss different plans, some with ordering constraints that are domain dependent, and others with domain-independent ordering constraints. In the *one-way rocket* domain, the goals of moving two objects to a different location interact, because the rocket can only move once. This is an interaction that is dependent on the domain definition. The *machine-shop scheduling* domain [Carbonell *et al.*, 1992] also constraints that holes in parts must be drilled before parts are polished, as the drilling operator deletes the shining effect. In this domain, the goals of polishing and making a hole in a part interact again due to the domain definition. In this same domain, when two identical machines are available to achieve two identical goals, these goals may interact, if the problem solver chooses to use just one machine to achieve both goals, as it will have to wait for the machine to be idle. If the problem solver uses the two machines instead of just one, then the goals do not interact. There is a variety of equivalent examples in the logistics transportation domain. In general it is not clear what use of resources is overall the best. As an example, in the logistics domain, suppose that the problem solver assumes that the same truck (or airplane) must be used when moving objects from the same location into the same (or close) destiny. This becomes however more complicated to generalize if there are capacity constraints for the carriers and the objects have different sizes. These examples motivate the complexity of handling goal interactions when the problem solver can find several solutions to a problem. [Pérez and Carbonell, 1993] is a current research effort on learning control knowledge to improve the quality of the plans generated by the problem solver.

Figure 5.4 shows the overall procedure that determines the sets of interacting goals that index the independent subparts of a case.

Input : A partially ordered plan $\mathcal{P}$ expressed as an adjacency
matrix of a directed graph (V, E), with $V = \{op_0, op_2, \ldots, op_{n+1}\}$, where
$\mathcal{P}[i, j] = 1$, if there is an edge from op_i to op_j), and the initial goal
statement $\mathcal{G} = G_1, G_2, \ldots, G_k$.

Output : The set of interacting goals.

procedure **Find_Interacting_Goals**($\mathcal{P}$, $\mathcal{G}$):
1. *connected_components* ← **Find_Connected_Subgraphs**($\mathcal{P}_{1,n}$)
2. *set_interacting_goals* ← $\emptyset$
3. for each *component* in *connected_components* do
4.   *interacting_goals* ← $\emptyset$
5.   for each v in *component* do
6.   *goal_edge_label* ← **Get_Goal_Edge_Label** (v, op_{n+1})
7.   if *goal_edge_label*
8.   then *interacting_goals* ← *interacting_goals* ∪ { *goal_edge_label* }
9.   *set_interacting_goals* ← *set_interacting_goals* ∪ {{*interacting_goals*}}
10. Return *set_interacting_goals*

Figure 5.4: Finding the set of interacting goals.

The procedure **Find_Interacting_Goals** in Figure 5.4 gets as an argument the partially ordered solution which represents the constraints on the ordering of the plan steps represented as a matrix $\mathcal{P}$. Step 1 finds the connected components of the directed graph $\mathcal{P}$ using a depth-first search algorithm to find the spanning forest of an undirected graph. The complexity of this step is $O(n*e)$ [Aho *et al.*, 1974] where n is the number of vertices, i.e., the number of steps in the plan and e is the number of edges, i.e., the dependencies among the plan steps. The remaining steps of the algorithm compute the set of interacting goals from the set of connected components. The algorithm that generates the partially ordered graph labels each edge with the particular goal conjunct, if any, that each operator achieves. Steps 5-8 use this labeling information to determine which goals are achieved by each connected component.

The complexity of the overall algorithm is determined by the complexity of step 1 as the other steps perform constant access operations for each connected component of the graph. The maximum number of connected components is k which is the number of goal conjuncts in the goal statement $\mathcal{G}$. The complexity of step 1 is $O(n*e)$ where e is the number of edges, and n is the number of vertices of the partial graph. The complexity of the algorithm above is therefore $O(max(n * e, k))$.

5.2   Identifying the relevant initial state

In addition to the goal statement, a problem solving situation is specified in terms of an initial state. It is a common concern to determine what are the *relevant* features of the initial state in order to solve a problem. This set of relevant features are the desired ones to use as indices to the case to be stored. There are two reasons why it is useful to reduce the set of features of the initial state to the set of relevant features:

1. The set of relevant features represents more accurately the semantic dependencies between the initial state and the goal statement (as the remaining features are not used to achieve the goal).

2. The set of relevant features is a subset of the total set of features. A smaller and more relevant set of features indexing a case increases the efficiency of the retrieval process.

We present a method to automatically identify the relevant features of the initial state.

5.2.1   Disambiguating the notion of "relevant"

We solved the problem of determining the set of relevant features of the initial state by noticing and using the following fact:

- The relevant initial state is not only a function of the goal statement, but it is also a function of the particular solution found to achieve that goal statement.

The following example illustrates this claim. Consider Figure 5.5 which shows in (a) the initial state and in (b) the goal statement of an example problem from the extended-STRIPS domain, say problem *strips2-17*. [3]

The rooms are numbered at their corners and the doors are named according to the rooms they connect. Doors may be open, closed, or locked. In particular, dr24 connects the rooms 2 and 4 and is locked. The door connecting the rooms 3 and 4, dr34, is closed and, for example, dr12 is open. The number of the boxes can be inferred by the attached description of the initial state. Note that box1 is in rm1. The problem solver must find a plan to reach a state where dr34 is open, and box1 is in rm2.

Assume that NoLimit solves the problem in Figure 5.5 by pushing box1 from rm1 into rm2, and then going to rm3 back through rm1 to open the door dr34. The actual solution searched and found would be the plan shown in Figure 5.6 (a).

In this way of solving the problem, for example, key24 for the locked dr24 does not play any role in reaching a solution. This door is therefore not a

---

[3]Problems are named for the purpose of identifying them when the organization of the case library is illustrated (see Section 5.3).

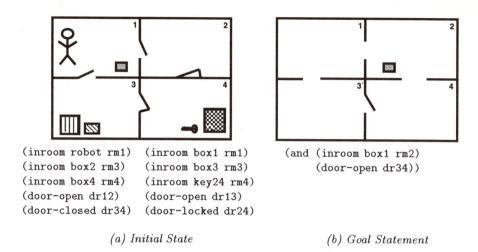

```
(inroom robot rm1)    (inroom box1 rm1)          (and (inroom box1 rm2)
(inroom box2 rm3)     (inroom box3 rm3)               (door-open dr34))
(inroom box4 rm4)     (inroom key24 rm4)
(door-open dr12)      (door-open dr13)
(door-closed dr34)    (door-locked dr24)
```

(a) Initial State   *(b) Goal Statement*

Figure 5.5: Problem situation in the extended-STRIPS domain (strips2-17); The goal statement is a partial specification of the final desired state: the location of other objects and the status of other doors remains unspecified.

relevant literal in the initial state if this particular problem solving episode is to be replayed. Also the other three boxes in the initial state, **box2**, **box3**, and **box4**, are not used to achieve the goal. Figure 5.6 (c) shows the set of literals in the initial state that are relevant to each particular goal conjunct for this particular solution. The initial state is *foot-printed* according to the goal conjuncts and the solution found, i.e., each literal in the initial state is associated with the list of goals that it contributed to achieve.

However NoLimit could have encountered a different solution to this problem, namely to push **box1** along on its way to door **dr34**, open it, and push **box1** through **dr24** into **rm2**, after unlocking this door. The actual solution searched and found would be the plan shown in Figure 5.6 (b). In this way of solving the problem, for example, (**inroom key24 rm4**) specifying the location of **key24** for the locked **dr24** is a *relevant* literal in the initial state of this problem if this problem solving episode is to be replayed. Figure 5.6 (c) shows the actual foot-print of the initial state for this solution.

We introduce the definition of relevancy not as an absolute concept, but as a concept relative to the particular goal and solution. Definition 2 introduces the set of relevant features of the initial state in terms of the goals they contributed to achieve in a particular solution.

Definition 2 Relevant features of the initial state:

Given an initial state $S = s_1, s_2, \ldots, s_m$, the conjunctive goal $\mathcal{G} = G_1, G_2, \ldots, G_k$, and a particular plan $\mathcal{T} = op_1, op_2, \ldots, op_n$, the literal s_i is **relevant** *to the problem situation with respect to the solution $\mathcal{T}$, iff s_i is in the* **foot-print** *of some goal conjunct G_j, i.e., iff s_i contributes to achieve the goal G_j in the plan $\mathcal{T}$.*

```
(GOTO-BOX box1)
(PUSH-THRU-DOOR box1 dr12)
(GO-THRU dr12 rm1)
(GOTO-DOOR dr13)
(GO-THRU dr13 rm3)
(GOTO-DOOR dr34)
(OPEN-DOOR dr34)
        (a)
```

```
(GOTO-BOX box1)
(PUSH-THRU-DOOR box1 dr13)
(PUSH-TO-DOOR box1 dr34)
(OPEN-DOOR dr34)
(PUSH-THRU-DOOR box1 dr34)
(GOTO-KEY key24)
(PICK-UP key24)
(GOTO-DOOR dr24)
(UNLOCK-DOOR dr24)
(OPEN-DOOR dr24)
(GOTO-BOX box1)
(PUT-DOWN key24)
(PUSH-THRU-DOOR box1 dr24)
        (b)
```

	Relevant State for Each Plan and Goal			
Complete Initial State	Foot-print for plan (a)		Foot-print for plan (b)	
	(inroom box1 rm2)	(door-open dr34)	(inroom box1 rm2)	(door-open dr34)
(inroom robot rm1)	√	√	√	√
(inroom box1 rm1)	√		√	
(inroom box2 rm3)				
(inroom box3 rm3)				
(inroom box4 rm4)				
(inroom key24 rm4)			√	
(door-open dr12)	√			
(door-open dr13)		√	√	√
(door-locked dr24)			√	
(door-closed dr34)		√	√	√
(arm-empty)	√		√	
(pushable box1)	√		√	
(connects dr12 rm1 rm2)	√			
(connects dr13 rm1 rm3)		√	√	√
(connects dr24 rm2 rm4)			√	
(connects dr34 rm3 rm4)		√	√	√

(c)

Figure 5.6: Two different solutions for the problem in Figure 5.5: Plans (a) and (b); and their corresponding foot-printed initial states as shown in table (c). The literals of the initial state in the foot-printed initial state for a particular plan and goal are marked with a √.

The next section formally introduces the procedure to automatically generate the foot-printed initial state from the derivational trace of the plan.

5.2.2 Foot-printing the initial state

The foot-printed features of the initial state are instantiated and identified from the final solution. This is similar to the chunking process in SOAR [Laird *et al.*, 1986]. Chunking happens at each problem solving impasse instead of just at the end of the problem solving episode as in our foot-printing. The algorithm in Figure 5.7 uses the derivational trace to identify the set of weakest preconditions necessary to achieve each goal conjunct of the goal statement. Then recursively the algorithm creates the *foot-print* of a user-given goal conjunct by doing a goal regression, i.e., projecting back its weakest preconditions into the literals in the initial state [Waldinger, 1981, Mitchell *et al.*, 1986].

Input : A totally ordered plan $T = op_0, op_1, \ldots, op_n, op_{n+1}$, and the goal statement $G = G_1, G_2, \ldots, G_k$.

Output : The foot-printed initial state.

procedure **Foot_Print_Initial_State**(T, G):
1. for $i = 1$ to k do
2. $op_r \leftarrow$ **Last_Op_Responsible_For_Precond** (G_i, n)
3.   **Recursively_Foot_Print** (G_i, G_i, **preconds** (op_r), op_r)

procedure **Last_Op_Responsible_For_Precond** (*goal*, *i*)
1. $op_a \leftarrow$ nil
2. *op_count* $\leftarrow i$
3. while (not op_a)
4.   if (or (and (**positive-goal-p** *goal*) (*goal* $\in$ **adds**(op_{op_count})))
          (and (**negative-goal-p** *goal*) (*goal* $\in$ **dels**(op_{op_count}))))
5.   then $op_a \leftarrow op_{op\_count}$
6.   else *op_count* $\leftarrow$ *op_count* -1
7. Return op_a

procedure **Recursively_Foot_Print** (*user_goal, literal, set_of_preconds, op_r*)
1. if $r = 0$
2.   then **Set_Foot_Print** (*literal, user_goal*)
3.   else for each *precond* $\in$ *set_of_preconds* do
4. $op_a \leftarrow$ **Last_Op_Responsible_For_Precond** (*precond*, r)
5.   **Recursively_Foot_Print** (*user_goal, precond,* **preconds** (op_a), op_a)

Figure 5.7: Foot-printing the initial state.

The literals in the initial state are *categorized* according to the goal conjunct they contributed to achieve. This episodic goal regression acts as a lazy explanation of the successful path [Cain *et al.*, 1991, Hickman and Larkin, 1990, Pazzani, 1990] It also emphasizes a goal oriented behavior [Kedar-Cabelli, 1985, Hammond, 1989], by focusing only on the goal-relevant portions of the initial state according to the stored derivational trace.

Several learning methods share the explanation provided by the subgoaling chain supplied by the underlying domain theory. In that sense, foot-printing is similar to explanation-based indexing techniques [Barletta and Mark, 1988, Hickman and Larkin, 1990, Pazzani, 1990] and chunking [Laird *et al.*, 1986]. A distinction between the methods is the level of generalization, abstraction, or scope of the explanation obtained. Foot-printing explains the episodic final solution while chunking explains each problem solving impasse. Explanation-based indexing, as used in [Barletta and Mark, 1988], uses goal regression to abstract domain features from the instantiated observables defining a solution episode. Foot-printing uses goal regression to reduce the set of instantiated features of the initial state.

The algorithm in Figure 5.7 uses the totally ordered plan as a list of the annotated applied operator decision nodes of the case. As presented in Section 4.1.2, these nodes have annotated slots with the corresponding lists of preconditions, additions, and deletions to the state, which are returned respectively by the access slot functions **preconds**, **adds**, and **dels**. Remember that **adds**(op_0) returns the initial state $\mathcal{S}$, and **preconds**(op_{n+1}) returns the goal statement $\mathcal{G}$.

Step 2 of the procedure **Foot_Print_Initial_State** finds the operator responsible, op_r, for adding each goal conjunct G_i. The procedure **Last_Op_Responsible_For_Precond** follows the solution from the operator begin analyzed back to the initial operator op_0, and stops when it finds an operator that adds the goal (or deletes it, in case of a negated goal). Notice that the procedure terminates always successfully because the given $\mathcal{T}$ is a solution to the problem. Therefore each goal is added by some previous operator in the plan. The procedure **Recursively_Foot_Print** implements the goal regression and sets the foot-printed initial state literals for each goal conjunct, *user_goal*, from the user-given goal statement.

The algorithm **Foot_Print_Initial_State** runs in polynomial time in the length of the plan. The procedure **Last_Op_Responsible_For_Precond**, if implemented as shown above, makes the overall algorithm run in $O(n^2)$. An alternative implementation where additional bookkeeping is done at search time, accomplishes the same procedure in constant time. Every time an operator is applied, the problem solving algorithm attaches links from the literals added (deleted) by the operator to the operator. Literals are themselves linked to goal decision nodes, and these pointers to the adding operators are stored attached to the preconditions of the applied operator nodes. For that implementation, the procedure **Last_Op_Responsible_For_Precond** returns the last operator adding a precond in constant time, i.e., the access slot time added to the time of returning the maximum index of the operators in the slot, as more than one operator may add the same precond and the procedure returns only the last one. The complexity of the overall algorithm is then $O(pn)$, where p is the total number of preconditions.

The foot-printed features of the initial state are instantiated and identified from the final solution. This is similar to the chunking process in SOAR [Laird *et al.*, 1986]. Chunking happens at each problem solving impasse instead of just at the end of the problem solving episode as in our foot-printing. The algorithm to foot-print the initial state uses the derivational trace to identify the set of weakest preconditions necessary to achieve each goal conjunct of the goal statement [Veloso and Carbonell, 1993a]. Then recursively the algorithm creates the *foot-print* of a user-given goal conjunct by doing a goal regression, i.e., projecting back its weakest preconditions into the literals in the initial state [Waldinger, 1981, Mitchell *et al.*, 1986]. The literals in the initial state are *categorized* according to the goal conjunct they contributed to achieve. This episodic goal regression acts as a lazy explanation of the successful path [Cain *et al.*, 1991, Hickman and Larkin, 1990, Pazzani, 1990]. It also emphasizes a goal oriented behavior [Kedar-Cabelli, 1985, Hammond, 1989], by focusing only on the goal-relevant portions of the initial state according to the stored derivational trace. Several learning methods share the explanation provided by the subgoaling chain supplied by the underlying domain theory. In that sense, foot-printing is similar to explanation-based indexing techniques [Barletta and Mark, 1988, Hickman and Larkin, 1990, Pazzani, 1990] and chunking [Laird *et al.*, 1986]. A distinction between the methods is the level of generalization, abstraction, or scope of the explanation obtained. Foot-printing explains the episodic final solution while chunking explains each problem solving impasse. Explanation-based indexing, as used in [Barletta and Mark, 1988], uses goal regression to abstract domain features from the instantiated observables defining a solution episode. Foot-printing uses goal regression to reduce the set of instantiated features of the initial state.

5.3 Organization of the case library

The previous sections presented the algorithms to identify the set of appropriate indices in terms of the goal statement and initial state. The goal statement $\mathcal{G}$ is partitioned into the sets of interacting goals, say $\mathcal{G}_i$. The initial state is foot-printed for the different goal conjuncts. Definition 3 introduces the foot-printed initial state of a set of interacting goals.

Definition 3 Foot-printed initial state for a set of interacting goals:
The foot-printed initial state for a set of interacting goals is the union of the foot-printed initial states for each individual goal in the set.

Figure 5.8 summarizes the previous sections by sketching a case multiply indexed by the sets of interacting goals and the corresponding foot-printed initial states. The goal statement $\mathcal{G}$ is partitioned into m sets of interacting goals, $\mathcal{G}_i, i = 1, \ldots, m$. The subgoaling links annotated at the case steps identify the set of steps of the case that achieve a particular set of interacting goals $\mathcal{G}_i$. As will be presented in Chapter 7, the replay mechanism may reuse only subparts of a case indexed by a particular set of interacting goals by following those subgoaling links, ignoring the steps of the case that are not related to that set of goals.

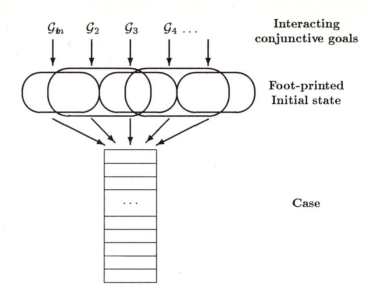

Figure 5.8: Case indices: Interacting goals and foot-printed initial state.

After the identification of the appropriate set of indices for a case, this section presents the data structures that support the indexing of the cases in the case library. The data structures are presented to support the efficient access to the case library.[4]

Parameterizing the problem solving situation

The analogical reasoner does not perform an eager generalization of the problem solving episode. The problem solving episode is however parameterized to facilitate the substitution of roles among similar situations.

Definition 4 Parameterized literal:

A **parameterized literal** *(either from the goal statement or from the foot-printed initial state) is a literal where its arguments are converted into variables of the immediate parent class in the type hierarchy.*

For example, consider Figure 5.9 which shows the type hierarchy of the extended-STRIPS domain.

The name of each variable is a concatenation of the class of the variable and some arbitrary number. At retrieval time variables are bound to objects of the same class. Some examples of parameterized goals follow:

Examples:

```
(door-open dr12) -> (door-open <door54>)
((inroom key24 rm2) (inroom box2 rm2)) ->
    ((inroom <key27> <room7>) (inroom <box63> <room7>))
(next-to robot box3) -> (next-to <agent13> <box59>)
```

---

[4]The reader may skip this section on a first pass through the book and return to it after getting familiar with the overall storage and retrieval procedures.

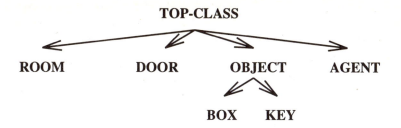

Figure 5.9: The class hierarchy in the extended-STRIPS domain.

A literal can be further parameterized to the classes of its arguments as shown in definition 5.

Definition 5 Class-parameterized literal:
A **class-parameterized literal** *is a literal with its arguments replaced by their immediate class names.*

Examples:

```
(door-open dr12) -> (door-open DOOR)
((inroom key24 rm2) (inroom box2 rm2)) ->
    ((inroom KEY ROOM) (inroom BOX ROOM))
(next-to robot box3) -> (next-to AGENT BOX)
```

Note that the class parameterization loses the information of the particular relationships among the arguments of the literals. In the second example above, ((inroom key24 rm2) (inroom box2 rm2)) is class-parameterized to ((inroom KEY ROOM) (inroom BOX ROOM)) missing the information that it is the key and the box are in the same room, rm2.

These two levels of parameterization are used to effectively prune the set of candidate analogs. In particular, at retrieval time, the comparison at the class parameterization level selects the set of cases that unify in terms of the arguments class (see Chapter 6).

The goal statement indexing structures

The several data structures that implement the goal and initial state indexing are designed to answer efficiently different requests from the analogical reasoner. Chapter 6 presents a detailed analysis of the efficiency resulting from these data structures. This and the next sections introduce the data structures used and briefly present the requests from the analogical reasoner that benefit from these particular data structures.

CLASS-GOAL-PARAMETERIZED-GOAL This hash table maps the class-parameterized goals to a list of the corresponding parameterized goals.

PARAMETERIZED-GOAL-INITIAL-STATE This hash table associates the parameterized goals with the discrimination network that stores the initial state pointers to all the cases that solved a problem with those parameterized goals.

GOAL-INTERACTIONS This vector stores, at position i, a list of the class-parameterized goals with i many conjuncts.

CLASS-GOAL-PROBLEM This hash table associates with the individual class-parameterized goals the list of problems that solved a corresponding instantiated goal.

Illustrating example

As an example consider the problem *strips2-5* shown in Figure 4.5 with goal statement (and (door-closed dr34) (next-to robot box3)) and consider that in the case to be stored the two goals interact. Consider also problem *strips2-17* shown in Figure 5.5 with goal statement (and (door-open dr34) (inroom box1 rm2)) and consider again that the two goals interact. For the purpose of better illustration, consider an additional problem *strips3-9* with goal statement (and (next-to robot box4) (inroom box4 rm1) (<door-closed dr12)). Assume that the solution found to this problem breaks the goal statement into two sets of interacting goals, namely {(door-closed dr12), (next-to robot box4)} and {(inroom box4 rm1)}. Figure 5.10 summarizes the three problems.

Interacting goals	Parameterized	Class-Parameterized
((door-closed dr34) (next-to robot box3))	((door-closed <door57>) (next-to <agent13> <box7>))	((door-closed DOOR) (next-to AGENT BOX)
((door-open dr34) (inroom box1 rm2))	((door-open <door39>) (inroom <box24> <rm44>))	((door-open DOOR) (inroom BOX ROOM))
((door-closed dr12) (next-to robot box4)) ((inroom box4 rm1))	(door-closed <door57>) (next-to <agent13> <box7>)) ((inroom <box25> <room78>))	(door-closed DOOR) (next-to AGENT BOX)) ((inroom BOX ROOM))

Figure 5.10: Parameterized goals in the example problems, strips2-5, strips2-17, and strips3-9.

The problems are inserted into the case library in the order *strips2-5, strips2-17* and *strips3-9*. The parameterization of the last problem *strips3-9* uses the same variables that are used in the first problem *strips2-5* because they share a set of interacting goals. The algorithm that assigns the variables to the goal statement accesses the *CLASS-GOAL-PARAMETERIZED-GOAL* hash table to match with identical previously stored problems.

Figure 5.11 (a) shows the contents of the hash table *CLASS-GOAL-PARAMETERIZED-GOAL* after the three problems are inserted. Note that this situation is very simple and is considered just for illustration of the data structures.

Class-parameterized	Parameterized goals
((door-closed DOOR) (next-to AGENT BOX))	(((door-closed <door57>) (next-to <agent13> <box7>)))
((door-open DOOR) (inroom BOX DOOR))	(((door-open <door39>) (inroom <box24> <room44>)))
((inroom BOX ROOM))	(((inroom <box25> <room78>)))

(a) *CLASS-GOAL-PARAMETERIZED-GOAL*

Parameterized goals	State-net-names
((door-closed <door57>) (next-to <agent13> <box7>))	"state-net-1"
((door-open <door39>) (inroom <box24> <room44>))	"state-net-2"
((inroom <box25> <room78>))	"state-net-3"

(b) *PARAMETERIZED-GOAL-INITIAL-STATE*

No. of interactions	List of class-parameterized goals
1	((inroom BOX ROOM))
2	(((door-closed DOOR) (next-to AGENT BOX)) ((door-open DOOR) (inroom BOX ROOM)))

(c) *GOAL-INTERACTIONS*

Class-parameterized	Problems
(door-closed DOOR)	(strips2-5 strips3-9)
(next-to AGENT BOX)	(strips2-5 strips3-9)
(inroom BOX ROOM)	(strips2-17 strips3-9)
(door-open DOOR)	(strips2-17)

(d) *GOAL-PROBLEM*

Figure 5.11: Indexing data structures.

Figure 5.11 (b) shows the contents of the hash table *PARAMETERIZED-GOAL-INITIAL-STATE*. The parameterized goals are associated with the discrimination networks that store the indexing foot-printed initial state. In particular note that ''state-net-1'' stores the indices for two cases, namely problem *strips2-5* and *strips3-9*. Note that the goal conjunct is sorted alphabetically.

Figure 5.11 (c) shows the contents of the vector *GOAL-INTERACTIONS*. There are two two-goal interacting cases and one one-goal.

Figure 5.11 (d) shows the relevant entries of the hash table *GOAL-PROBLEM* after problems *strips2-5*, *strips2-17*, and *strips3-9* are stored into memory. For example, the hash key (inroom BOX ROOM) has value the list (strips2-17 strips3-9), because these two problems have an instantiation of that literal in their goal statement, respectively (`inroom box1 rm2`) and (`inroom box4 rm1`).

The retrieval procedure benefits from these data structures

The organization of memory is functionally dictated by the needs of the other modules of the analogical reasoner. In particular the case library is accessed to retrieve similar problem solving episodes that the replay procedure should be able to use in order to reduce its search space. Therefore in the next Chapters 6 and 7 it becomes clear why the particular data structures are chosen.[5] In a nutshell the retrieval procedure accesses the vector *GOAL-INTERACTIONS* to find the potential goals that can guide a subset of the new goals. From the list of goals returned by this hash table the retrieval procedure accesses the *CLASS-GOAL-PARAMETERIZED-GOAL* for the possible set of goals that match their arguments at the class level. This hash table returns the parameterized goals that the retriever matches against the new goals. It then proceeds to match the initial state in the adequate state network returned by accessing the hash table *PARAMETERIZED-GOAL-INITIAL-STATE*. The underlying justification for the design of these data structures is the goal to achieve, in close to constant time by hashing, an effective reduction of the number of candidate analogs from the large case library.

The initial state discrimination network

There are many problem solving situations for which the parameterized goal statements are identical and the initial states are different. These different initial states are organized into a discrimination network to index efficiently these cases that share completely the goal statement, but differ in the relevant initial state. Though in fact the structure is a network as nodes have several incident nodes, consider for convenience that the network is a tree where nodes are repeated for common paths.

Each network has a root frame of class "state-root" as shown in Figure 5.12 that summarizes the contents of the network. The nodes of the network are frames of class "state" also shown in Figure 5.12. Their content is a set of literals in the foot-printed initial state of the cases indexed by the network.

The following properties and definitions describe the semantics of the discrimination tree:

Property 1: A node n of the tree points directly to a case c, iff $c \in cases(n)$ and $\forall k \in children(n) : \neg(c \in cases(k))$. Let n be the *pointer-node* for case c. So the case c is in the list of cases of the node n but not in any of the lists of cases of the node children of n.

Property 2: The foot-printed initial state for a case c is the union of the contents of the tree nodes in the path from the *pointer-node* of c to the root of the tree.

---

[5] A description of an initial version of the memory data structures can be found in [Veloso and Carbonell, 1993b].

```
(def-frame state-root (:is-a tofu)
   :prob-names nil        ;list of the problem names stored
                          ;in the state discrimination net
   :goal nil              ;conjunctive goal for all the cases in the net
   :relevance-bias nil    ;ordering of relevance of the literals
   :cases nil             ;list of all the cases in net
   :children nil          ;points to only one state frame.
   )

(def-frame state (:is-a tofu)
   :content nil           ;list of literals of the foot-printed
                          ;initial state
   :parent nil            ;parent node, state-root frame or state frame
   :children nil          ;list of the children state frames
   :cases nil             ;list of cases in the node's subtrees
   )
```

Figure 5.12: The frame structure of the nodes of the discrimination net for the initial state.

Property 3: The organization of the tree is such that the content of a node is more relevant than the contents of its children nodes. Sibling nodes are equally relevant.

Properties 1 and 2 define the structure of the nodes as the foot-printed initial states that index the cases. The foot-printed initial state was identified as the subset of the features of the complete initial state that are relevant to a particular problem solving episode. However even these already relevant features can be ranked in a scale of relevance. The parent-child relationship between nodes in the initial state discrimination tree capture this ranking which is used by the similarity metric as it will be presented in Chapter 6. Therefore property 3 establishes that the structure of the network is such that the literals closer to the root are more relevant than the ones at the leaves. The case library is dynamically organized to reflect this degree of relevance of the literals in the initial state. This reorganization is based on the feedback that the analogical replay mechanism provides to the case library on the utility of the suggested guidance. The degree of relevance of the literals for each particular state network is stored in the slot **relevance-bias** of the root of the tree (see Figure 5.12). Example:

```
(make-frame 'state-net-1 state-root
   :prob-names '(strips2-5 strips3-9)
   :goal '((door-closed <door57>) (next-to <agent13> <box7>))
   :relevance-bias ' ((connects . 1) (pushable . 1)
      (arm-empty . 2) (door-open . 2) (door-closed . 2)
      (door-locked . 2) (inroom . 2))
```

```
:cases '(case-strips2-5-0 case-strips3-9-0)
:children '(state-11 state-12)
)
```

Figure 5.13 sketches the network structure of **state-net-1** which indexes the two solutions for the problems *strips2-5* and *strips3-9* (see Figures 5.10 and 5.11).

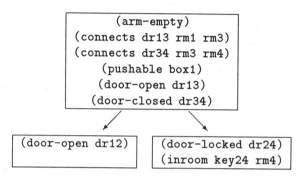

Figure 5.13: A sketch of a simple initial state discrimination tree. The figure shows the contents of the nodes and the parent-child relationships.

5.4   The complete storage algorithm

Figure 5.14 shows the complete storage procedure.

Input :   A problem specified by the goal statement $\mathcal{G}$, the initial state $\mathcal{S}$, and the corresponding derivational trace and plan $\mathcal{T}$.

Output :   The updated case library.

procedure **Store_Case**($\mathcal{G}, \mathcal{S}, \mathcal{T}$):
1. *partial_order* ← **Build_Partial_Order** ($\mathcal{T}$, s)
2. *sets_interacting_goals* ← **Find_Interacting_Goals** (*partial_order*, $\mathcal{G}$)
3. *foot_printed_initial_state* ← **Foot_Print_Initial_State** ($\mathcal{T}, \mathcal{G}$)
4. for each *set_interacting_goals* $\in$ *sets_interacting_goals*
5.   *foot_print_set* ← **Union_Foot_Prints**
            (*foot_printed_initial_state, set_interacting_goals*)
6.   *sorted_par_goal* ← **Sort_and_Parameterize_Goal** (*set_interacting_goals*)
7.   *state_net* ← **GetHash_or_New** (*sorted_par_goal*)
8.   **Insert_New_Case** (**Root_of** (*state_net*), *foot_print_set, sorted_par_goal*)
9.   **Update_Indexing_Tables**
10.   **Update_Case_Header**

Figure 5.14: The complete storage algorithm.

- Step 1 produces the partially ordered plan by using the procedure **Build-_Partial_Order** which builds the partial order analyzing the dependency structures of the totally ordered plan produced by NoLIMIT.
- Step 2 finds the sets of interacting goals using the procedure **Find_Interacting_Goals** which determines the connected components of the partial order and identifies these with the corresponding interacting goals.
- Step 3 computes the foot-printed initial state by using the procedure **Foot-_Print_Initial_State** which identifies the relevant features of the initial state by goal regressing in the derivational trace of the solution.
- Steps 4-8 handle each one of the set of interacting goals and proceed to the multiple indexing of each case. Step 5 determines the foot-printed initial state for each set of interacting goals. Step 6 parameterizes and sorts alphabetically the conjunctive goal.
- Steps 7-8 insert the new foot-printed initial state into the corresponding discrimination network returned by the procedure **GetHash_or_New** at step 7. The procedure **Insert_New_Case** is described below in detail.
- Finally steps 9-10 update the indexing data structures. The case header records the resulting parameterization from the complete insertion process of the case.

Figure 5.15 sketches the overall organization of the case library illustrated with goals from a logistics transportation domain.

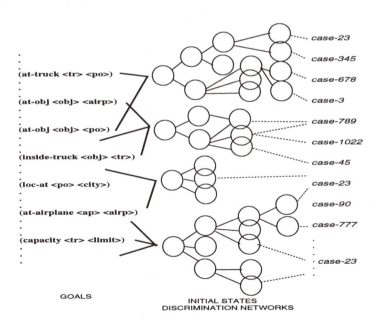

Figure 5.15: Prodigy/Analogy's case library organization. The goals at the left are indexed by a hash table (not shown).

The goals are used in a first level of indexing followed by the discrimination network of the initial state. The leaves of this indexing structure point to the cases.

In summary, organizing the case library consists of designing appropriate data structures to store the set of indices such that the set of candidate analogs at retrieval time can be pruned as efficiently as possible. We use two levels of indexing — a hash table and a discrimination network — to store the features in the goal statement and in the initial state shared among the cases. There are many problem solving situations for which the parameterized goal statements are identical and the initial states are different. These different initial states are organized into a discrimination network to index efficiently these cases that completely share the goal statement, but differ in the relevant initial state.

When a new case is inserted into the discrimination network, the underlying concern is to follow the relevance-bias making sure that the properties of the discrimination network remain invariant. Figure 5.16 shows formally the procedure to insert a new case into the discrimination network.

Input : A state net node, the new foot-printed initial state, and the sorted parameterized interacting goals.

Output : The updated discrimination state network.

procedure **Insert_New_Case** (*state_net_node, new_state_goal, sorted_par_goal*)
1.when *new_state_goal* do
   ;;*Compare the contents of state_net_node against the new_state_goal*
2. *old_left* ← *state_net_node* \ *new_state_goal*
3. *intersect* ← *state_net_node* ∩ *new_state_goal*
4. *new_left* ← *new_state_goal* \ *state_net_node*
5. if **Highest_Relevant** (*intersect*)
6.   then **Set_State_Node_Contents** (*state_net_node, intersect*)
7.   if *old_left*
8.   then **Create_New_State_Node** (*new_left*)
9.   else
       matching_child ← **Find_Matching_Child** (*state_net_node, new_left, sorted_par_goal*)
8.   **Insert_New_Case** (*matching_child, new_left, sorted_par_goal*)
9.   else **Create_New_State_Node** (*new_left*)

Figure 5.16: Algorithm to insert a new case into memory.

The procedure recursively gets as an input the contents of a node in the discrimination state net, *state_net_node*, the new foot-printed initial state, *new_state_goal*, and the parameterized goals, *sorted_par_goal*. The *new_state_goal* and the *state_net_node* may have literals in common. Steps 2-4 of the procedure identify the intersection and differences between these two sets of literals. Step 5 checks if the literals in the intersection are of higher relevance than the literals in both complementing subsets. The procedure **Highest_Relevant** uses the `relevance-bias` stored at the root of the network to compute the relative relevance of the literals. Steps 6-9 maintain the structure of the tree to guarantee that the contents of each parent node are of equal or higher relevance than the literals in its children nodes.

Figure 5.17 illustrates the three different situations described that can occur at insertion time. In (a) a particular node **OLD** is sketched with its children subtrees **A** and **B**. Part (b) of the figure shows the new situation **NEW** intersecting the node **OLD** (after matching and unification). Part (c) shows the different resulting new configurations of the discrimination tree.

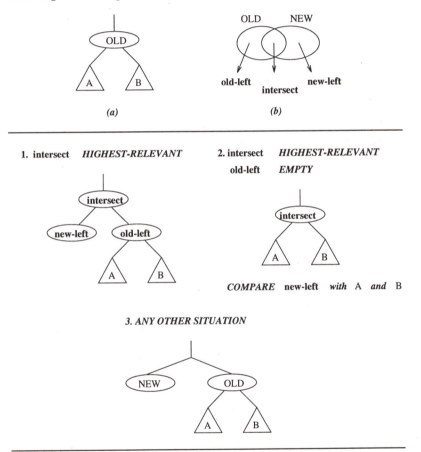

Figure 5.17: Inserting a new case into the state net; (a) The initial discrimination network; (b) The NEW state literals intersect the OLD state literals at the node; (c) The three possible situations: 1. The highest-relevant literals are part of the intersection of NEW and OLD, 2. Same as 1. but in addition there are no OLD literals left, 3. Any other situation.

Part (c) 1. and 2. illustrate the situation in which the literals in the intersection of `OLD` and `NEW` are more relevant than either the literals in `old-left` or `new-left`. The situation (c) 2. shows the more common frequent situation in which `old-left` is empty and therefore the literals in `new-left` are recursively inserted into the subtrees `A` and `B`. Finally part (c) 3. shows the resulting tree in any other situation where the intersection between the `OLD` and the `NEW` literals of the initial state is not more relevant than any of other left subsets. For this situation both the `NEW` and `OLD` nodes become siblings of each other.

We developed some preliminary algorithms to dynamically reorganize the discrimination networks based on the feedback that the analogical replay mechanism provides to the case library on the utility of the suggested guidance. We are currently exploring further the impact of the dynamic reorganization of the case library in the overall performance of our learning system.

5.5   Summary

This chapter presented the indexing of the cases, the data structures supporting the organization of the case library, and the complete storage algorithm.

The storage algorithm involves the identification of the set of indices for a case and the selection of appropriate data structures to organize the acquired knowledge in the case library.

The interacting goals are identified by partially ordering the totally ordered solution found. The connected components of the partially ordered plan determine the independent fragments of the case each corresponding to a set of interacting goals. Each case is multiply indexed by the sets of interacting goals. The relevant literals of the initial state are foot-printed for each goal conjunct in the goal statement by goal regressing through the episodic plan found.

Chapter 6

Efficient Case Retrieval

The previous chapter described how a case is multiply indexed by the set of interacting goals and by the relevant features of the initial state. It also presented the data structures that support the indexing of the case library. There is an important question to address next: How can past experience be retrieved efficiently from the case library?

This chapter describes the retrieval procedure. It follows the path of a new given problem through the case library until a set of similar past cases is identified. The chapter is organized in five sections. The first section states the general retrieval problem and motivates the need for an *efficient* algorithm especially in large case libraries. Section 2 introduces different similarity metrics with increasing degrees of problem-context sensitivity. The third section presents the designed and implemented retrieval algorithm, discusses its implementation, and illustrates the procedure with an example from the logistics transportation domain. Section 4 discusses how the cost of retrieving the similar cases can be offset by the expected search effort savings. Finally, Section 5 summarizes the chapter.

6.1 The ground for the retrieval procedure

Consider that a new problem is proposed to the problem solver specified in terms of a goal statement and an initial state. Instead of simply trying to solve the new problem from its domain theory (if one is available), PRODIGY/ANALOGY tries to find if it has solved any *similar* problems before. Two aspects motivate our problem solving strategy of looking first for similar past experience rather than proceeding to search for a solution to the problem straight from the domain theory.

1. Solving a problem from a domain theory involves searching through the problem state space. The search is exponential on the length of the solution. For large and complex problems this search may be unacceptable. Therefore the problem solver looks for previous problem solving experience

that it can use in addition to, or instead of, its domain theory to generate a solution to the new problem.

2. The analogical problem solver explores the transfer of problem solving experience among similar situations. It tries to learn not only from the exact same past problem solving experience but from similar situations.

The retrieval phase consists of identifying the similar problem solving situations that will potentially be helpful to the replay mechanism guiding its reconstruction process and reducing the problem solving search effort involved. Several questions drive the design of the retrieval procedure:

- What are similar problem solving situations?

  - What features should be compared?
  - How to rank the partially matched situations that differ and match in different features sets?

- What is a reasonable amount of effort to invest in searching for similar situations?

  - Should it be guaranteed that the retrieved analogs are the *best* matched problems in the case library?
  - Can anything be predicted in terms of the amount of problem solving savings expected from a particular similar case?

The first set of questions on the suitability of various similarity metrics motivates a major part of the research in analogy and case-based reasoning. In this work I face similar questions, but answers are provided in a more relaxed manner, i.e., from an integrated machine learning and problem solving perspective. The concept of *similar* is defined in terms of the problem solving experience.

The second set of questions, as raised in this work, is driven by the scaling up of the case library and the integration with the base problem solver. When the case library increases considerably in size and in complexity of the stored cases, the matching time, even for role substitution at the indexing level, may become very expensive if there is no concern for how the learned knowledge is organized. When the number of cases in the case library is small, it is feasible to guarantee a best match. In fact, a problem solver that is not integrated with any kind of other domain knowledge needs to guarantee that the similar past problem to be adapted does not differ considerably from the new situation, so that the knowledge-weak adaptation phase may succeed. In this work the integration with the base level problem solver allows the system to relax on retrieving a guaranteed best match, and requires instead a reasonable match that overcomes the weaknesses of the specifications of the domain theory.

Overall, both sets of questions proved very challenging to answer. The approach developed in this work to efficiently retrieve similar cases is successfully validated through empirical results as shown in Chapter 8. Later this chapter also presents a simple analysis of the trade-off between the retrieval and the problem solving search costs.

This section discusses the techniques developed to address the issues raised above. It further defines formally the concepts and presents the algorithms designed.

6.1.1 What are similar problem solving situations?

Consider a new problem solving situation with goal statement $\mathcal{G} = G_1, G_2, \ldots, G_k$ and initial state $\mathcal{S}$ also given as a conjunction of literals. When retrieving past cases, the system compares the features from these two distinct sets, i.e. the goal and initial state features. As the analogical reasoner expects to learn from situations that **partially match** the new situation, it considers as reasonable candidate analogs, past cases that share only subsets of the features of the goal statement and/or of the initial state.

The immediate question that arises is that of how to rank the partially matched situations: What is "best": To share more features *all together* independently from whether they are in the goal or initial state feature sets? To share more *goal* features? To share more features from the *initial state*? The common sense intuitive answer is to consider as the "best" match, the situation that shares *the most relevant* features. Many attempts have been made to define relevance, most of which are successful in special purpose systems [Ashley and Rissland, 1987, Hinrichs and Kolodner, 1991, Rissland and Skalak, 1991]. The new similarity metric developed in this work relaxes the need to guarantee that the "best" match is returned. The method however guarantees that the match is *reasonable* in the sense that it is expected to reduce problem solving search time when the replay mechanism constructs a new solution guided by the retrieved similar cases.

The retrieval procedure could simply search for cases to cover each goal conjunct individually. However the interactions among multiple goal conjuncts both in terms of operator choices and operator orderings are responsible for a major part of the problem solving search effort and the quality of the solutions encountered. Furthermore each case stored in the case library is indexed through the corresponding sets of interacting goals. The case library is a source of acquired knowledge of experienced goal interactions. Therefore when trying to retrieve cases to cover a set of multiple goals, the retrieval procedure tries to find cases with similar interacting goals instead of choosing separate one-goal cases for each individual goal. The used similarity metric accounts for the combined match degree of the interacting goal conjuncts and the corresponding foot-printed initial state. I also propose a method where the levels of relevance used by the similarity metric are dynamically updated by interpreting the feedback that the replay mechanism returns on the utility of the guidance provided.

6.1.2 How can retrieval be efficient in a large case library?

Previous researchers have identified a variety of situations where a learning system may face a *utility* problem, i.e., a decrease in performance when the amount of learned knowledge increases [Minton, 1988b]. In the context of this work, this utility problem could be stated as:

- Does the performance of the overall analogical reasoner degrade with an increase in the number of cases in the case library?

In particular in terms of the retrieval procedure, the question reduces to whether the retrieval procedure can be efficient even for large case libraries. In PRODIGY/ANALOGY I follow the view that "learning" consists of a global process whose final result *must* be a performance improvement. Therefore learning does not uniquely consist of compiling experience into new reusable knowledge. The learning process needs to incorporate the additional phase of efficiently organizing the learned knowledge. Hence, the case library in PRODIGY/ANALOGY is appropriately indexed to allow the efficient retrieval of candidate analog cases. The potential utility problem is then avoided or considerably reduced.

In order to design an efficient retrieval algorithm, we used the following strategies:

- Reduce the number of candidates to be subject to detailed matching and unification by using several levels of indexing filtering.

- Even if the case indices are efficiently selected, complete matching or unification may be unacceptable especially in complex problems with a large set of features. Therefore thresholds are set for the match degree expectation, for the allowed retrieval time, and for the degree of guiding coverage returned.

The overall technique to avoid the utility problem relies on efficient data structures (hash tables) for the indices that prune the set of candidate analogs early, and on setting thresholds for the amount of effort allowed in the overall retrieval procedure. This approach is possible because of the powerful integration of the analogical component into the base-level problem solver. The integration allows the system to reason from partially matched situations, as the analogical replayer will solve a new problem more efficiently by using the guiding similar past cases in addition to its domain theory, than by searching solely using from the domain theory.

The idea of setting thresholds may seem simple. It becomes however interesting when the problem solver is a **learning** system in addition to being a static problem solver. The challenge is to let the overall system accumulate experience and learn better correlations among the acquired knowledge.[1] The learning component enables the system to converge towards improving the quality of the retrieved analogs with bounded retrieving capabilities.

---

[1] We did not explore other issues on memory organization, such as forgetting acquired experience. However, the storage algorithm keeps a rudimentary count on the frequency of reuse of a case and also a measure of the complexity of the search space explored in the problem solving episode corresponding to a case. Further research can draw upon these stored indices to define principles to drive the eventual forgetting of unused experience.

In summary, this work initiates this novel line of reasoning by which the analogical problem solver restates the retrieval question from: "Which are the *best* similar past cases that are available?" to the question: "Which are the *reasonably* similar past cases that can be retrieved within limited bounded resources, within the allocated time for retrieval and partial match degree?". This work is an initial step in this approach within the problem solving and machine learning framework.

6.2 Defining a similarity metric

Let P be a new problem proposed to the problem solver with goal statement $\mathcal{G}^P$, and initial state $\mathcal{S}^P$, both given as conjunctions of literals. A *literal* is a predicate applied to any number of argument values, i.e., literal = (predicate argument-value*). As an example, (at-truck tr13 po57) is a literal where at-truck is the predicate and tr13 and po57 are its instantiated arguments.

The retrieval procedure identifies a set of past cases that jointly **cover** the goal statement. Definition 6 introduces what is meant by a case covering a goal conjunct.

Definition 6 Coverage and unification:
  Let $\mathcal{G}^P = G_1^P, G_2^P, \ldots, G_k^P$ be the conjunctive goal statement of problem P with conjuncts $G_1^P, G_2^P, \ldots, G_k^P$. A past case C with goal statement $\mathcal{G}^C = G_1^C, G_2^C, \ldots, G_l^C$ **covers** a goal G_i^P, or G_i^P is **covered** by the case C, iff there is some G_j^C such that G_i^P and G_j^C unify.
  A literal l **unifies** a literal l', if
  • The predicate of l is the same as the predicate of l'.
  • Each argument of l is of the same class (type) as its corresponding argument of l'.
In this case, there is a substitution $\sigma = \{arg_1/arg_1', \ldots, arg_k/arg_k'\}$, such that $l = \sigma(l')$.

As an example of the unification of literals, the literal (in-room key12 room1) unifies with the literal (in-room key13 room4), where key12 and key13 are both of class KEY and room1 and room4 are both of class ROOM, under the substitution $\sigma = \{$(key12 . key13), (room1 . room4)$\}$.

Selecting a set of past cases that cover the new problem involves the establishment of a *similarity metric* by which the algorithm can decide whether it is *better* to cover the problem with one set of cases or another.

There are several options of possible similarity metrics. Below three different ones are introduced with increasing degrees of problem-context sensitivity. First definition 7 introduces the match value of two conjunctions of literals under some substitution as the number of literals that unify under that substitution.

Definition 7 Match value of two conjunctions of literals:
  A conjunction of literals $L = l_1, \ldots, l_n$ unifies a conjunction of literals $L' = l_1', \ldots, l_m'$ under a substitution σ with **match value** δ^σ, if there are δ **many** literals in the intersection of L and $\sigma(L')$.

6.2.1   A direct similarity metric

The simplest comparison between a new problem and a past case is to just equate the features of the goal statement and initial state flatly by counting the number of shared features. Definition 8 establishes this direct similarity metric between two problems.

Definition 8 Direct similarity metric:

  Let P and P' be two particular problems, respectively with initial states $\mathcal{S}^P$ and $\mathcal{S}^{P'}$, and goals $\mathcal{G}^P$ and $\mathcal{G}^{P'}$. Let $\delta_\mathcal{G}^\sigma$ be the match value of $\mathcal{G}^P$ and $\mathcal{G}^{P'}$ and $\delta_\mathcal{S}^\sigma$ be the match value of $\mathcal{S}^P$ and $\mathcal{S}^{P'}$, under some substitution σ.

  The two problems P and P' **directly match** *with* **match value** $\delta^\sigma = \delta_\mathcal{G}^\sigma + \delta_\mathcal{S}^\sigma$ *for substitution σ.*

In this metric all the features of both the goal statement and the initial state are credited for the similarity of the problems. The immediate advantage of this metric is its conceptual simplicity. It does not require any particular understanding or encoding of what is more relevant. All the knowledge available is uniformly weighed. The empirical experiments showed that this similarity metric is adequate for simple and well-defined problems where the initial state is reduced to a small set of useful features.

The partial match value of two problems is substitution dependent. As an example, consider the goal $\mathcal{G}$ ={(inroom key12 room1), (inroom box1 room1)}, and the goal $\mathcal{G}'$ ={(inroom key13 room4), (inroom key14 room2), (inroom box53 room4)}. Then $\mathcal{G}$ directly matches $\mathcal{G}'$ with match value $\delta^\sigma = 2$ under the substitution σ ={(key12 . key13), (room1 . room4), (box1 . box53)}, and match value $\delta^{\sigma'} = 1$ under the substitution σ' ={(key12 . key14), (room1 . room2)}. This direct similarity metric does not consider any relevant correlations between the initial states and the goal statements.

6.2.2   Global foot-printing similarity metric

The problem of matching conjunctive goals turns out to be rather complex. As conjunctive goals may interact, it is not at all clear that problems are more similar based simply on the *number* of literals that match the initial state and the goal statements. Noticing that matching conjunctive goals involves reasoning over a large lattice of situations, a new similarity metric is developed that refines the indexing based on the derivational trace of a past solution.

When the complexity of the specification of the initial state increases it becomes impossible and inadequate to consider evenly all the features. As a past case corresponds to problem solving experience, it is possible to identify the relevant features of the initial state of the past case. Section 5.2 extensively showed a method to automatically identify these relevant features from the derivational trace of the case. According to that algorithm the initial state is foot-printed into the sets of literals that contribute to achieve the different goal conjuncts of the goal statement. Definition 9 is built upon the previous direct similarity metric but increases the problem-context sensitivity as it takes into account the reduced foot-printed as opposed to the complete initial state.

When assigning a match value to two problems, the global foot-printing similarity metric considers not only the *number* of goals that match, but also uses the matched goals themselves to determine the match degree of the initial state.

Definition 9 Global foot-printing similarity metric:
Let P be a new problem and P' be a previously solved problem, respectively with initial states S^P and $S^{P'}$, and goals G^P and $G^{P'}$. Let δ_G^σ be the match value of G^P and $G^{P'}$, under substitution σ, and let $G_1, \ldots, G_m$ be the matched goals.

Let $S_{fp}^{P'}$ be the foot-printed initial state of problem P' for the set of matched goals $G_1, \ldots, G_m$. Let δ_S^σ be the match value of S^P and $S_{fp}^{P'}$, under substitution σ.

The two problems P and P' **globally foot-print match** *with* **match value** $\delta^\sigma = \delta_G^\sigma + \delta_S^\sigma$ *for substitution σ.*

The purpose of retrieving a similar past case is to provide a problem solving episode to be replayed for the construction of the solution to a new problem. The similarity metric captures the role of the initial state in terms of the different goal conjuncts for a particular solution found. Situation details are not similar per se. They are similar as a function of their relevance in the solution encountered. When the foot-printed literals are taken into account for the measure of the similarity among problems, the retrieved analogs may provide reasonable guidance at replay time, as the foot-printed initial state is in the subgoaling chain of the goal statement in the particular solution to be replayed. If the new situation shares some of these features, the problem solver should encounter the same or parts of the past search space. The case may not be fully-sufficient due to the partial match, but, because of the shared foot-printed literals of the initial state, the case does not work against the goal, except for unexpected or uncovered goal interactions.

6.2.3 Interacting foot-printing similarity metric

There is an issue to resolve about using parts of a case for partially matched goal situations. If the shared goals are not from the same set of interacting goals of the candidate guiding case, then the question is why to use this guiding case instead of using a set of individual cases to cover each of the goals. Definition 10, considers not only the *number* of goals and initial state literals that match, but also uses the matched goals themselves to determine the match degree of the initial state. This metric extends the previous one by requiring that if a case covers totally a set of goals, then these are interacting goals.

Definition 10 Interacting foot-printed similarity metric:
Let P be a new problem and P' be a previously solved problem, respectively with initial states S^P and $S^{P'}$, and goals G^P and $G^{P'}$. Let δ_G^σ be the match value

of $\mathcal{G}^P$ and $\mathcal{G}^{P'}$, under substitution σ, such that **the matched goals** $G_1, \ldots, G_m$ **cover completely one or more sets of interacting goals**.

Let $\mathcal{S}_{fp}^{P'}$ be the foot-printed initial state of problem P' for the set of matched goals $G_1, \ldots, G_m$. Let $\delta_{\mathcal{S}}^{\sigma}$ be the match value of $\mathcal{S}^P$ and $\mathcal{S}_{fp}^{P'}$, under substitution σ.

The two problems P and P' **interactively foot-print match** *with* **match value** $\delta^{\sigma} = \delta_{\mathcal{G}}^{\sigma} + \delta_{\mathcal{S}}^{\sigma}$ *for substitution σ.*

Chapter 8 shows empirical results comparing the direct and the global foot-printing similarity metrics. The tests were run in the extended-STRIPS and the machine-shop scheduling domains. The results obtained show that the analogical problem solver performs better when the global foot-printing similarity metric is used than when the direct one is used. The extensive tests in the logistics transportation domain use the interacting foot-printing similarity metric. This metric was found to be the most adequate to handle the large and complex problems in that domain. The term "foot-printing similarity metric" with no qualification refers from now on to the interacting foot-printing similarity metric.

The purpose of retrieving a similar past case is to provide a problem solving episode to be replayed for the construction of the solution to a new problem. The similarity metric captures the role of the initial state in terms of the different goal conjuncts for a particular solution found. Situation details are not similar per se. They are similar as a function of their relevance in the solution encountered. When the foot-printed literals are taken into account for the measure of the similarity among problems, the retrieved analogs provide expected adequate guidance at replay time, as the foot-printed initial state is in the subgoaling chain of the goal statement in the particular solution to be replayed. If the new situation shares some of these features, the problem solver encounters the same or parts of the past search space. The case may not be fully-sufficient due to the partial match, but, because of the shared foot-printed literals of the initial state, the case does not work against the goal, except for unexpected or uncovered goal interactions. These will be new learning opportunities as new cases to store and reuse.

6.3   The retrieval procedure

Consider that each past case C stored in the case library is indexed by the corresponding foot-printed initial state and goal statement, respectively $\mathcal{S}^C$ and $\mathcal{G}^C$. When a new problem P is given to the system in terms of its goal statement $\mathcal{G}^P$ and initial state $\mathcal{S}^P$, retrieving one (or more) analog consists in finding a *similar* past case by comparing these two inputs $\mathcal{G}^P$ and $\mathcal{S}^P$ to the indices of the past case, $\mathcal{G}^C$ and $\mathcal{S}^C$.

Figure 6.1 shows the retrieval procedure where the underlying strategy is to get guidance from cases that cover the largest possible set of interacting goals. The algorithm focuses on retrieving past cases where the problem solver experienced equivalent goal interactions, as these are expectedly responsible for a large part of the problem solving search effort.

Input : A new problem with goal statement $\mathcal{G} = G_1, G_2, \ldots, G_k$ and initial state $\mathcal{S}$.

Output : A set of similar cases.

procedure **Retrieve_Similar_Cases** ($\mathcal{G}$, $\mathcal{S}$):
1. *covering_cases* ← ∅; *no_int_goals* ← k; *uncovered_goals* ← $\mathcal{G}$;
2. *past_case* ← nil; *continue_retrieval_p* ← true
3. while *uncovered_goals* or *continue_retrieval_p*
4.   *past_case* ← **Find_Another_Analog** (*no_int_goals*, *uncovered_goals*, *past_case*)
5.   if *past_case* then
6.   *(matched_goals, goal_substitution)* ← **Match_Goals** (*past_case*, $\mathcal{G}$)
7.   *(similarity_value, total_substitution)* ← **Match_Initial_States** (*past_case, matched_goals, goal_substitution*, $\mathcal{S}$)
8.   if **Satisfied_with_Match** (*similarity_value*)
           then
9.   *uncovered_goals* ← *uncovered_goals* \ *matched_goals*
10.   *covering_cases* ← *covering_cases* ∪ {*past_case*}
11.   if (*no_int_goals* > 1) and (number of *uncovered_goals* <= *no_int_goals*)
       then
12.   *no_int_goals* ← **Decrease_Interacting_Scope** (*no_int_goals*, *uncovered_goals*)
13.   else if (*no_int_goals* = 1) or **Stop_Retrieval_p** (*past_case*, *uncovered_goals, no_int_goals*)
14.   then *continue_retrieval_p* ← nil
15. Return *covering_cases*

Figure 6.1: Retrieving similar past cases.

Initially step 1 sets the number of goals that the algorithm tries to cover simultaneously, i.e., *no_int_goals*, to the total number k of goal conjuncts. All the conjunctive goals are also declared uncovered. A goal remains uncovered throughout the procedure until a case is found that covers it (see definition 6). The procedure **Find_Another_Analog** at step 4 incrementally searches in the case library for a case that covers *no_int_goals* many of the still uncovered goals. This algorithm uses efficient data structures to perform an incremental generation of candidate analogs. Suppose that a case is returned. Then steps 6 and 7 evaluate the similarity value between the new and past situations. The goals are considered covered at step 9, if the procedure is satisfied with the match value as determined at step 8. Step 10 adds the *past_case* to the list of *covering_cases*. Step 11-14 establish the termination and continuation conditions. In particular, the procedure at step 12 decreases the scope of interactions to be considered according to the number of remaining *uncovered_goals* and no more interactions of size *no_int_goals* are found. The retrieval effort may be interrupted by the procedure **Stop_Retrieval_p** when a threat is recognized in its potential benefits with respect to problem solving search savings (see [Veloso and Carbonell, 1989]).

To illustrate a general run of the procedure, suppose that there are three goals in the new problem, $\mathcal{G} = G_1, G_2, G_3$. The procedure goes through the following steps:

- At step 4 the procedure tries to find cases indexed by three interacting goals that unify with the three goals G_1, G_2, G_3.

- Suppose that it does not find any case indexed by the conjunction of the three goals G_1, G_2, G_3. Step 12 decreases the scope of the interaction from 3 to 2, if no other factors are taken into account.

- Step 4 again tries to find two-interacting goal problems that unify with some combination of the new goals, i.e., $(G_1, G_2), (G_1, G_3)$, or (G_2, G_3).

- Suppose that a past case is returned that unifies with (G_1, G_2). Steps 6 and 7 calculate the similarity value between the foot-printed initial state of the past case and the new initial state. Suppose that the match is not considered satisficing at step 8. This means that the two goals G_1 and G_2 are not considered covered. The algorithm proceeds back to step 4.

- Step 4 incrementally finds the next similar case from the case just found. Suppose that another case is returned that unifies with the two goals (G_2, G_3) with a satisfying match degree. The goals G_2 and G_3 are considered covered.

- Only G_1 is left uncovered at step 9 and step 12 decreases the scope of interaction now to one (as there is only one goal left to cover).

- Step 4 attempts finally to find a case indexed by the goal G_1. If no case is found, it terminates.

- The *covering_cases* returned cover all or part of the complete goal statement.

6.3.1   Indexing data structures

The retrieval procedure is composed of several phases corresponding to the different procedure calls as shown in Figure 6.1. The complexity of each of the particular procedures, namely **Find_Another_Analog** at step 6, **Match_Goals** at step 8, and **Match_Initial_States** at step 9, is determined by their particular implementation.

The underlying general principle developed in this work for the implementation of the matching problem is to hash on static indices. By using the hash tables presented in the previous chapter, the algorithm accesses the static attribute information in constant time to compute the role substitutions at different levels of the class hierarchy. **Find_Another_Analog** and **Match_Goals** match therefore only an already reduced number of the cases for a particular degree of goal interaction. Both matching algorithms, **Match_Goals** and **Match_Initial_States** are incremental and generate one new match as a function of the last match generated.

The empirical results shown in Chapter 8 show that the cost of retrieval increases close to linearly with the complexity of the problem, when a threshold for the match value is used.

In summary the implementation conforms the following characteristics:

- Indexing hash tables reduce the set of candidate analogs in constant time.

- The matching algorithm is incremental to allow stopping retrieval if some "reasonable" partial match is found.

- No effort to retrieve the *best* set of candidate analogs from the case library.

6.3.2 Illustrative example

The retrieval algorithm is now applied step by step pursuing the example presented in the overview chapter in Section 2.3.[2]

Figure 6.2 shows formally the contents of the several data structures for the indices to the case library, after the five problems **ex1**, **ex2**, **ex3**, **ex4**, and **mult1** have been solved and stored, as sketched in Figure 6.3. Variables are in angle brackets. The name of the variables identifies the class they belong to, namely p for PACKAGE (or OBJECT), ap for AIRPORT, t for TRUCK, po for POST-OFFICE, and a for AIRPLANE.

Consider that a new problem, **mult2** is proposed to the system. Figure 6.4 shows this new problem solving situation with the class distribution of the instances, the initial state, and the goal statement with three goal conjuncts, namely (inside-airplane ob5 p18), (inside-truck ob13 tr1), and (at--truck tr4 p20)).

Stepping through the internals of the retrieval procedure

At the start of the procedure, *no_int_goals* is set to 3, as there are three goal conjuncts in the goal statement (*no_int_goals* captures the level of goal interaction that the procedure is looking for). All the goals are uncovered and *covering_cases* is empty.

The procedure **Find_Another_Analog** accesses the vector *GOAL-INTER-ACTIONS* to find out what three-goal interacting problems are stored in the case library. As *GOAL-INTERACTIONS*[3] is nil and therefore no *past_case*

---

[2]The reader does not need to review the example of the overview chapter, as Figure 6.3 reproduces here the contents of the case library as at the end of the overview examples.

Class-parameterized	Parameterized goals
((inside-truck OBJECT TRUCK))	((inside-truck <p35> <t42>))
((inside-airplane OBJECT AIRPLANE))	((inside-airplane <p25> <a70>))
((at-obj OBJECT AIRPORT))	((at-obj <p69> <ap17>))
((inside-airplane OBJECT AIRPLANE) (inside-truck OBJECT TRUCK))	((inside-airplane <p58> <a25>) (inside-truck <p41> <t6>))

(a) *CLASS-GOAL-PARAMETERIZED-GOAL*

Parameterized goals	State-net-names
((inside-truck <p35> <t42>))	state-net-1
((inside-airplane <p25> <a70>))	state-net-2
((at-obj <p69> <ap17>))	state-net-3
((inside-airplane <p58> <a25>) (inside-truck <p41> <t6>))	state-net-4

(b) *PARAMETERIZED-GOAL-INITIAL-STATE*

No. of Interactions	List of class parameterized goals
1	(((inside-truck OBJECT TRUCK)) ((inside-airplane OBJECT AIRPLANE)) ((at-obj OBJECT AIRPORT)))
2	(((inside-airplane OBJECT AIRPLANE) (inside-truck OBJECT TRUCK)))

(c) *GOAL-INTERACTIONS*

Class-parameterized	Problems
(inside-truck OBJECT TRUCK)	(ex1 ex3 ex4 mult1)
(inside-airplane OBJECT AIRPLANE)	(ex2 mult1)
(at-obj OBJECT AIRPORT)	(ex3 ex4)

(d) *GOAL-PROBLEM*

Figure 6.2: Indexing data structures for the example of Chapter 2.

is returned, step 12 sets *no_int_goals* to 2, i.e., the procedure proceeds searching for two-goal interacting past cases.

The procedure **Find_Another_Analog** accesses the vector *GOAL-INTER-ACTIONS* again and *GOAL-INTERACTIONS*[2] returns the class-parameterized conjunctive goal ((inside-airplane OBJECT AIRPLANE) (inside--truck OBJECT TRUCK)) which unifies at the class level with two of the goals of the new problem, namely (inside-airplane ob5 p18) and (inside-truck ob13 tr1). The procedure **Find_Another_Analog** takes this conjunctive goal to access the hash table *CLASS-GOAL-PARAMETERIZED-GOAL* which

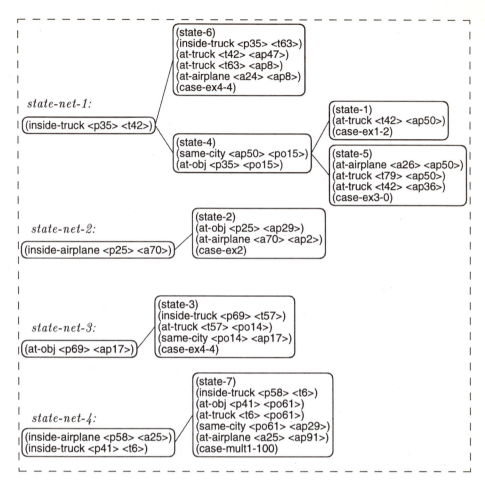

Figure 6.3: Contents of the case library after problems **ex1** (case-ex1-2), **ex2** (case-ex2-1), **ex3** (case-ex3-0), **ex4** (case-ex4-4), and **mult1** (case-mult1-100) have been solved and stored.

returns the parameterized goal ((inside-airplane <p58> <a25>) (inside-- truck <p41> <t6>)). This is considered the first *past_case* (although in reality it may correspond to a set of cases indexed by this conjunctive goal.)

Step 6 calls the procedure **Match_Goals** which returns *matched_goals* set to ((inside-airplane ob5 pl8) (inside-truck ob13 tr1)) and the *goal_sub- stitution* set to ((<p58> . ob5) (<a25> . pl8) (<p41> . ob13) (<t6> . tr1)). The unification requires that the variables be of the same class as the substituting instances (see definition 6).

With this goal substitution the initial state is matched according to the interacting foot-printed similarity metric. The discrimination state net which

```
(has-instances              (state (and              (goal (and
    OBJECT ob5 ob13)           (at-obj ob5 a20)          (inside-airplane ob5 p18)
(has-instances                 (inside-truck ob13 tr4)   (inside-truck ob13 tr1)
    TRUCK tr1 tr4)             (at-truck tr4 a20)        (at-truck tr4 p20)))
(has-instances                 (at-truck tr1 a5)
    AIRPLANE p18)             (at-airplane p18 a20)
(has-instances                 (same-city a5 p5)
    AIRPORT a5 a11 a20)       (same-city a11 p11)
(has-instances                 (same-city a20 p20)))              (c)
    POST-OFFICE p5 p11 p20)      (b)
(has-instances
    CITY c5 c11 c20)
        (a)
```

Figure 6.4: A new example - mult2: (a) class distribution of instances, (b) initial state, (c) goal statement.

stores the cases solving this goal is given by accessing the hash table *PARAME-TERIZED-GOAL-INITIAL-STATE* which returns state-net-4. This network has only one case stored denominated case-mult1-100, as shown in Figure 6.3. This case corresponds to the solution obtained by solving the problems mult1 by derivational analogy (see Chapter 2).

The procedure **Match_Initial_States** tries to match the stored foot-printed initial state, which is the contents of the state net node state-7 (see Figure 6.3), against the new initial state. Figure 6.5 (a) shows the past initial state after applying the already set *goal_substitution* and in (b) it shows the new initial state.

Unifying the two initial states returns only one extra substitution namely ((<ap91> . a20)) with the similarity value of 1 out of 5 literals in the past initial state. Assume that there is a threshold of 60% of match required to consider that the match between the past and new initial state is satisfiable. The match obtained is 1 out of 5, equivalent to only a match of 20%. **Satisfied_with_Match** returns therefore nil. The two goals are not considered yet covered by this case and the search for a better coverage continues.

As there are no other two-goal interacting cases, step 12 decreases the value of *no_int_goals* to 1, which means that the procedure is now going to search for one-goal cases to cover the three goal conjuncts.

By accessing *GOAL-INTERACTIONS*[1], **Find_Another_Analog** considers the three one-goal cases stored in the case library, namely ((inside-truck OBJECT TRUCK)), ((inside-airplane OBJECT AIRPLANE)), and ((at-obj OBJECT AIRPORT)). By accessing the hash table *CLASS-GOAL-PARAMETER-IZED-GOAL* on the first goal, *past_case* is returned as ((inside-truck <p35> <t42>)).

Step 6 calls the procedure **Match_Goals** which returns *matched_goals* set to (inside-truck ob13 tr1) and the *goal_substitution* set to ((<p35> . ob13) (<t42> . tr1)). The state net state-net-1 is returned by *PARAMETER-IZED-GOAL-INITIAL-STATE* of (inside-truck <p35> <t42>) (see Figure 6.2).

```
goal_substitution:
 ((<p58> . ob5) (<a25> . p18) (<p41> . ob13) (<t6> . tr1))


State net node state-7                    New initial state:
after goal_substitution:

(inside-truck ob5 tr1)                    (at-obj ob5 a20)
(at-obj ob13 <po61>)                      (inside-truck ob13 tr4)
(at-truck tr1 <po61>)                     (at-truck tr1 a5)
(same-city <po61> <ap29>)                 (at-truck tr4 a20)
(at-airplane p18 <ap91>)                  (at-airplane p18 a20)
                                          (same-city p5 a5)
                                          (same-city p11 a11)
                                          (same-city p20 a20)
             (a)                                  (b)
```

Figure 6.5: (a) Foot-printed past initial state of a candidate analog after applying the goal substitution; and (b) the new initial state (b).

The procedure **Match_Initial_States** matches the new initial state against the stored foot-printed initial state first at the top level state net nodes, namely state-6 and state-4 (see Figure 6.3). These nodes are closer to the root, which means that their literals are more relevant than the literals at the nodes further away from the root. Figure 6.6 (a) shows the past initial state after applying the already set *goal_substitution* and in (b) it shows the initial state for the new problem.

The two initial states unify with the substitution ((<t63> . tr4) (<ap47> . a5) (<ap8> . a20) (<a24> . p18)). The similarity value is a match of four literals out of the total four literals in the past foot-printed initial state. With the same threshold of 60% to consider satisfiable a match value of a past case, the procedure **Satisfied_with_Match** returns true. The goal (inside--truck ob13 tr1) is considered covered by case case-ex4-4. The cycle at step 3 proceeds to try to cover the other goals.

An identical situation occurs for the goal (inside-airplane ob5 p18). As an exercise the reader can confirm that this goal is covered by case case-ex2-1 stored at state-net-2 with the *total_substitution* set to ((<p25> . ob5) (<a70> . p18) (<ap29> . a20)). The match value is 50% as only one of the two literals matches, namely (at-obj ob5 a20). In the past case the object and the airplane are at different airports while in the new problem they are at the same airport. The match value is not above the preestablished threshold of 60%, but it is above an also preestablished minimum covering threshold of 30%. The goal is considered covered by this case as there are no other candidates covering cases.

```
goal_substitution:
      ((<p35> . ob13) (<t42> . tr1))


State net node state-6              New initial state:
after goal_substitution:

(inside-truck ob13 <t63>)           (at-obj ob5 a20)
(at-truck tr1 <ap47>)               (inside-truck ob13 tr4)
(at-truck <t63> <ap8>)              (at-truck tr1 a5)
(at-airplane <a24> <ap8>)           (at-truck tr4 a20)
                                    (at-airplane p18 a20)
                                    (same-city p5 a5)
                                    (same-city p11 a11)
                                    (same-city p20 a20)
              (a)                             (b)
```

Figure 6.6: (a) Foot-printed past initial state of another candidate analog after applying the goal substitution; and (b) the new initial state.

Finally the goal (at-truck tr4 p20) is not covered by any past case. Figure 6.7 shows a trace of the final returned set of covering cases.

```
<cl> (retrieve-analogs 'mult2)

 Analogs to prob mult2:
 (((inside-airplane ob5 p18) case-ex2-1
   ((<p25> . ob5) (<a70> . p18) (<ap29> . a11))
     1 0.5 2 "state-net-2")
  ((inside-truck ob13 tr1) case-ex4-4
   ((<p35> . ob13) (<t42> . tr1) (<t63> . tr4)
    (<ap47> . a5)  (<ap8> . a20) (<a24> . p18))
      4 1.0 5 "state-net-1")
  ((at-truck tr4 p20) 'no-case))
nil
<cl>
```

Figure 6.7: Retrieving similar past cases for problem mult2.

Each goal is associated with a guiding case, if one was found. For each goal the figure shows additionally the substitution, the number of literals matched in the initial state, the match degree, the total number of literals matched in the goal and initial state, and the discrimination network for the guiding case.

6.4 Trading off retrieval and search costs

In pure general-purpose problem solvers, the cost of search is exponential in the length of the solution. In pure CBR systems the cost of retrieval is very high as the system fully relies on retrieving the *best* case in memory to maximize its chance of successful adaptation. This section explores the trade-offs of balancing the cost of retrieving and the residual problem solving cost.

The organization of the memory is such that the indices for the cases are less relevant as their indexing features move away from the root of the discrimination network. For a given a new problem P with initial state $\mathcal{S}^P$ and goal $\mathcal{G}^P$, the absolute maximum possible match value is simply $absolute\_max\_match =$ length $(\mathcal{G}^P) +$ length $(\mathcal{S}^P)$.

In general, the purpose of the integration of analogy and search is to reduce the size of the search space in terms of the number of the nodes searched and consequently achieve an improvement in running time. The desired behavior of the analogical reasoner is captured by the inequality:

$$t_{retrieval} + t_{replay} \ll t_{domain-search}$$

where $t_{retrieval}$ is the retrieval time or effort, t_{replay} is the replay (or adaptation) time, and $t_{domain-search}$ is the time to search direct and uniquely using the domain theory. Harandi and Bhansali [Harandi and Bhansali, 1989] confirmed that analogy would be useful if the time to find analogs is small and the degree of similarity is high. Hickman, Shell, and Carbonell [Hickman *et al.*, 1990] also showed that internal analogy can reduce the search cost. I show here that there is an optimal range of retrieval time to spend searching for candidate analogs. Intuitively the deeper that memory is searched, the more confidence on the retrieved analogs and expectedly the less search required by the problem solver. However searching memory also takes time. Is there, hence, an optimal amount of effort to spend searching memory?

The memory is organized in such a way that the confidence on the match degree increases monotonically with retrieval time [Kolodner, 1984, Schank, 1982] though not necessarily in a linear manner. This also means that there is always one (or more) case(s) available to return when retrieval is halted. If the retrieval time increases, then more cases are compared or more matching can be done for a particular case. To capture this effect in a simple way, let

- t_r be the time spent to retrieve a similar past case,
- δ_{t_r} be the match value between the case retrieved and the new problem,
- m be the absolute_max_match as introduced above, and
- d be the percentage of deviation from the absolute_max_match of the match value of the case retrieved if the retrieval time is null (or close to null).

To capture the fact that the match degree increases with the time the algorithm spends retrieving, the retrieval time is expressed as:

$$\delta_{t_r} = m(1 - dC^{-\alpha t_r}), \qquad (6.1)$$

where C and α are constants.

Figure 6.8 sketches three possible curves for the match value as a function of the retrieval time. Curves 1 and 2 show situations where the initial match is poor, i.e., with low match degree. However for curve 1 the rate of match-degree improvement is very low (low α) while for curve 2 the match degree increases rapidly with the retrieval time. Situations 1 and 2 depict two different rates of improvement for the match result while traversing down the discrimination net. Curve 3 plots a situation where the initial match is immediately high and continues to improve gradually towards the maximum.

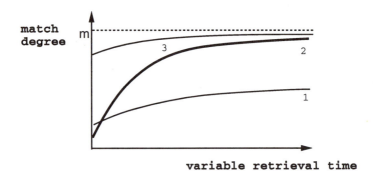

Figure 6.8: Three different curves for the match value as a function of the retrieval time.

In the situations captured by the curves 1 and 3, the system should not invest a long time in retrieving a *better, or best* similar past case. In both cases termination occurs because the rate of improvement, α, is low. In case 1, the system should solve the problem using the basic problem solver search, because there are no good cases. In case 3 it should immediately start derivational replay on the retrieved high-match case, rather than waste time seeking a marginally better one. Situation 2 illustrates the case where retrieval time is more wisely invested. Given the fact that the match degree is on average directly related to search savings in problem solving, one can show that there is an optimal amount of effort to spend searching memory.

PRODIGY's search tree can be viewed as an OR-tree, branching alternatively among possible goal orderings and possible operators to achieve a goal. Let b be the average branching factor of the search tree, l be the solution length for a given problem, and S be the search effort without analogy. Then the complexity of S is [Hickman *et al.*, 1990], $S = \mathcal{O}(b^{\mathcal{O}(l)})$. (From now on the *order of* notation, $\mathcal{O}$, is not used for simplicity of notation.) Assume that the effect of analogical reasoning is captured in a decrease of the average branching factor [Hickman *et al.*, 1990]. This reduction of the search effort is in direct relationship with the match degree of the guiding case(s). Let $S_{analogy}$ be the search spent with analogy. Then, for some linear function f,

$$S_{analogy} = ((1 - f(\delta_{t_r}))b)^l. \tag{6.2}$$

The goal of the integrated analogical reasoner is to improve the effort to reach a solution: problem solving search time plus memory search time. The objective is to find the situation when this sum is much smaller than brute-force problem solving search without any analogical guidance. This goal is captured in the inequality below, where it is not represented, for simplicity, the function f introduced in eq. 6.2:

$$t_r + ((1 - \delta_{t_r})b)^l \ll b^l. \tag{6.3}$$

Substituting eq. 6.1 into the eq. 6.3, the final equation as a function of the retrieval time t_r is:

$$t_r + (1 - m(1 - dC^{-\alpha t_r}))^l b^l \ll b^l \tag{6.4}$$

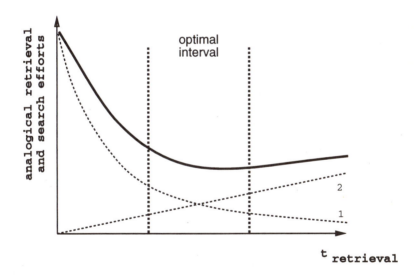

Figure 6.9: Retrieval time (curve 2) plus analogical search effort (curve 1).

Figure 6.9 sketches the left hand side of inequality 6.4.[3] The analysis of this qualitative curve leads to the conclusion that there is an optimal retrieval time interval, which is a function of the dynamic match rate α. Retrieval should stop when a given threshold is reached, namely when the derivative of the expected search savings approaches the incremental memory search cost.

---

[3] This smooth curve does not correspond to data from any particular domain. It captures solely the qualitative behavior of the search effort according to our analytical analysis.

6.5   Summary

The major points to retain from the retrieval procedure are:

- The similarity metric considers the foot-printed initial state and the goal interactions of the past cases.

- Hash tables prune the set of candidate analogs as early as possible.

- The matching is done incrementally until a "reasonable" similar set of past cases is found according to a previously set threshold for the partial match.

Chapter 7

Analogical Replay

This chapter presents the last phase of the analogical problem solving cycle, i.e., the replay mechanism. The previous chapters build up the framework to reach this point where the base-level problem solver is extended with the ability to solve problems by replaying the problem solving episodes of the set of the retrieved similar past cases.

The chapter is organized in five sections. The first section presents an informal description of the replaying procedure. The section outlines the method, and discusses its advantages in terms of the problem solving search reduction and in terms of the memory reorganization. Section 2 states formally the replay algorithm as an extension to the base-level problem solver presented in Chapter 3. The section shows how the similar past cases guide the problem solving steps. The replaying functionality converts the base-level problem solver from a generator and explorer of different search directions to a tester of the validity of past choices, while still being able to generate solutions if the cases don't cover the problem adequately. The third section offers examples on the reuse of a few justifications. Section 4 discusses the method proposed to dynamically reorganize the memory indices based on the feedback that the analogical problem solver may provide on the utility of the guidance received. Finally Section 5 summarizes the chapter with a revision of the techniques developed.

7.1 Replaying past problem solving episodes

The previous chapters 4 and 5 showed how the derivational traces of the problem solving episodes, i.e., the cases, are generated and stored into the case library. Chapter 6 further presented the process to retrieve past cases similar to a new problem solving situation. The next step consists of extending the problem solver to an analogical reasoner by incorporating into its algorithm the functionality of replanning from past problem solving episodes. These are supplied to the analogical planner as a sequence of decision nodes annotated with the justifications supporting the choices that succeeded or failed.

The general replay mechanism involves therefore a complete interpretation of the justification structures in the context of the new problem to be solved, and the development of adequate actions to be taken when transformed justifications are no longer valid. When solving new problems similar to past cases, one can envision two approaches for derivational replay:

A. *The satisficing approach* - Minimize planning effort by solving the problem as directly as possible, recycling as much of the old solution as permitted by the justifications.

B. *The optimizing approach* - Maximize plan quality by expanding the search to consider alternatives of arbitrary decisions and to re-explore failed paths if their causes for failure are not present in the new situation.

This work so far implements in full the satisficing approach, although work on establishing workable optimizing criteria may make the optimizing alternative viable (so long as the planner is willing to invest the extra time required). Satisficing also accords with observations of human planning efficiency and human planning errors [Newell and Simon, 1972].

7.1.1   Outline of the replay procedure

In the satisficing paradigm, the system is fully guided by its past experience. The syntactic applicability of an operator is always checked by simply testing whether its left hand side matches the current state. Semantic applicability is checked by determining whether the justifications hold (e.g., whether there is still a reason to apply this operator). For all the choice points, the problem solver tests the validity of the justifications (its semantic applicability, or rather its "desirability" in the new situation). In case the choice remains valid in the current problem state, it is merely copied, and in case it is not valid the system has two alternatives:

1. Replan at the particular failed choice, e.g., establishing the current subgoal by other means (find an equivalent operator, or equivalent variable bindings) substituting the new choice for the old one in the solution sequence, or

2. Re-establish the failed condition by adding it as a prioritized goal in the planning, and if achieved simply insert the extra steps into the solution sequence.

In the first case (substitution), deviations from the retrieved solution are minimized by returning to the solution path after making the most localized substitution possible.

The second case occurs for example, when the assumptions for the applicability of an operator fail. The system then tries to overcome the failed condition, and if it succeeds, it returns to the exact point in the derivation to proceed as if nothing had gone wrong earlier. If the extra steps performed do not interfere with the already replayed case steps, the extension occurs without further problems. It may also happen that future steps in the case continue to fail and the case is abandoned.

The two situations may also be described in terms of their effect in how the cases are followed. When the justifications hold, the past choices are transferred to the new context. The cases are advanced to propose the next potentially useful steps. When the justifications are not valid, then the two alternatives described above may correspond to the following actions in the guiding cases:

1. Suspend the guiding case if some extra planning work is needed. For example, this corresponds to the situation where an operator was applied in the past case, and now in the new problem, it cannot be applied yet, as one of its preconditions is not true in the state yet. The replay procedure diverges from the guiding case and tries to replan or recursively tries to find another case that can guide the reachievement of the particular preconditions.

2. Advance the guiding case when some of the past planning work is not necessary. For example, this corresponds to the situation where the past case subgoals in a literal that is now already true in the state. The replay procedure tries to advance the case to the next step that can be replayed.

Figure 7.1 outlines the replay procedure.

The partial match between the past and new situations in principle could lead to divergence from the set of guiding cases. This does not occur however when the adequate foot-print similarity metric is used. The foot-printed initial state which is compared to the new situation captures the relevant features of the initial state in terms of the goals to be achieved and as a function of the solution to be replayed. While the case library is not rich enough in a diversity of cases, the retrieval procedure generally returns a smaller set of guiding cases rather than a larger set of not suitable ones.

Justification structures also encompass the record of past failures in addition to just the subgoaling links [Bhansali, 1991, Kambhampati, 1989, Mostow, 1989]. This allows both the early pruning of current alternatives that were experienced to have failed in the past, and the exploration of alternatives for which the past reason of failure does not exist in the current situation. Furthermore, the replay mechanism in the context of casual commitment as opposed to least commitment allows naturally to combine guidance from several past problem solving episodes. Replicated adapted decisions can be interleaved and backtracked upon. The multiple past similar solutions are merged freely adding or deleting steps as necessary at any stage of the planning.

7.1.2 Advantages of replaying

The replay algorithm is implemented as an extension to the base-level planner. It consists mostly of interrupting the planner at its decision points so it may make

- Select a case to follow: follow the justifications and the selected strategy to merge the guidance from the multiple source similar cases.

- Get the relevant operators for the goals from past cases.

- Prune alternative failures from the current search path if the justifications of the past failures hold.

- Check syntactic applicability of an operator by testing whether its left hand side matches the current state.

- Semantic applicability of decisions is checked by determining whether the justifications hold.

- If choice is not valid, choose the suitable action:

  - Suspend the guiding case if some extra planning work is needed, and
    - Retrieve additional case(s) for problem encountered.
    - Or base plan using the domain theory.
  - Advance the guiding case for the past planning work that is not necessary.
  - Change the focus of attention by selecting another guiding case.

Figure 7.1: Outline of the replay procedure.

choices similar to the ones taken in the past guiding plans. The problem solving procedures are augmented with the functionality to use the control guidance provided by the similar problem solving episodes in addition to the available domain theory.

When using only its domain theory, the problem solver spends a large search effort matching the current problem solving state against its domain theory to resolve what is the next suitable problem solving step.

A guiding case records the *sequence* of decisions that directed the problem solver through the search space in the past similar problem solving episode. The analogical problem solver follows the guiding cases keeping pointers to the individual steps transferred. The subsequent steps to the current last transposed ones of each of the individual guiding cases are the steps that the analogical reasoner considers as the new possible next steps. Hence the matching cost of deciding which domain knowledge applies is drastically reduced to a well-defined test on the appropriateness of the proposed new steps. Through the similar cases returned by the retriever the analogical problem solver gets guidance for each individual step of the complete reconstruction process.

The replay functionality transforms therefore the problem solver, from a module that costly generates possible operators to achieve the goals and searches through the space of alternatives generated, into a module that tests the validity of the choices proposed by the past experience and follows equivalent search directions.

In addition, the past cases also provide information about all the alternatives available beyond the successful one. The ones that were explored in the past and failed have the record of their failure reason. When the transfer of the same choice fails, the replay procedure considers the alternatives explored in the past and prunes the ones that failed whose failure reasons hold. This pruning step corresponds to a reduction in the branching factor of the new search tree.

As an example, consider Figure 7.2 which shows the transfer of choices from two past decision nodes.

NEW   PAST

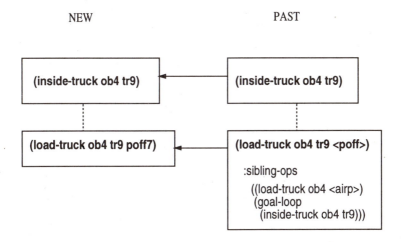

Figure 7.2: Transfer from past decision nodes - an example from an operator transfer.

The past goal node (inside-truck ob4 tr9) is transferred to the new context. This node was achieved in the past by loading the object ob4 into the truck tr9 at some post office that is not instantiated yet, <poff>. Recall that the retrieval procedure returns a partial instantiation for the variables of the past guiding cases. Now at replay time, the algorithm checks whether this operator is still relevant to the goal. It fully instantiates the operator by following any justifications available. In this case there is only the implicit **post-office** type of the variable <poff>. The replay algorithm chooses an instance of this class and adds the bindings (<poff>.poff7) to the current partial instantiation.

In addition to providing the operator that achieves the goal, the past case also provides information about all the other alternatives available. The ones that were explored in the past and failed have the record of their failure reason. In particular in the sketched example of Figure 7.2, the alternative operator of loading the object into the truck at an airport was explored and failed in the past, because the problem solver encountered a goal loop with the goal (inside-truck ob4 tr9). As this same goal is present in the current active search path of the new search tree, the replay procedure prunes that alternative from the new operator node. This early pruning step signifies a reduction in the number of alternatives corresponding therefore to a decrease in the branching factor of the new search tree.

In summary, the replay procedure provides the following two major benefits to the problem solving procedure:

- Proposal and validation of choices versus generation and search of possible alternatives operators and goal orderings.
- Reduction of the number of plausible alternatives – past failed alternatives are pruned up front by validating the failures recorded in the past cases.

7.1.3 Feedback to memory

The analogical problem solver has the potential to interpret the utility of the guidance provided by the similar retrieved cases. The degree of success that it experiences transferring the past choices to the new context allows the problem solver to deliberate on the appropriateness of the similarity metric used. Figure 7.3 sketches four situations that may happen during the transfer process.

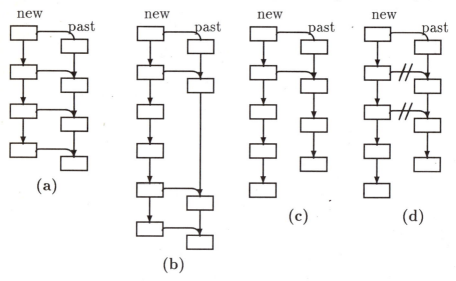

Figure 7.3: Four situations to encode the utility of the guidance received: (a) Fully-sufficient: past case is fully copied; (b) Extension: past case is used but additional steps are performed in the new case; (c) Locally-divergent: justifications do not hold and invalidate transpose part of the past case; (d) Globally-divergent: extra steps are performed that undo previously transferred steps.

If a case was *fully-sufficient* under a particular substitution, the memory manager generalizes its data structure over this match updating the indices to access these cases. If the new problem is an *extension* of the previous case, the conditions that lead into the adaptation and extension work are used to differentiate the indexing of the two cases. The situations where the two cases *diverge* represent a currently incorrect memory concept of similarity or lack of knowledge. The case is *locally-divergent* when some justifications do not hold and invalidate the transfer of remaining of the case. The case is *globally-divergent* if the new situation requires extra steps that undo some of the previously transposed steps.

The fact that the retrieval mechanism suggests a past case as most similar to the new problem and the problem solver cannot fully use the past case or even extend it, indicates either the sparsity of better cases in memory, or a similarity function that ignores an important discriminant condition. The memory manager either specializes variables in the memory data structures due to previous overgeneralization or completely sets apart the two cases in the decision structure used for retrieval.

The system learns by experience with its performance evolving from eventual global and local divergent transfers to extension or fully-sufficient cases.

Each case is retrieved as a guiding case for a set of goals from the goal statement. Therefore each case *covers* a set of goals. A case is *abandoned* when all the goals it covers are achieved. Until all the covered goals are achieved, the corresponding guiding case is always considered as a source of possible guidance and the problem solver keeps it active. The covered goals may be achieved by transferring all the steps of the guiding case or there may be local or global divergences. If a divergence is found, the guiding case stays active but suspended at the diverging step. The replay algorithm continues to test for additional transfer. When a local divergence is resolved the transfer continues successfully. If the divergence is global, the case remains suspended and the problem solver is not able to return back to it until all the covered goals are achieved by different means. At this point the suspended case is abandoned as its covered goals are achieved.

7.2 The replay algorithm

Chapter 3 presented the base level problem solver, NoLimit, which searches for a solution to a problem by using the available domain theory. As the complexity of the problems and domains increases, NoLimit becomes less efficient as the size of the search space expands exponentially with the length of the solution. NoLimit must then rely on control knowledge to direct its problem solving activity pruning the search space. This book explores a method to automatically acquire control guidance by compiling and reusing successful problem solving episodes annotated with the failures encountered and the reasoning process experienced. NoLimit's base level problem solving ability is then enlarged with the capability to generate and reuse this episodic control guidance.

Chapter 4 extends NoLimit's problem solving procedures with the functionality to generate the annotated search episodes. This section presents formally how these problem solving procedures are augmented with the mastery to use the control guidance provided by the similar problem solving episodes in addition to the available domain theory.

Figure 7.4 shows the main problem solving procedure as previously also shown in Figure 3.7 and discussed in Section 3.3.

Input : A search tree
  $T = (N, E)$, sets $\mathcal{A}_N$, $\mathcal{F}_N$, $\mathcal{S}_N$ of the active, failed, and suspended search tree nodes, and act, the active leaf node.

Output : An expanded search tree
  $T' = (N', E')$, new sets $\mathcal{A}_{N'}$, $\mathcal{F}_{N'}$, $\mathcal{S}_{N'}$ of the new active, failed, and suspended search tree nodes, and an updated active leaf node.

procedure **Problem_Solving_Step** $(N, E, \mathcal{A}_N, \mathcal{F}_N, \mathcal{S}_N, act)$:
1. $children\_set \leftarrow$ **Generate_Children** (T, act)
2. if $children\_set = \emptyset$
    then
3.   Return **Backtrack_Path** $(N, E, \mathcal{A}_N, \mathcal{F}_N, \mathcal{S}_N, act,$ **no-choices**, $children\_set)$
    else
4. $N' = N \cup children\_set$
5. $E' = E \cup \{(act, n) : n \in children\_set\}$
6. $T' = (N', E')$
7. $termination\_reason \leftarrow$ **Check_Termination_Reason** $(\mathcal{A}_N, act)$
8.   case $termination\_reason$
9.   success
10.   Return **Success** $(N, E, \mathcal{A}_N, \mathcal{F}_N, \mathcal{S}_N, act)$
11.   failure
12.   Return **Backtrack_Path** $(N, E, \mathcal{A}_N, \mathcal{F}_N, \mathcal{S}_N, act,$
            $termination\_reason, children\_set)$
13.   shift_attention
14.   Return **Backtrack_Path** $(N, E, \mathcal{A}_N, \mathcal{F}_N, \mathcal{S}_N \cup children\_set, act,$
            $termination\_reason, \emptyset)$
15.   otherwise
16. $S'_N = S_N \cup children\_set$
17.   Return **Pursue_Active_Search_Path** $(act, children\_set, T')$

Figure 7.4: Problem solving stepping.

This top level stepping procedure remains unchanged and the replay ability is added to its two constituent phases, namely the **expand** and the **commit** ones, captured mainly by the steps 1 and 17 respectively. The next section describes how the replay of the guiding cases transforms the expansion phase from a generation task into a testing one. The following section presents the commit phase driven by the episodic past experience.

7.2.1   Generation of new search directions

When no similar guiding cases are available, the problem solver spends a large search effort matching the current problem solving state against its domain the-

ory to resolve what is the suitable next problem solving step. Even when individual control rules are present to help pruning the search tree, it is still a
recognized problem [Minton, 1988a] to determine which control rules apply to
the particular problem solving circumstance.

A guiding case records the sequence of decisions that directed the problem
solver through the search space in the past similar problem solving episode.
The analogical problem solver follows the guiding cases keeping pointers to the
individual steps transferred. The subsequent steps to the current last transposed
ones of each of the individual guiding cases are the steps that the analogical
reasoner considers as the new possible next steps. Hence the matching cost of
deciding which domain knowledge applies is drastically reduced to a well-defined
test on the appropriateness of the proposed new steps. Through the similar cases
returned by the retriever the analogical problem solver gets guidance for each
individual step of the complete reconstruction process.

Input : A search tree $T = (N, E)$, the active leaf node *act*.

Output : A set of the search children available.

procedure **Generate_Children** (T, *act*):
1. $\mathcal{D} \leftarrow$ the domain theory.
2. case *act*
3.   goal node

> 3a.   *guiding_case* ← **Link_To_Past_Case** (*act*)
> 3b.   if *guiding_case*
> 3c.   then *child* ← **Validate_Op_Past_Case** (*guiding_case*, *act*)
> 3d.   if *child*
> 3e.   then Return *child*

4.   else Return **Compute_Relevant_Instantiated_Operators** (*act*, T, $\mathcal{D}$)
5.   otherwise
6.   *pending_goals_set* ← **Compute_Pending_Goals** (*act*, T)
7.   *applicable_operators_set* ← **Identify_Applicable_Operators** (*act*, T)
8.   Return *pending_goals_set* and *applicable_operators_set*

Figure 7.5: Generating the children for a problem solving search tree.

The procedure **Generate_Children** returns the set of possible choices to
pursue in the problem solving search tree.

There is a functional distinction between the generation of children search
nodes for a goal node and for the other kind of nodes. When the problem solver
commits to pursue a specific goal (the active leaf node is that goal), then the
next step is to find the operator that is relevant to this goal. This operator can
be obtained from the past guiding case for the goal, if there is one such case.
Hence the expansion phase for a goal node (generating its relevant operator) is
guided by the past case and the commit phase is mostly passive as the choice
is determined at generation time. The next step after an operator is chosen or

applied is a new goal to pursue or a new operator to apply. These new steps are "independent" from the last search node. The expansion phase for a chosen or applied operator is not guided by the past cases as the set of pending goals and the set of applicable operators is directly computed from the active search path. The commit phase however is strongly guided by the past cases determining the new next step.

The boxed steps 3a through 3e in Figure 7.5 show the extension to this procedure that enables it to return the operator relevant to a goal from the guiding case. When the active leaf node, *act*, is a goal node, step 3a determines whether *act* is linked to a past case, i.e., whether the decision to work on that goal was guided from a past case. If this is the situation, step 3c tries to validate the relevant operator chosen in the past case. If the justifications for the past choice are no longer valid, then the procedure **Validate_Op_Past_Case** returns a null child as checked at step 3d. In this situation the problem solver proceeds to generate the children search steps from its domain theory (step 4) as the base-level NoLimit does.

If the active leaf node is not a goal node, then the generation of children progresses by computing the set of pending goals and applicable operators. This step does not involve any matching (unification) effort. It consists of a look up along the active search path for the operators selected to determine either the corresponding preconditions that are not yet true in the current state or to identify the operators that can be immediately applied as their preconditions are already achieved. The past cases guide the decision making step (commit phase) of choosing what goal to pursue next from the set of pending goals or which operator to apply from the set of applicable operators. The next section shows the procedure **Pursue_Active_Search_Path** that is extended to follow this guidance for the commit phase of the algorithm.

Figure 7.6 shows the procedure that validates a relevant past operator by checking whether the annotated justifications still hold in this new problem solving situation.

Step 1 of the procedure identifies the specific guiding step from the guiding case to which the active search node is linked. When the retrieval procedure returns the set of similar past cases, it also identifies a role substitution by which the past and new situations are found similar (see Chapter 6). However as only the goal statements and initial states are used to determine the similar past cases, this role substitution provides in general a partial instantiation for the parameterized variables of the past case. Therefore the role substitution available also partially instantiates the relevant past operator. Step 2 completes the instantiation, if needed, and applies the obtained substitution to the past choice. The argument to the procedure **Apply_And_Extend_Substitution**, namely **choice** (*guiding_step*), is the value of the slot **:choice** of the past search node, *guiding_step*.

To illustrate the partial instantiation provided by the retrieval procedure being extended at replay time, consider the two problems sketched below:

Input :   The active *guiding_case* and the active goal node *act*.

Output :   The relevant operator used in the past case validated if its
justifications still hold; otherwise nil.

procedure **Validate_Op_Past_Case** (*guiding_case, act*):
1. *guiding_step* ← **Pointer_To_Active_Step** (*guiding_case*)
2. *candidate_op* ← **Apply_And_Extend_Substitution**
(**choice** (*guiding_step*))
3. if **Relevant_To** (*candidate_op, act*)
then
4.   if **Justifications_Hold** (**why-this-operator** (*guiding_step*),
candidate_op)
5.   then **Advance_Case** (*guiding_step, guiding_case*)
6.   Return *candidate_op*
7.   else **Advance_Case** (*guiding_step, guiding_case*)
8.   Return nil

Figure 7.6: Validating the past chosen operator.

```
Past case:                          New situation:
  (goal (inside-truck <ob5> <tr9>))   (goal (inside-truck ob11 tr14))

  (foot-printed-state                 (state (and  ...
   (inside-airplane <ob5> <pl7>)       (inside-airplane ob11 pl10)
   (at-truck <tr9> <po11>)             (at-truck tr14 a99)
   (same-city <po11> <a49>)            (at-airplane pl10 a3)
   (at-airplane <pl7> <a45>))          ...))
```

Suppose that the retrieval procedure returns the following substitution: (-
(<ob5>.ob11), (<tr9>.tr14), (<pl7>.pl10), (<a45>.a3)). Figure 7.7 shows
a fragment of the trace of the replay run. After step 3 the replay algorithm
accesses the relevant operator used in the past case, namely (**load-truck ob11
tr14 <ap63>**). One of the arguments of this operator is not instantiated by
the partial instantiation returned by the retrieval module, namely the variable
<ap63>. The substitution is completed at replay time. As the variable is of the
class **airport**, the substitution is completed with the bindings (**<ap63>.a99**)
and reused in the future case steps, as shown in the steps 4 and 5.

Returning to the presentation of the algorithm of Figure 7.6, step 3 tests if
the operator is still relevant to the goal at the active leaf node. The operator is
relevant if one of its effects unifies with the goal, which means that the goal is
achieved when the operator applies to a state which is an element of the class
of states represented by the set of its preconditions. At step 4, the procedure
Justifications_Hold tests whether the reasons for the choice of this operator
still hold in the current new situation. The operator decision node records the
reasons why-this-operator was selected in the past. Finally steps 5 or 7 advance

. . .

```
Following case-step case-rep3-4-2.

3. tn3 (inside-truck ob11 tr14)

Getting candidate past chosen-op snode.
Case step to compare (load-truck ob11 tr14 <ap63>)
Following case!
Following case-step case-rep3-4-3.

4. tn4 (load-truck ob11 tr14 a99)

No applicable-op (or forget about it, because decision is SUBGOAL)
Checking for a case to follow.
These are the available cases ((case-rep3-4 . case-rep3-4-4))
Only one pending goal: (at-obj ob11 a99).
Found case step for unique goal case-rep3-4-4.
Case was advanced one more search cycle
        to step case-rep3-4-6: (at-truck tr14 a99).
Following case-step case-rep3-4-4.

5. tn5 (at-obj ob11 a99)
```

. . .

Figure 7.7: Role substitution added at replay time.

the case to the next potentially transferable step.

Chosen Op Node :choice :sibling-relevant-ops :why-this-operator :relevant-to	**:choice** is used to get the pointer to the operator description; **:sibling-relevant-ops** is used to prune the alternative operators if the reasons of failure experienced in the past still hold; **:why-this-operator** is used to test whether the choice agrees with the explicit direction provided in the past; **:relevant-to** is used to identify the goal(s) that dictated the selection of this operator.

Figure 7.8: Reuse of the justifications of a chosen operator node.

Figure 7.8 summarizes the reuse of the justifications annotated at a decision node corresponding to the choice of an operator. The next section shows how a past goal choice or a past choice to apply an operator determines the choices in the new context.

7.2.2 Pursuing the search

After the procedure **Generate_Children** identifies the possible next search steps, the problem solver faces a "committing" phase to decide which particular step to pursue. Figure 7.9 shows the procedure **Pursue_Active_Search_Path**.

Input : A search tree $T = (N, E)$, the active leaf node *act*, and the set of children nodes, *children_set* returned by **Generate_Children**.

Output : A new active leaf node.

procedure **Pursue_Active_Search_Path** (*act*, *children_set*, T):
1. case *act*
2.   goal node
    2a.   if is-linked-to-past-case (*act*) and *children_set*
    2b.   then *new_active_leaf* ← unique *child* in *children_set*
3.   else *new_active_leaf* ← **Controlled_Choice** (**operator**, *children_set*,T)
4.   otherwise
    4a.   *guiding_cases* ← **Active_Guiding_Cases**
    4b.   if *guiding_cases*
    4c.   then *new_active_leaf* ←
                ← **Validate_Step_Past_Case** (*guiding_cases*, *act*, *children_set*)
    4d.   if not *new_active_leaf*
          then
5.   *applicable_ops* ← { $n \in$ *children_set*: n is an applicable operator }
6.   *pending_goals* ← { $n \in$ *children_set*: n is a goal }
7.   *apply_or_subgoal* ← subgoal
8.   if *applicable_ops* $\neq \emptyset$ then
9.   *apply_or_subgoal* ← **Controlled_Choice** (**apply_or_subgoal**,
                                      children_set, T)
10.   if *apply_or_subgoal* = apply then
11.   *new_active_leaf* ← **Controlled_Choice** (**apply**, *children_set*, T)
12.   **Apply_Operator** (*new_active_leaf*)
13.   if *apply_or_subgoal* = subgoal and *pending_goals* $\neq \emptyset$
          then
    13a. if **Worth_Recursively_Retrieve** (*pending_goals*)
    13b.   then **Get_Additional_Guiding_Cases** (*pending_goals*, **Current_State**)
    13c.   go to step 4a
    13d. else
14.   *new_active_leaf* ← **Controlled_Choice** (**goal**, *children_set*, T)
15. if *new_active_leaf*
16.   then **Update_Node_Status** (*new_active_leaf*, T)
17.   else **Backtrack_Path** (T, *act*,$\emptyset$)

Figure 7.9: Committing in the active search path.

The boxed steps 2a-2b, 4a-4d, and 13a-13d show the functionality added to the base procedure to consider the past cases to guide the choice of the next step to pursue.

When the active search node is a goal node, the procedure **Generate_Children** validates the operator that is found relevant to the goal in the past guiding case. The commitment is therefore done at generation time and steps 2a and 2b return the choice already selected in this situation. Steps 4a through 4d handle the complementary situations where the active search node is either a chosen or applied operator node. The problem solver incurs first on the validation of a past choice at step 4c. When this validation procedure **Validate_Step_Past_Case** does not find a justified past choice, as tested at step 4d, then the algorithm proceeds as if it were not guided (steps 5-13 and 14-17).

If the problem solver encounters a new unguided subgoal, steps 13a-13d show that the replay algorithm may recursively invoke the retrieval of additional guiding cases for the current set of pending goals. The procedure **Worth_Recursively_Retrieve** at step 13a decides whether this recursive invocation of guidance is worth pursuing. This decision may be as elaborated as desired and may be based on a prediction of the complexity of the new goal encountered. In particular in the experiments run in this work, the problem solver has a predefined ranking of the goals that dictates the decision of the recursive retrieval. It is a challenging future work extension to this work to apply machine learning techniques to support the automatic improvement also of this level of decision making.

Figure 7.10 shows the procedure that accomplishes the validation of the goal and applied operator choices at the past cases.

The procedure consists of two interleaved phases of **merging** and **validating** the candidate possible steps from the several guiding cases.

Merging multiple guiding cases

The replay procedure uses a set of guiding cases as opposed to necessarily a single past case (see Chapter 6). This enhancement constitutes a powerful technique to get guidance from complementary individual past cases. The replay of multiple cases proves to be highly useful for complex problems that may be solved by resolving minor interactions among simpler past cases. Following several cases however poses an additional decision making step of choosing which case to pursue. Resolving at this level of decision making may be seen as an instance of meta-level reasoning in a higher level of abstraction than the domain level decisions, such as which operator to apply, or which goal to pursue next in order to solve a user given problem situation. Although developing a learning method for meta-level decision making is beyond the immediate focus of this work, we explored a few different strategies to merge the guidance from the several cases from the set of similar cases. Figure 7.11 presents the procedure to choose a case from the set of guiding cases which shows four different merging strategies:

Serial: The cases are merged serially one after the other. The particular initial merging ordering of cases is randomly chosen. The procedure **Link_To_Past_Case** at step 3 returns the last case that has been followed. When

---

Input : The set of *guiding_cases*, the active leaf node *act*, and the set of children nodes, *children_set* returned by **Generate_Children**.

Output : A new active leaf node from a guiding case.

procedure **Validate_Step_Past_Case** (*guiding_cases, act, children_set*)

1. *merging_strategy* ← **Active_Case_Merging_Strategy** (*guiding_cases, children_set*)

2. *guiding_case* ← **Choose_Case** (*merging_strategy, guiding_cases, act, children_set*)

3. *guiding_step* ← **Next_Case_Step** (*guiding_case*)

3. case *guiding_step*

4.   goal-decision

5.   *candidate_goal* ← **Apply_Substitution** (choice (*guiding_step*))

6.   if **Justifications_Hold** (**why-this-goal** (*guiding_step*), *candidate_goal*)

7.   then **Advance_All_Cases** (*guiding_case, guiding_cases*)

8.   Return *candidate_goal*

9.   else *merging_strategy* ← exploratory

10.   *guiding_cases* ← *guiding_cases* \ {*guiding_case*}

11.   go to step 2

12. applied-operator-decision

13.   *candidate_applied_op* ← **Apply_Substitution** ((choice (*guiding_step*)))

14.   if **Applicable_Operator** (*candidate_applied_operator*)

15.   **Justifications_Hold** (**why-this-operator** (*guiding_step*), *candidate_applied_op*)

16.   then **Advance_All_Cases** (*guiding_case, guiding_cases*)

17.   Return *candidate_applied_op*

18.   else *merging_strategy* ← exploratory

19.   *guiding_cases* ← *guiding_cases* \ {*guiding_case*}

20.   go to step 2

21. otherwise Return nil

Figure 7.10: Validating a new step from a past case.

all the steps of a case are reused or the case is abandoned then the next case in the serial order is returned and followed.

Round-robin: This is an opposite strategy to the serial one. The cases are maximally interleaved by following a step of each case at a time. The particular initial merging ordering of the cases is also randomly chosen. The procedure **Next_Case_After** returns the next case in the merging ordering after the case that is linked to the current active search node or after the last guided search node, if the current node is unguided.

Eager: When there are applicable operators in the *children_set*, i.e., in the set of possible next problem solving actions, this eager merging strategy looks

for the past cases that are suspended at steps where any of these particular operators were applied in the past. Step 1 of the procedure **Vali-
date_Step_Past_Case** (see Figure 7.10) sets this eager merging strategy
as the active one in this eventuality, i.e., when there applicable operators in
the set of children search steps. The procedure **Find_Applying_Op_Case**
at step 7 finds the guiding case that points at an applicable operator from
the *children_set*. The justification structures at the past cases can provide
information about a successful order to apply several applicable operators.

Exploratory: Finally this strategy merges the cases in a random order. The
procedure **Randomly_Pick_Case** returns a case arbitrarily chosen from
the set of guiding cases.

Input :   The set of *guiding_cases*, the active leaf node *act*, and the set of
children nodes, *children_set* returned by **Generate_Children**, and the
current *merging_strategy*.

Output :   A new case to follow.

procedure **Choose_Case** (*merging_strategy, guiding_cases, act, children_set*)
1. case *merging_strategy*
2.   serial
3.   Return **Link_To_Past_Case** (*act*)
4.   round-robin
5.   Return **Next_Case_After** (*guiding_cases*, **Link_To_Past_Case** (*act*))
6.   eager
7.   Return **Find_Applying_Op_Case** (*guiding_cases, children_set*)
8.   exploratory
9.   Return **Randomly_Pick_Case** (*guiding_cases*)

Figure 7.11: Strategies to choose a case to pursue from the set of guiding cases.

It is interesting to briefly discuss these different merging strategies. The
question to be addressed is twofold: Which of the merging strategies is more
advantageous to help reduce the problem solving base search effort? And which
of the merging strategies allows the learner to accumulate richer cases in terms of
the interactions among goals? To debate these issues, consider the two extreme
situations in terms of goal interactions, namely:

A,   where the set of goals covered by the different guiding cases are all
independent from each other, and

B,   where there are strong interactions among the goals covered by the
different cases.

In terms of the expected reduction of the problem solving search effort, for
situation **A** all the merging strategies are equivalent as the goals do not interact.
On the other hand, for situation **B**, the merging strategy used produces funda-
mentally different results in search reduction. A serial strategy delays to an

extreme the detection of goal interactions. A round-robin strategy may be able to spot the goal interactions rather early and contribute to avoid long undesirable serial search paths. This strategy provides the maximum benefits but only if the correct initial case ordering is selected. The exploratory strategy balances these two strategies by allowing cases to both be serialized or interleaved.

In terms of the accumulation of a wide variety of cases, the learner masters from a rich problem solving experience. Ideally the learner benefits most from an integral understanding of the complete search space as a result of its entire exploration by the problem solver identifying all the failing and succeeding paths. This situation however is not desirable in terms of problem solving efficiency. For both situations **A** and **B**, the problem solver ends up finding the correct solution after the necessary search. The learner captures and compiles the existing goal interactions. The issue is which of the strategies allows a richer exploration of the search space to learn from success and failures. The serial merging strategy is indifferent for situation **A** for both search reduction and learning usefulness. For situation **B** both the serial and the round-robin strategies are equally useful from the learning perspective, as they depend heavily on the initial case ordering. In a nutshell this discussion leads into the conclusion that the exploratory strategy secures the trade-off between handling situations **A** and **B** successfully both from the search reduction and learning utility point of views. In the experiments run in this work, the merging strategy is fixed to be the exploratory one. The choices are picked up randomly from the set of available alternatives, if no additional guidance can be applied.

The procedure **Validate_Step_Past_Case** in Figure 7.10 shows that the justifications stored at the case nodes may override an a priori choice of case merging strategy. In fact, steps 9-11 and equivalently steps 18-20 set the exploratory merging strategy when the justifications of the selected node do not hold in the new context. Therefore these two phases of choosing a case and validating the past case step in the procedure **Validate_Step_Past_Case** are bound together.

Validating the justifications structure

We discuss now the validation phase of the procedure **Validate_Step_Past_Case** shown in Figure 7.10. After a particular case is chosen to be pursued at step 2, steps 6 through 8 validate the choice proposed if this is a goal decision. Figure 7.12 summarizes the reuse of the justifications annotated at the different slots of a goal decision node of a guiding case.

Steps 15 through 17 validate the step proposed when this is an applied operator node. In this situation checking the validity of following the same step simply involves to check whether the preconditions of the operator are true in the new state, so the operator can also be applied. Figure 7.13 summarizes the reuse of the justifications annotated at an applied operator node.

Chapter 4 introduced the language that is used to specify the justifications in particular at the why- slots. The power of the replay mechanism stems exactly from the ability to understand and reinterpret the annotations at the past

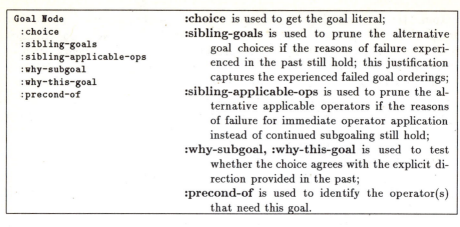

Goal Node	:choice is used to get the goal literal;
:choice	:sibling-goals is used to prune the alternative goal choices if the reasons of failure experienced in the past still hold; this justification captures the experienced failed goal orderings;
:sibling-goals	
:sibling-applicable-ops	:sibling-applicable-ops is used to prune the alternative applicable operators if the reasons of failure for immediate operator application instead of continued subgoaling still hold;
:why-subgoal	
:why-this-goal	
:precond-of	:why-subgoal, :why-this-goal is used to test whether the choice agrees with the explicit direction provided in the past;
	:precond-of is used to identify the operator(s) that need this goal.

Figure 7.12: Reuse of the justifications of a goal node.

Applied Op Node	:choice is used to get the pointer to the operator description;
:choice	:sibling-goals is used to prune the alternative goal choices if the reasons of failure experienced in the past still hold;
:sibling-goals	
:sibling-applicable-ops	:sibling-applicable-ops is used to prune the alternative applicable operators if there was more than one applicable operator; orderings of this justification captures the experienced particular orderings of applying operators that failed in the past case;
:why-apply	
:why-this-operator	
:chosen-at	
:preconds	:why-apply, :why-this-operator is used to test whether the choice agrees with the explicit search direction pursued in the past;
:adds	
:dels	:chosen-at is used to get a pointer to the step where the operator is chosen; when advancing a case to a suitable next step, the applied operator steps corresponding to operators not chosen are skipped;
	:preconds is used to test the syntactic applicability of the operators by checking whether these preconditions are true in the current world state;
	:adds, :dels is not directly used by the replay mechanism, at decision making time; this information to identify the dependencies among the final steps of the solution.

Figure 7.13: Reuse of the justifications of an applied operator node.

decision nodes. The generation and replay phases of the analogical process are strongly interconnected. The generation procedure successfully identifies the reasons that support the decisions made only if it associates with these justifications a meaning that can be checked at replay time. Figure 7.14 summarizes the actions of the procedure **Justifications_Hold** (see Figures 7.6 and 7.10) which interprets the language of the annotations at the why- slots which can each take the values select, prefer, reject, case, function, and why-user.

The why-user and the function slot values are associated with a user-given, or otherwise known, function definition that at replay time is used as a predicate to validate the past choice.

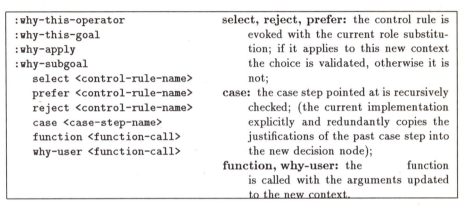

Figure 7.14: Reuse of the justifications at the why-slots.

When the justifications are valid in the new context the choice is returned to the problem solving stepping function that proceeds exploring an equivalent search path to the one followed in the guiding cases. When a justification is not valid in the new context, the validation procedure either tries to pursue a different case or returns nil, i.e., no past choice is supported by its justifications in the new problem solving context.

7.2.3 Advancing the cases

When the transfer occurs from a past guiding case to the new problem solving episode the past guiding cases are advanced to their new possible steps. In principle only one guiding case should be advanced, namely the one from which the transfer effectively occurred. However it is often the situation that the guiding cases share some common steps and therefore the algorithm advances all the cases that share the transferred guiding step. Figure 7.15 shows the algorithm to accomplish this move forward in the guiding cases.

Chapter 5 showed how a case is indexed by all the sets of interacting goals and Chapter 6 presented how a case is retrieved for any of those sets to cover a new set of goals. The subgoaling structure is used to identify the steps of the case that are in use and can potentially be useful in the reconstruction process.

Definition 11 Potentially useful step of a guiding case:
*A step of a guiding case is a **potentially useful** step, iff the step is in the subgoaling structure of any of the goals covered by the guiding case.*

Input :   The set of *guiding_cases* and the current *guiding_case*.

Output :   The set of *guiding_cases* with the pointers to the candidate next
steps.

procedure **Advance_All_Cases** (*guiding_case, guiding_cases*)
1. *current_used_step* ← **Current_Case_Step** (*guiding_case*)
2. **Advance_Case** (*current_used_step, guiding_case*)
3. foreach *case* ∈ (*guiding_cases* \ {*guiding_case*})
4.   *active_case_step* ← **Current_Case_Step** (*case*)
5.   if **choice** (*current_used_step*) = **choice** (*active_case_step*)
6.   then **Advance_Case** (*active_case_step, case*)

procedure **Advance_Case** (*current_step, guiding_case*)
1. *next_current_step* ← **Next_Case_Step** (*current_step, guiding_case*)
2. *covered_goals* ← **Goals_Covered_by_Case** (*guiding_case*)
3.   case *next_current_step*
4.   goal-decision-node
5.   if **Is_in_Subgoaling_Chain** (*next_current_step, covered_goals*)
6.   then **Current_Case_Step** ← *next_current_step*
7.   else **Advance_Case** (*next_current_step, guiding_case*)
8.   chosen-operator-node
9   if **Is_Relevant_To** (*next_current_step, covered_goals*)
10.   then **Current_Case_Step** ← *next_current_step*
11.   else **Advance_Case** (*next_current_step, guiding_case*)
12.   applied-operator-node
13.   if **Is_Relevant_To** (**chosen-at** (*next_current_step*), *covered_goals*)
14.   then **Current_Case_Step** ← *next_current_step*
15.   else **Advance_Case** (*next_current_step, guiding_case*)
16.   otherwise ;case was advanced to the end
17.   **Case_Abandoned** (*guiding_case*)

Figure 7.15: Advancing the guiding cases to the next potentially useful steps.

Step 5 of the procedure **Advance_Case** in Figure 7.15 determines whether
a goal node is a potentially useful step by determining whether the goal is in
the subgoaling chain of any of the covered goals. Similarly step 9 finds that an
operator node is a potentially useful step, if it is relevant to some potentially
useful goal. Finally step 13 settles that an applied operator node is potentially
useful if the operator node where it was chosen at, was found useful. The
procedure follows recursively a case until it finds a potentially useful step. If
no such step is found and the case is advanced unsuccessfully until its last step,
step 17 declares that the case is abandoned, i.e., the case is removed from the
set of active cases for the current active search path.

Failing and backtracking

The analogical problem solver may still encounter failures due to some goal interactions not previously experienced and therefore unguided, or due to the partial match between the new and past situations. The backtracking algorithm finds the search nodes with alternative choices. Due to the recording of the failures as justifications at the case nodes, the branching factor on the number of possible alternatives is drastically reduced by the past validated failures. When a new choice point is found, the pointers to the transferable steps of the guiding cases are updated and set back to the new problem solving state from which the search proceeds.

7.3 Examples

This section presents some examples that illustrate some aspects of the replay procedure (other examples can be found in [Veloso and Carbonell, 1993a]), including the reuse of the subgoaling structure, of the record of failures, and of the justifications at the why-slots; and the exploratory merging of guiding cases.

Following one case - the subgoaling structure and failures

Figure 7.16 illustrates how the subgoaling structure and the failure records at a stored case can help guiding the reconstruction process for a similar new problem. First let me introduce the basic representation used in the figure. The left side of Figure 7.16 shows a sequence of nodes labeled cn1 through cn21 that correspond to a past stored case. The sequence of nodes, n1,..., n21, on the right side of Figure 7.16 represents the new problem solving episode. Both sequences represent successful search paths. The arrows across the nodes show the transfer occurred from the nodes of the past case to the new situation.

The past case was stored with instances generalized to variables of the same class as presented in Chapter 5. When a case is retrieved as similar to a new situation, the partial match found between the old and new situations defines partial bindings to the variablized past case. The past generalized problem consists of moving an object <ob9> from the post office <po35> at some city, to an airport <ap17> at a different city. In the past initial state there is a truck <tr35> at the post office <po35>, and an airplane <pl3> at the airport <ap17>. Concretely, the relevant past initial state is: (at-obj <ob9> <po35>) (at-truck <tr35> <po35>) (at-airplane <pl3> <ap17>) (same-city <po35> <ap35>). The goal statement is the simple goal (at-obj <ob9> <ap17>).

Assume that this case is retrieved to guide a new problem where an object ob0 is also to be moved from a post office p0 to an airport a2 at a different city. In this new initial state however a truck tr0 is at the airport a0 and there is an airplane pl0 also at a0. Concretely, the initial state is: (at-obj ob0 p0) (at-truck tr0 a0) (at-airplane pl0 a0) (same-city p0 a0), and the goal statement is: (at-obj ob0 a2). The retrieval procedure returns the substitution ((<ob9>.-ob0), (<po35>.p0), (<ap35>.a0), (<ap17>.a2)) as a partial match between

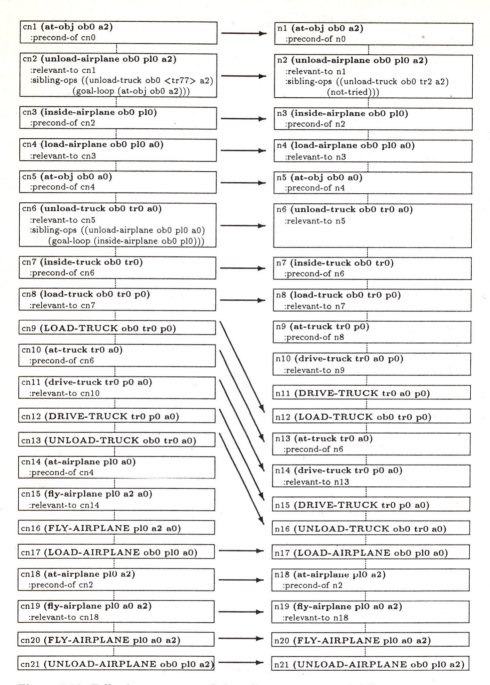

Figure 7.16: Following one case – Subgoaling structure and failures.

that past case and the new situation. Note that neither the truck <tr35> nor the airplane <p13> get bindings from this partial match. However the replay mechanism assigns new bindings as the match between the two situations becomes clearer along the solution reconstruction process. The case is instantiated with the additional substitutions (<tr35>.tr0) and (<p13>.p10) which are set dynamically at transfer time as discussed earlier.

The same goal that was chosen at node cn1 is now chosen at the node n1. At node cn2 the past case records that the operator (unload-airplane ob0 <p13> a2) was successfully chosen and that the operator (unload-truck ob0 <tr77> a2) failed. This information guides the decision at node n2 of choosing (also successfully) the relevant operator (unload-airplane ob0 p10 a2) instead of (unload-truck ob0 tr2 a2). The substitution (<p13>.p10) is set and applied to the case. The transfer continues interleaving the choices of goals and relevant operators in the same subgoaling chains. At node cn6 the alternative choice of (unload-airplane ob0 p10 a0) is pruned from the new case, because the justification for failure in the past holds in the new situation. The goal (inside-airplane ob0 p10) is present in the new search path at node n3. As this goal is not achieved yet at the current node n6, a goal-loop would also occur. The justification is validated and the alternative choice is pruned.

As noticed above, the problems diverge in the location of the truck and airplane. In fact at node cn9, the past decision of loading the truck at the post office cannot be immediately transferred as the operator (load-truck ob0 tr0 p0) is not applicable in the new problem. The new solution diverges then from the past case at nodes n9, n10, and n11, where the conditions for applying that operator are set, namely by driving the truck tr0 from the airport a0 to the post office p0. The past case is stopped at the node cn9. The past decision is tested at each new step to see whether it is justified. This happens at node n12 where the transfer continues. A somehow symmetric situation occurs when, at the node cn14, the goal (at-airplane p10 a0) is not a pending goal in the new problem, as the airplane was initially already at the airport a0. In this situation, the past case is advanced and the steps in the subgoaling structure of that goal are skipped. The transfer is pursued at node cn17 and the reconstruction process terminates successfully.

Following multiple cases - merging and reuse of justifications

Figure 7.17 shows a new problem and two past cases selected for replay. The cases are partially instantiated to match the new situation. Further instantiations occur while replaying. The new problem to be solved consists of a two-goal conjunct, namely to load an object ob3 into an airplane p15,n and to load an object ob8 into a truck tr2. The goal conjunct is (and (inside-airplane ob3 p15) (inside-truck ob8 tr2). The literals (inside-truck ob3 tr2) (at-truck tr2 p4) (at-airplane p15 a12) (at-obj ob8 p4) are in the new initial state.

The two cases retrieved cover one goal each and their initial states partially match the new initial state. In the case that covers the goal (inside-airplane

Past cases	New problem

(goal (inside-airplane ob3 pl5))
(relevant-state (at-obj ob3 <ap3>)
        (at-airplane pl5 a12))

(goal (inside-truck ob8 tr2))
(relevant-state (at-obj ob8 p4)
        (at-truck tr2 <ap7>))

(goal (inside-airplane ob3 pl5)
        (inside-truck ob8 tr2))

(initial-state
        (inside-truck ob3 tr2)
        (at-truck tr2 p4)
        (at-airplane pl5 a12)
        (at-obj ob8 p4))

Figure 7.17: Instantiated past cases cover the new goal and partially match the new initial state. Some of the case variables are not bound by the match of the goals and initial state.

ob3 pl5), the object ob3 is at an airport, while in the new situation ob3 is inside of truck tr2. In the case that covers the goal (inside-truck ob8 tr2), truck tr2 is an airport, while in the new situation tr2 is at the post-office p4. These partially-matched cases provide useful guidance for the replay procedure as shown below.

Figure 7.18 illustrates the replay episode that generates a solution to the new problem. The new situation is shown at the right side of the figure and the two past guiding cases at the left.

The transfer occurs by interleaving the two guiding cases, performing any additional work needed to accomplish remaining subgoals, and skipping past work that does not need to be done. In particular, the case nodes cn3' through cn5' are not reused, as there is a truck already at the post office in the new problem. The nodes n9-14 correspond to unguided additional planning done in the new episode. Note that extra steps may be inserted at any point, interrupting and interleaving the past cases, and not just at the end of the cases. At node n7, PRODIGY/ANALOGY prunes out an alternative operator, namely to load the truck at any airport, because of the recorded past failure at the guiding node cn2'. The recorded reason for that failure, namely a goal-loop with the goal (inside-truckob8 tr2), is validated in the new situation, as that goal is in the current set of open goals, at node n6. The two cases are merged using a bias to postpone additional planning needed. Different merges are possible.[1]

To illustrate the reuse of a justification at a why- slot, notice the transfer from node cn4 to the new node n4. The past decision node cn4 is annotated with the justification :why-this-op (applicable) for the reason why this operator was chosen. At the new node n4, the replay procedure chooses bindings for an airplane and an airport that make the operator fly-airplane applicable.

A different situation could occur if the initial decision were made based

---

[1] The replay mechanism can randomly decide on which case to pursue. This randomness usually occurs in a small percentage of the decisions, as most of them are guided by the justifications stored, in particular by the subgoaling chaining. The experiments run show interestingly that the random behavior allows innovative merging of past cases leading to solutions of a better quality in several situations (see Chapter 8, Section 8.2.5).

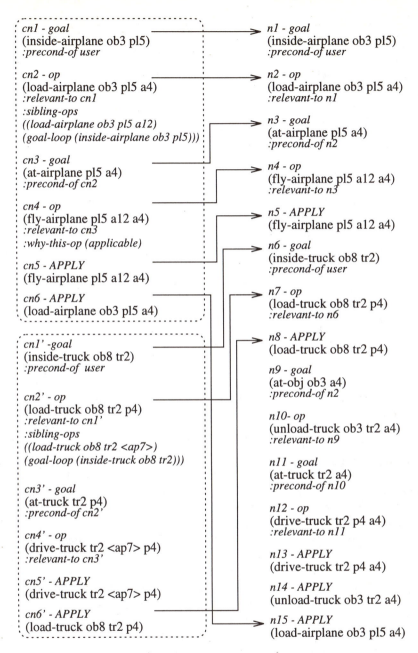

Figure 7.18: Derivational replay of multiple cases.

on applying a control rule. Suppose that the justification at node **cn4** was
:why-this-op (select bindings fly-direct). fly-direct refers to the name
of a control rule that binds the source airport of the operator FLY-AIRPLANE to

the airport where the airplane is currently at. An example of a possible such control rule is the following:

```
(CONTROL-RULE FLY-DIRECT
  (<airplane> <destination-airport> <source-airport>)
  (preconds
   (and (current-op-p 'FLY-AIRPLANE)
        (current-goal (at-airplane <airplane> <destination-airport>))
        (true-in-state (at-airplane <airplane> <source-airport>))))
  (effects (select bindings ((<loc-from> . <source-airport>)))))
```

When the replay procedure would try to get guidance from this node to the new situation, it finds that the source airport is not bound by the partial bindings returned by the retrieval procedure. Using the justification annotated, the replay mechanism would set the source airport to the current location of the airplane. This binding would be obtained by attempting to validate the justification, applying the same control rule proposed in the current new state. This binding information could equivalently have been provided by an external user by using the why-user slot, or could be obtained by the bindings returned by the retrieval procedure. The why- slots may also be used to provide information on particular goal, operator, or binding selections to increase the quality of the plans produced by the problem solver.

7.4   Feedback: problem solver to memory

After the analogical problem solver finds a solution to a new problem directed by the retrieved similar past cases, it can evaluate the utility of the guidance provided by those past cases. In general the analogical problem solver acts as a tester of the accuracy of the similarity metric that dictated the selection of the particular set of guiding cases. This section presents a simple way of improving the similarity metric among problems based on a rudimentary feedback from the analogical problem solver on the utility of the guiding cases retrieved. This elementary technique was developed mostly for the purpose of demonstrating that the problem solver has access to enough knowledge from which to reason about the utility of the guidance. The approach, even if elementary, presents the novelty that the problem solver may act automatically as a tester and learner of the similarity metric. We find an interesting future work direction (see Chapter 10) to explore more sophisticated techniques to incrementally learn an accurate similarity metric based on the feedback given by the problem solver. In a nutshell the supporting method for the closed-loop approach proposed in this work consists of allowing the analogical problem solver to supply feedback on the relative relevance of the literals of the initial state with respect to the goals that they contribute to achieve.

7.4.1   The method explored

At retrieval time, the new problem is described by a goal statement and an initial state. As the problem solver did not solve the problem yet, it does not know which features of the initial state will be relevant, i.e., foot-printed, to solving the problem, i.e., to achieving the goal statement. On the other hand the cases stored in the case library against whom the retriever compares the new problem, are indexed through the foot-printed initial state. However not all the features in the foot-printed initial state may be equally relevant in terms of the search effort invested in solving the corresponding achieved goals. This is why the foot-printed initial state that indexes the cases is organized in a discrimination tree. This structure captures different levels of relevance by their depth with respect to the root of the tree. Chapter 5 presented the formal procedure to organize the case library. In a nutshell the insertion of a new case into the discrimination network conforms a particular order of relevance, stored in the variable *relevance-bias* at each network. The problem solver changes this bias according to the utility of the guidance at replay time, and the discrimination network is reorganized when this bias changes.

7.4.2 Illustrative example

Figure 7.19 shows a problem where an object ob1 must be located at an airport a7 and is initially inside of a truck tr5 which is at the airport a7.

```
(has-instances          (state (and                 (goal
   (OBJECT ob1)             (inside-truck ob1 tr5)       (at-obj ob1 a7))
   (TRUCK tr5)              (at-truck tr5 a7)
   (AIRPLANE pl3)           (at-airplane pl3 a7)
   (AIRPORT a7)             (same-city a7 p7)))
   (POST-OFFICE p7)
   (CITY c7))
        (a)                      (b)                         (c)
```

Figure 7.19: An example problem - in-truck: (a) class distribution of instances, (b) initial state, (c) goal statement.

Suppose that there is a case in the case library, say case-in-airplane, as shown in Figure 7.20, where an object must also be located at an airport, as indicated by the goal (at-obj <ob23> <a35>). As this case was previously solved it is indexed by the foot-printed initial state that shows that the two relevant literals to achieve the goal are both that the object is inside of an airplane, (inside-airplane <ob23> <pl44>), and that the location of the airplane is at the airport destination, i.e., (at-airplane <pl44> <a35>).

Consider that the initial relevance bias known by the retriever weighs equally all the literals, i.e.,

```
:relevance-bias
    ((at-truck . 0) (at-airplane . 0) (inside-truck . 0)
     (inside-airplane . 0) (at-obj . 0) ....).
```

The retriever returns the case-in-airplane as a similar past-case under the substitution ((<ob23>.ob1) (<a35>.a7) (<pl44>.pl3)) for which the match is partial as the initial state of the new problem only matches one literal of the

```
class of variables:   (foot-printed-initial-state      (goal
   (OBJECT <ob23>)        (and                             (at-obj <ob23> <a35>))
   (TRUCK <tr51>)            (inside-airplane <ob23> <p144>)
   (AIRPLANE <p144>)        (at-airplane <p144> <a35>)))
   (AIRPORT <a35>)
   (POST-OFFICE <p35>)
   (CITY <c35>)
         (a)                          (b)                        (c)
```

Figure 7.20: An example case - in-airplane: (a) class of variables, (b) foot-printed initial state, (c) goal statement.

past case, namely `(at-airplane <p144> <a35>)` corresponding to the literal `(at-airplane p13 a7)` in the new initial state. The literal `(inside-truck ob1 tr5)` has one of its arguments matching a past variable, namely `ob1` is matched to `<ob23>`.

When replaying the past case, the analogical problem solver finds the guiding case not useful, as in the past case the operator chosen and applied is simply to unload the airplane. This choice fails in the new problem, because a goal loop is encountered when trying to put the object at the airplane again in order to load it into the airplane. Based on this fact the analogical problem solver returns to memory that the guidance was not useful which is interpreted as weighing as more relevant the difference between the past case and the new problem. Only the two literals `(at-airplane p13 a7)` and `(inside-truck ob1 tr5)` partially matched the past foot-printed initial state. The foot-printed literal `(inside-airplane <ob23> <p144>)` was not matched. As the case was not found useful, the difference between `inside-truck` and `inside-airplane` is found more relevant, than what is in common, namely `at-airplane`. The new relevance-bias becomes:

```
:relevance-bias
   ((inside-truck . 1) (inside-airplane . 1) (at-airplane . 0)
    (at-truck . 0) (at-obj . 0) ....).
```

The relative relevance of the other literals to each other will be incrementally learned through experience.

It is clear that, in general, deciding whether a guiding case is useful to the construction of a solution to a new problem situation is more complex than illustrated in the example above. It is a very challenging direction for future work to define the criteria for usefulness and in particular to try to automate the learning of this decision. In this work, we used a fixed preestablished threshold on the fraction of a guiding case that is successfully transferred.

7.5   Summary

This chapter presented the replay mechanism. It motivates the problem and describes the approach developed. The replay algorithm is designed as an extension to the base-level planner. It involves a complete reinterpretation of the justifications structures in the new problem solving context, as well as the development of appropriate actions to be taken when transformed justifications are no longer valid.

The base-level problem solver alternates between generating alternatives to solve a problem and searching the space created by these alternatives. In contrast, the analogical reasoner tests previous alternatives, attempting to pursue the successful ones. The branching factor of the search space may also be reduced when the replay mechanism validates previous failures and prunes them from the new search space.

The replay mechanism can integrate guidance from multiple past similar cases. The chapter also discusses different merging strategies.

Chapter 8

Empirical Results

The previous chapters described the design and implementation of a complete problem solver which integrates reasoning from first principles (domain theory) and analogical reasoning from accumulated episodic experience (cases, i.e., derivational traces). We achieved the integral implementation to provide comparative empirical evidence evaluating the utility of recycling and organizing past experience in the derivational analogy framework. Furthermore, there had never been a comprehensive empirical evaluation of a complete analogical reasoner automatically generating, storing, retrieving, and replaying multiple cases in a large case library.[1] Hence it became rather challenging to scale up the system by testing the performance of the algorithms designed in a large case library for a complex domain task.

This chapter presents the empirical results obtained from running the system in a diversity of domains including a complex logistics transportation domain with a growing case library of more than 1000 cases in it.

The chapter is organized in five sections. The methodology we followed in this work was to build the full system incrementally by designing and developing one by one each of its functional modules. The first section shows results acquired in different stages of this incremental process. They illustrate specific aspects of the approach, including the diversity of tasks that the system can address, the reduction in problem solving search time, and the sensitivity to two different similarity metrics. The following sections show empirical results on the performance of the full system in the logistics transportation domain. Section 2 motivates the scaling up process, introduces the domain, and presents how the experiments were conducted. Section 3 shows a variety of results demonstrating that the integrated analogical problem solver performs significantly better than the base level problem solver along various dimensions. The results include the demonstration of a significant increase in the solvability horizon of the problem solver and of high positive transfer reducing significantly the combined memory

---

[1][Golding, 1991] is a recent thesis that applied case-based and rule-based reasoning to problem solving. The thesis was tested for the task of name pronunciation with a case library of 5000 names. See Chapter 9 for additional comparisons.

retrieval and problem solving times. Section 4 summarizes and discusses the results.

8.1   Diversity of tasks

The algorithms designed and developed are completely domain independent, meaning that the integrated analogical problem solver can be applied to any domain for which the problem solving task can be encoded in NoLimit's representation language.[2]

The system has been applied to several domains along its development. Figure 8.1 gives a perspective of the domains tested. It also indicates the stage of the system development when the domain was introduced.

Domain description	Development stage	Cases
Matrix manipulation: This domain consists of several operations on matrices to perform Gaussian elimination.	• Initial generation of the justification structures at the decisions nodes; • Initial design of the memory model.	4 - 5
one-way rocket: Simple transportation domain where objects can be moved among two locations in rockets that move only in one direction.	• Nonlinear problem solving as full interleaving of goals; • Initial replay mechanism, guidance from a single case	5 - 10
Extended STRIPS and **Machine-shop scheduling**: Traditional domains [Minton et al., 1989]	• Analysis of similarity metrics; • Retrieval from a linearly organized case library; • Replay of single cases.	100
Logistics transportation: In this domain packages move in trucks and airplanes among locations from different cities.	• Scaling up; Advanced memory organization; • Complete indexing of cases; • Incremental retrieval; • Replay of multiple cases.	> 1000

Figure 8.1: A perspective on the diversity of tasks and the stage of the framework in which they were introduced.

This section shows empirical results obtained from experiments in the *one-way-rocket* domain, and in the extended-STRIPS and machine-shop scheduling domains. [Carbonell and Veloso, 1988] shows the initial version of the justification structures applied to the matrix manipulation domain to accomplish

---

[2]This is equivalent to PRODIGY2.0's description language [Minton et al., 1989] with some syntactic modifications and an additional class hierarchy for the entities in the domain. PRODIGY4.0 follows also NoLimit's extended representation and its complete specification is in [Carbonell et al., 1992].

Gaussian elimination. The next section presents results from the logistics transportation domain.

8.1.1   The *one-way-rocket* domain

The *one-way-rocket* domain was introduced in Section 3.1.1 (see Figure 3.3). Consider the problem introduced in Figure 3.4, Section 3.1.1, to illustrate briefly the derivational replay process and its reduction in search time.

Figure 8.2 shows the results obtained when solving the problems of moving two, three, and four objects from *locA* into *locB* by base level search and by analogy.

First, each of the problems is solved by base level search. The column labeled "Base Search" in Figure 8.2 shows the average running times obtained by running NoLimit without analogy in the two- (2objs), three- (3objs), and four-object (4objs) problems, respectively. The system generates cases from the derivational traces of the solutions to each of these problems.

Then the analogical problem solver is tested on solving new problems consisting of moving two, three, and four objects, guided by each one of the accumulated cases.

New Prob	Base Search	Replayed cases		
		Case 2objs	Case 3objs	Case 4objs
2objs	4.5s	2s	2s	2s
3objs	14.75s	4.75s	3.25s	3.25s
4objs	117.5s	7.75s	7.75s	5.75s

Figure 8.2: Results in a simple transportation domain.

The rest of the table in Figure 8.2 shows the replaying time for the six possible combinations. For example, the analogical reasoner takes 4.75 seconds solving the 3objs problem by analogy with the 2objs problem. The diagonal values, i.e., the k-objs problem replaying the k-objs problem (with k=2,3,4), correspond to the situations where the new problem is structurally the same as the guiding case. They differ in respect to variable instantiation. For example, this means that the 2objs problem solved previously involves moving objects obj-x and obj-y, and the new 2objs problem involves moving two other objects, say obj-w and obj-z. For these situations the analogical reasoner gets guidance for all its decision points and does not have to perform any additional planning.

The solution is replayed whenever the same step is a possible step and the justifications hold. For example, in using the two-object case as guidance to the three- (or four-) object problem, the failure justification for moving the rocket, namely no-relevant-ops (at ROCKET locA), is tested and this step is not replayed until all the objects are loaded into the rocket. The improvements obtained are high as the new cases are extensions of the previous cases used for guidance. Maximal improvement is achieved when the case and the new problem differ substantially (two-objects and four-objects respectively).

These results also show that it is better to approach a complicated problem, like the four-object problem, by first generating automatically a reduced problem [Polya, 1945], such as the two-object problem, then gain insight solving the reduced problem from scratch (i.e., build a reference case), and finally solve the original four-object problem by analogy with the simpler problem. The running time of this 2-step process still adds up to less than trying to solve the extended problem directly, without analog for guidance: 4.5 s + 7.75 s = 12.25 seconds, for solving the two-object from scratch (4.5 s) + derivational replay of the two-object for the four-object problem (7.75 s) versus 117.5 seconds for solving the four-object problem from scratch.

Notice that whereas our work implements the nonlinear problem solver, the case generation module, and the analogical replay engine, it does not yet address the equally interesting problem of automated generation of simpler problems for the purpose of gaining relevant experience. That is, PRODIGY/ANALOGY will exploit successfully the presence of simpler problems via derivational analogy, but cannot create them as yet.

8.1.2   The extended-STRIPS and machine-shop domains

These two domains are substantially more complicated than the *one-way* rocket one. The results show the sensitivity of the benefits of the replay as a function of two different similarity metrics.

A first experiment uses the direct similarity metric to evaluate the partial match between problems, not considering therefore any relevant correlations between the initial states and the goal statements.

NoLimit without analogy ran over a set of problems in the extended-STRIPS and in the machine-shop scheduling domains.[3] A library of cases was accumulated from the derivational traces of the search episodes of solving this set of problems. In order to factor away other issues in memory organization, the case library was simply organized as a linear list of cases. Then the same set of problems was solved by derivational analogy using a *same-out* testing strategy, in which the retrieval module does not return the exact same problem if it is present in the case library. As the problems are randomly generated and independent from each other, the same-out strategy is equivalent to training the system with a randomly generated set of problems and then testing the system with a different randomly generated one.

Figures 8.3 (a) and (b) show the results obtained from a set of 40 problems in the machine-shop scheduling, and from a set of 45 problems in the extended-STRIPS robot planning domains, respectively.

The graphs plot the cumulative number of nodes searched. The dashed curves represent the initial runs without analogy using NoLimit's base-level search

---

[3] This set is a sampled subset of the original set used by [Minton, 1988a].

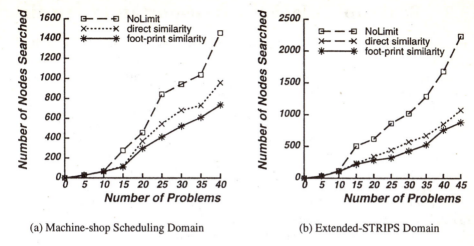

(a) Machine-shop Scheduling Domain   (b) Extended-STRIPS Domain

Figure 8.3: Comparison between the number of nodes searched with NoLimit's base-level search algorithm and with the analogical reasoner following the guidance of cases found similar according to two different similarity metrics.

algorithm. The dotted curves represent the number of nodes searched while following the guidance of cases found similar using the direct similarity metric. These dotted curves show that analogy achieved an improvement over base search (dashed curves): a factor of 1.5 fold-up for the machine-shop scheduling domain and 2.0 fold-up for the extended-STRIPS domain. In general the direct similarity metric lead to acceptable results. However a closer analysis of analogical problem solving episodes shows that the straightforward similarity metric does not always provide the best guidance when there are several conjuncts in the goal statement.

The problem of matching conjunctive goals turns out to be rather complex. As conjunctive goals may interact, it is not at all clear to decide that problems are more similar based simply on the *number* of literals that match the initial state and the goal statements. The foot-print similarity metric refines the account of the relevance of the literals of the initial state with respect to their contribution to achieving each goal conjunct (see chap:retrieval).

We ran new experiments using the global foot-print similarity metric in the extended-STRIPS and machine-shop scheduling domains. The solid curves in Figures 8.3 (a) and (b) show the results for these two domains using the global foot-print similarity metric. These new results show an improvement of the analogical reasoner over base search of a factor of 2.0 fold-up for the machine-shop scheduling and scheduling domain and 2.6 fold-up for the extended-STRIPS domain. The curves obtained do not represent the best improvement expected, as the set of forty problems used does not completely cover the full range of problems in either domain.

8.2   Scale up: A logistics transportation domain

To scale up the system in both the size and diversity of domains, we built a 1000-case library in a complex logistics transportation domain. In this domain, packages are to be moved among different cities. Packages are carried within the same city in trucks and across cities in airplanes. In the version of the domain used in the experiments, the trucks and the airplanes have unlimited capacity. At each city there are several locations, e.g., post offices and airports. This transportation domain represents scale up in both the length of the solution and the size of the search space over other domains used. This transportation domain represents scale up in both the length of the solution and the size of the search space over the other domains described above in the previous sections.

The logistics transportation is a complex domain. In particular, there are multiple operator and bindings choices for each particular problem, and those choices increase considerably with the size or complexity of the problem. For example, for the goal of moving an object to an airport, the problem solver does not have direct information from the domain operators on whether it should move the object inside of a truck or an airplane. Objects can be unloaded at an airport from both of these carriers, but trucks move within the same city and airplanes across cities. So if the object must go to an airport within the same city where it is, it should be moved in a truck, otherwise it should be moved in an airplane. The specification of these constraints is embedded in the domain knowledge and not directly available. The city at which the object is located is not immediately known, as when the object is inside of a carrier or a building, its city location is specified indirectly. PRODIGY/ANALOGY provides guidance at these choices of operators and bindings through the successful and failed choices annotated in past similar problem solving episodes.

The empirical tests with this large case library demonstrate the scaling properties of the memory organization, of the match/retrieval process, and of the reconstruction mechanism replaying multiple cases.

8.2.1   Generation of problems

To generate such a large collection of problems, we implemented tools to automatically create problems of different complexity in this domain. The user specifies the static information, namely the number of cities, and locations within the city, i.e., post offices and airports. The generator prompts the user for a maximum number of trucks, airplanes, and packages. It randomly selects subsets of the packages and the carriers provided. It then randomly assigns the initial locations for all these entities. At this generation level the complexity of the problem is controlled by the size of the initial world configuration as well as by the number of goal conjuncts in the goal statement. This number is also specified by the user. Figure 8.4 shows the trace of the generation dialogue and Figure 8.5 shows the actual set of problems created. The literals in the initial state shared by all the problems in the same set are stored in the variable `*state-common-set*`.

```
<cl> (create-probset)
There are 15 cities, each with 1 post office
and 1 airport.

Enter the specifications for a new set of problems:

    Enter problem set filename: set-new-3
    Number of problems in this set? 2
    Prefix for name of problems? new-3
    Number of goals per problem? 5
    Maximum number of packages? 30
    Maximum number of trucks? (additional to 15) 20
    Maximum number of planes? 15

nil
<cl>
```

Figure 8.4: Dialogue for the generation of a set of problems.

8.2.2   Set up of experiments

The set of problems reported here in the experiments consists of 1000 problems each with 1 to 20 goals and more than 100 literals in the initial state. The experiments do not test the dynamic reorganization of the case library. The relevance-bias followed by the case library manager to insert new cases into memory is fixed along the tests (see Chapter 5). The replay mechanism uses the exploratory merging strategy to combine guidance from multiple analog cases.

The underlying goal of the experiments is to compare the performance of the analogical and the base level problem solvers with respect to their efficiency to solve problems. The experiments vary two major factors:

- The CPU running time limit that the problem solver can spend solving a problem.
- The contents of the case library, i.e., the amount of knowledge learned and stored in memory.

The performance of the base-level problem solver is only affected by the first factor, i.e., the CPU time bound. The problems generated for the experiments in this logistics transportation domain are all in principle solvable from the domain theory. Therefore the base-level problem solver is not able to solve some of the problems, only because of the limited time that it is allowed to spend searching for a solution.

The performance of the analogical reasoner is affected by both factors. It is clearly inherent to the analogical reasoning process that the contents of the case library affect the performance of the analogical reasoner. The search is reduced as a function of the guidance received from the case library. The sensitivity to the CPU running time bound is due to the reconstruction of complex solutions and to the fact that the analogical problem solver also performs base-level search for the unguided parts of its search space.

The experiments are conducted in the phases presented below. At the end of the last phase, all 1000 problems are solved by the derivational analogy reasoner

```
(setf *instances-common-set* '(            (has-instances AIRPLANE
(has-instances CITY                          pl0 pl1 pl2 pl3 pl4 pl5 pl6)
  c0 c1 c2 c3 c4 c5 c6 c7 c8
  c9 c10 c11 c12 c13 c14 c15)               (state (and
(has-instances POST-OFFICE                   (at-truck tr16 po3) (at-truck tr17 po13)
  po0 po1 po2 po3 po4 po5 po6 po7 po8        (at-truck tr18 a4) (at-truck tr19 po7)
  po9 po10 po11 po12 po13 po14 po15)         (at-truck tr20 po8) (at-truck tr21 po15)
(has-instances AIRPORT                       (at-truck tr22 po15) (at-truck tr23 a4)
  a0 a1 a2 a3 a4 a5 a6 a7 a8                  (at-truck tr24 po12) (at-truck tr25 a7)
  a9 a10 a11 a12 a13 a14 a15)                (at-truck tr26 po4) (at-truck tr27 a10)
(has-instances TRUCK                         (at-truck tr28 a8) (at-truck tr29 a13)
  tr0 tr1 tr2 tr3 tr4 tr5 tr6 tr7 tr8        (at-truck tr30 po12) (at-truck tr31 po2)
  tr9 tr10 tr11 tr12 tr13 tr14 tr15)         (part-of tr16 c3) (part-of tr17 c13)
))                                           (part-of tr18 c4) (part-of tr19 c7)
                                             (part-of tr20 c8) (part-of tr21 c15)
(setf *state-common-set* '((state (and      (part-of tr22 c15) (part-of tr23 c4)
  (at-truck tr0 po0) (at-truck tr1 po1)      (part-of tr24 c12) (part-of tr25 c7)
  (at-truck tr2 a2) (at-truck tr3 a3)        (part-of tr26 c4) (part-of tr27 c10)
  (at-truck tr4 po4) (at-truck tr5 a5)       (part-of tr28 c8) (part-of tr29 c13)
  (at-truck tr6 po6) (at-truck tr7 po7)      (part-of tr30 c12) (part-of tr31 c2)
  (at-truck tr8 po8) (at-truck tr9 po9)      (inside-airplane ob0 pl6)
  (at-truck tr10 po10) (at-truck tr11 po11)  (at-obj ob1 po4) (at-obj ob2 po5)
  (at-truck tr12 a12) (at-truck tr13 po13)   (at-airplane pl0 a6) (at-airplane pl1 a10)
  (at-truck tr14 po14) (at-truck tr15 a15)   (at-airplane pl2 a11) (at-airplane pl3 a15)
  (part-of tr0 c0) (loc-at po0 c0) (loc-at a0 c0)   (at-airplane pl4 a14) (at-airplane pl5 a0)
  (same-city po0 a0) (same-city a0 po0)      (at-airplane pl6 a12)))
  (part-of tr1 c1) (loc-at po1 c1) (loc-at a1 c1)
  (same-city po1 a1) (same-city a1 po1)     (goal (and
  (part-of tr2 c2) (loc-at po2 c2) (loc-at a2 c2)   (inside-truck ob2 tr20) (inside-truck ob0 tr17)
  (same-city po2 a2) (same-city a2 po2)      (at-truck tr5 po5) (inside-airplane ob1 pl5)
  (part-of tr3 c3) (loc-at po3 c3) (loc-at a3 c3)   (at-truck tr25 po7)))
  (same-city po3 a3) (same-city a3 po3)    )
  (part-of tr4 c4) (loc-at po4 c4) (loc-at a4 c4)   ;****************************************
  (same-city po4 a4) (same-city a4 po4)
  (part-of tr5 c5) (loc-at po5 c5) (loc-at a5 c5)   (PROBLEM new-3-1
  (same-city po5 a5) (same-city a5 po5)    (has-instances OBJECT
  (part-of tr6 c6) (loc-at po6 c6) (loc-at a6 c6)     ob0 ob1 ob2 ob3 ob4 ob5 ob6 ob7 ob8
  (same-city po6 a6) (same-city a6 po6)      ob9 ob10 ob11 ob12 ob13 ob14 ob15 ob16
  (part-of tr7 c7) (loc-at po7 c7) (loc-at a7 c7)     ob17 ob18 ob19)
  (same-city po7 a7) (same-city a7 po7)    (has-instances TRUCK
  (part-of tr8 c8) (loc-at po8 c8) (loc-at a8 c8)     tr16 tr17 tr18 tr19 tr20)
  (same-city po8 a8) (same-city a8 po8)    (has-instances AIRPLANE
  (part-of tr9 c9) (loc-at po9 c9) (loc-at a9 c9)     pl0 pl1 pl2 pl3 pl4 pl5)
  (same-city po9 a9) (same-city a9 po9)
  (part-of tr10 c10) (loc-at po10 c10)      (state (and
  (loc-at a10 c10)                           (at-truck tr16 a8) (at-truck tr17 po9)
  (same-city po10 a10) (same-city a10 po10)  (at-truck tr18 a11) (at-truck tr19 a7)
  (part-of tr11 c11) (loc-at po11 c11)       (at-truck tr20 po15) (part-of tr16 c8)
  (loc-at a11 c11)                           (part-of tr17 c9) (part-of tr18 c11)
  (same-city po11 a11) (same-city a11 po11)  (part-of tr19 c7) (part-of tr20 c15)
  (part-of tr12 c12) (loc-at po12 c12)       (inside-truck ob0 tr6) (inside airplane ob1 pl5)
  (loc-at a12 c12)                           (inside-airplane ob2 pl2) (at-obj ob3 po3)
  (same-city po12 a12) (same-city a12 po12)  (inside-airplane ob4 pl1)
  (part-of tr13 c13) (loc-at po13 c13)       (inside-airplane ob5 pl5)
  (loc-at a13 c13)                           (inside-airplane ob6 pl5) (inside-truck ob7 tr10)
  (same-city po13 a13) (same-city a13 po13)  (inside-airplane ob8 pl1) (at-obj ob9 po9)
  (part-of tr14 c14) (loc-at po14 c14)       (inside-truck ob10 tr1) (at-obj ob11 a15)
  (loc-at a14 c14)                           (at-obj ob12 a9) (at-obj ob13 a13)
  (same-city po14 a14) (same-city a14 po14)  (at-obj ob14 po14) (inside-truck ob15 tr3)
  (part-of tr15 c15) (loc-at po15 c15)       (inside-truck ob16 tr4) (at-obj ob17 a6)
  (loc-at a15 c15)                           (at-obj ob18 a6) (inside-truck ob19 tr6)
  (same-city po15 a15) (same-city a15 po15)  (at-airplane pl0 a11) (at-airplane pl1 a8)
))))                                         (at-airplane pl2 a4) (at-airplane pl3 a4)
;****************************************    (at-airplane pl4 a10) (at-airplane pl5 a2)))

(PROBLEM new-3-0                            (goal (and
(has-instances OBJECT                        (inside-truck ob13 tr0) (inside-truck ob15 tr1)
  ob0 ob1 ob2                                (at-airplane pl3 a11) (at-obj ob12 a4)
(has-instances TRUCK                         (inside-airplane ob16 pl0)))
  tr16 tr17 tr18 tr19 tr20 tr21 tr22 tr23  )
  tr24 tr25 tr26 tr27 tr28 tr29 tr30 tr31)   ;****************************************
```

Figure 8.5: Set of problems created from the dialogue in Figure 8.4. The system creates random initial state configurations and goals that follow the user's specifications.

with a CPU time bound of 350 seconds.

1. First, 250 initial problems, considered simpler as their goal statements have less than 7 goals, are all run without analogy up to a CPU running time bound of 250 seconds. Each problem that is solved within this time bound was indexed appropriately, and stored into the case library.

2. The same set of 250 problems is then solved by derivational analogy up to the same CPU time bound of 250 seconds. Let P be one problem in this set. In this phase, P is solved by derivational analogy using the case library in the following way. There are two situations: either P was solved, or not solved, in the previous phase without analogy. If P was solved previously, then this means that the corresponding solution case for P, say *case-P*, is stored in the case library. In this situation, the retrieval procedure is explicitly blocked from considering *case-P* as a possible guiding case. The retrieval procedure returns guidance from other cases in the library. If P was not solved previously, and the problem is newly solved by derivational analogy, then it is stored in the case library at this phase. The guiding case library is then incremented also along this phase.

3. The other 750 problems have up to 20 goals. They are given to both problem solving configurations to be solved without and with analogy alternatively, in sets of 20 problems each, with the same CPU time bound of 250 seconds. Once again, the case library is used and incremented, in the same way as in phase 2.

4. Finally, after the three phases above, there were only a few (17) problems that had not been solved by analogy within the time bound of 250 seconds and there were many (566) problems that the base-level problem solver had not solved within the same time bound. In this final phase, we increased the CPU running time bound to 350 seconds. The 17 problems were tried again with analogy and the 566 problems were all tried again without analogy. The runs by analogy benefited both from the increase in the time bound and from the large case library that they could use. All these 17 problems were solved by analogy. Only a few extra problems (14 out of the 566) were solved without analogy.

8.2.3 The solvability horizon

The experiments focus on learning how to accomplish more efficiently the complex planning aspect of the problems. An unguided exploration of the search space drives the problem solver very easily into a chain of inconvenient or wrong decisions from which it is very hard to recover, since there is a very large number of alternatives at each choice point. Therefore although all the problems are solvable theoretically, in practice they become rapidly unsolvable within a bounded running time when their complexity increases.

One of expected and experienced contributions of the analogical reasoner is the increase that it affords in the solvability horizon of the problem solving task: Many problems that the base-level problem solver cannot solve within a particular search time limit are solved by the analogical reasoner within that limit or a lower one.

Figure 8.6 plots the number of problems solved without and with analogy for different CPU times bounds. Without analogy, i.e., by base search, No-LIMIT solves only 458 problems out of the 1000 problems even when the search time limit is increased up to 350 seconds. PRODIGY/ANALOGY can solve all the problems with the same time bound.

- A point (t, p) on the **dashed** curve of the graph of Figure 8.6 shows that the **base-level** nonlinear problem solver is able to solve p many problems when its allowed search running time is bound to t seconds for each individual problem. Examples are the points $(50, 355)$ and $(300, 451)$.
- A point (t', p') on the **solid** curve of the graph of Figure 8.6 shows that the **analogical** nonlinear problem solver is able to solve p' many problems when its allowed search running time is bound to t' seconds. Examples are the points $(50, 784)$ and $(300, 993)$.

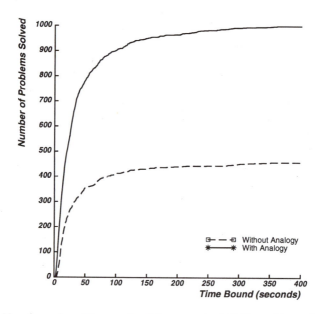

Figure 8.6: Number of problems solved from a set of 1000 problems for increasing running times bounds. By base-level search the problem solver solves only 458 problems while with analogy it solves the complete set of 1000 problems.

This graph shows by itself a very significant improvement achieved by solving problems by analogy with previously solved problems. However one may think that without analogy the system still can solve 458 problems out of the 1000 problems which represents 45.8% of the total number of problems. The interesting fact experienced was that the percentage of problems solved without analogy decreases very rapidly with the complexity of the problems. The experiments clearly showed this fact which is not explicitly represented in the graph of Figure 8.6. In order to show this increase in the solvability horizon of the problem solver as a function of the problem complexity, we face the question of how to define a complexity metric.

There are several dimensions along which problems differ and can be considered to compare the problems' relative complexity, to wit:

- The number of goal conjuncts;

- The number of literals in the initial state;

- The length of the solution, i.e., the number of steps in the final plan;

- The number of nodes searched in the problem solving episode;

- The search time expended solving the problem.

Initially the more complex sets of problems are generated by increasing the number of goal conjuncts. However the complexity of the individual goals varies significantly in particular with the specific corresponding initial state. It thus happens that some problems with more goals are less *complex* than other problems with a smaller number of goal conjuncts. This notion of *complexity* is more related to the length of the solution returned. However, even for problems with the same solution length, the problem solver may have found that one problem more difficult to solve than the other, for example both in terms of the cost of generating the alternatives available to solve the problem and the size of the search space. This discussion illustrates the hard question that is the one of defining an adequate measure of complexity of problem tasks. (This can be viewed as an instance of the general problem of studying problem complexity [Kolmogorov, 1965].) The arguments above lead to the definition of a complexity metric that encompasses more than one dimension of comparison. The generation of more complex problems can only be driven by the number of goal conjuncts and literals in the initial state. After a problem is solved however there is the additional problem solving information that helps ranking the problems according to their relative complexity.

Figure 8.7 shows the increase in the solvability horizon achieved by the analogical reasoner as a function of the problem complexity. The 1000 problems are all solved either without or with analogy and are sorted according to the following metric:

- Problem P is more complex than problem P' if the the solution for problem P is longer, i.e., has more steps, than the solution for problem P'.

- If the two solutions for P and P' are of the same length, then P is more complex than P' if P explored more search nodes than P'.

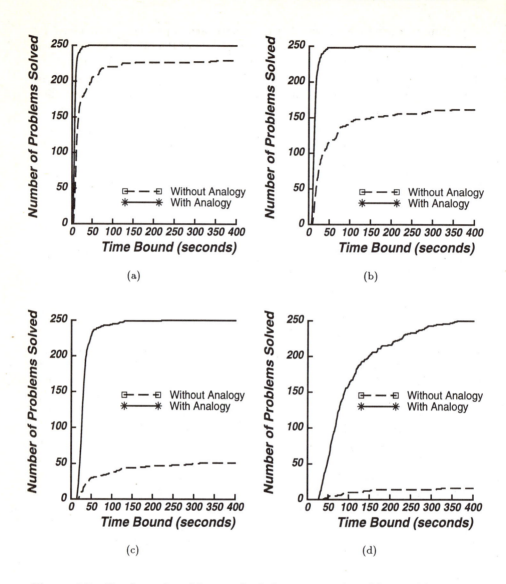

Figure 8.7: Number of problems solved for ranges of problems of increasing complexity. Problems in (a) are simple and easily solved without analogical guidance. Problem complexity increases through (b) and (c) and fewer problems are solved without analogy. Problems in (d) are rather complex with up to 20 goals and a large initial state. In (d) very few problems can be solved without analogy while all are solved using analogical reasoning.

Figure 8.7 shows four graphs each corresponding to 250 problems of increasing complexity from (a) through (d). The solid curves represent the results from the analogical reasoner while the dashed curves represent the results from the base-level problem solver.

The meaning of a point in these graphs is the same as the one introduced above for a point in the graph of Figure 8.6. The results shown in these graphs represent a major achievement of analogical problem solving. The gradient of the increase in the performance of the analogical problem solver over the base-level algorithm shows its large advantage when scaling up on the complexity of the problems to be solved.

The following sections provide several direct comparison of the performance of the base-level and the analogical problem solver along various dimensions. These comparisons are mostly done for the set of problems solved by both configurations. The comparisons are interesting but the reader should keep in mind the remaining 562 problems that are not even solved without analogy within the CPU running time bound of 350 seconds. The performance of the analogical reasoner while solving this set of 562 problems cannot be compared against a concrete base-level run as there is no such one. It is an improvement in the solvability horizon of the problem solver.

8.2.4   Cumulative running times

Previous comparisons between the performance of a problem solver before and after learning control knowledge [Minton, 1988a, Knoblock, 1991, Etzioni, 1990] were done by graphing the cumulative running times of the two systems over a set of problems.[4] To follow this precedent we also graph the cumulative performance of the two systems.

Figure 8.8 shows the cumulative running time for the set of problems (458) that were both solved by base search and by analogy. The curves are monotonically increasing because of the cumulative effect.

- A point (P, T) on the **dashed** curve of the graph of Figure 8.8 shows that the **base-level** nonlinear problem solver spends T seconds to solve all of the first sorted P many problems. Examples are the points $(100, 759.23)$ and $(458, 19852.48)$.
- A point (P, T') on the **solid** curve of the graph of Figure 8.8 shows that the **analogical** nonlinear problem solver spends T' seconds to solve all of the same P many problems. Examples are the points $(100, 586.12)$ and $(458, 6026.89)$.

The graph shows a final factor of 3.6 cumulative speed up of the analogical problem solver over the base NoLimit. The maximum individual speed up is of a factor of approximately 40. The graph compares the running times for the solved problems.

To make this comparison more similar to the ones performed previously in PRODIGY, we compute the cumulative running times accounting also for the problems not solved by the base level problem solver within the time bound of

---

[4]The next sections consider the retrieval times in addition to the running time for the analogical runs.

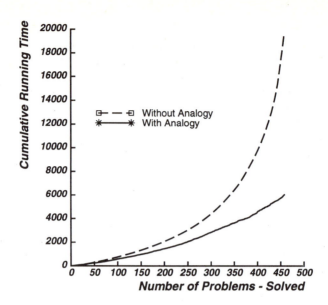

Figure 8.8: Cumulative running time for the 458 problems from a set of 1000 problems solved both by base-level search (without analogy) and by derivational analogy (with analogy).

350 seconds. Therefore for each unsolved problem, we add the running time until the time bound limit is reached, in the same way as it is done in [Minton, 1988a]. Figure 8.9 shows the curves obtained.

The 1000 problems solved by analogy correspond to a total of 39,479.11 seconds, while the total running time effort of the base level problem solver corresponds to 210,985.87 seconds. This represents a speed-up of a factor of approximately 5.3, and also means that the cumulative savings in running time for analogy is approximately 81.3%.

No direct comparison between earlier PRODIGY/EBL and current PRODIGY/-ANALOGY is possible because the former used a linear problem solver whereas the latter used a nonlinear one. Moreover the complexity of the problems was substantially greater for PRODIGY/ANALOGY. These factors mitigate towards a larger overall search space for the current work and therefore more room for learning, as observed with respect to improved average running time and solvability boundary.

8.2.5   Solution length

Another interesting issue to analyze is the comparison of the quality of the solutions produced by analogy and the ones returned by the base NoLimit. This study uses a measure of quality of plans which is based simply on the

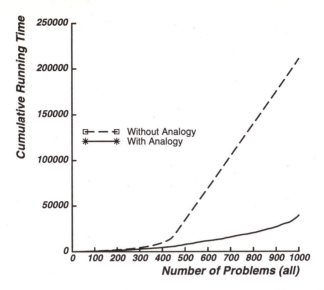

Figure 8.9: Cumulative running time for the set of 1000 problems. If a problem is not solved it is accounted for with the CPU time limit used of 350 seconds.

length of the solution.[5]

The study is done by finding the difference between the length in the solutions found by NoLimit and by analogy for each problem. Figure 8.10 shows a table summarizing the results obtained.[6]

Difference in solution length: ANALOGY versus NoLimit	Number of Problems	Percentage of problems
Longer 1-6 steps	79	17.25%
Equal	168	36.68%
Shorter 1-13 steps	211	46.07%

Figure 8.10: Comparison in solution length between the analogical and the base-level problem solvers.

These results show that in 82.75% (36.68% + 46.07%) of the solved problems the analogical reasoner produces plans of no worst quality than the ones

---

[5] In [Pérez and Carbonell, 1993] Pérez proposes to research in acquiring control knowledge from an expert to guide the problem solver to achieve plans of higher quality according to several dimensions.

[6] When the alternatives at the decision points are not heuristically ordered, NoLimit makes arbitrary choices in order not to favor any particular syntactic order dependent on the user specification of the domain. Along the experiments, some of the problems were rerun more than once (for example with different CPU time bounds). The solution considered without analogy is the shortest solution found by NoLimit in case different solutions of different lengths were found for the same problem.

produced by base-level search. In terms of the total 1000 solved problems by analogy, in 92% of the problems ((1000-79)/1000), PRODIGY/ANALOGY produces not worse plans than the base-level planner.

Before we ran this comparison, we did not have a clear feeling of what the outcome of this study would be. In fact we feared an eventually more balanced or even disadvantageous result for analogy in terms of plan quality. The reason for this expectation (which turned out to be ungrounded) is the exploratory strategy that we follow to merge the guidance from several cases at replay time. The method follows the principle that a learner benefits more from random exploration of its choices, if no preferences are available, than from following always a fixed exploration order. In particular this principle applies to the replay of multiple cases in the random interleave of the several guiding cases when no other preferred choice is known. Hence the exploratory merging strategy leads to novel explorations of the search space allowing the problem solver to encounter "surprising" successes or failures from which it can learn by enriching its library of problem solving experience. Though supported by this learning argument, it was not clear to us what were the effects of the approach in the quality of the specific final solution delivered by the analogical problem solver. The results in Figure 8.10 show the rewarding fact that the overall replay algorithm of multiple guiding cases produces solutions of equal or better quality in a large majority of the situations.

8.2.6   Retrieval and replay times

The previous results shown account for the running time of the analogical replay mechanism. This section presents additional results that include both the retrieval and replay times.

In an initial study to compare the retrieval versus the replay times, we selected arbitrarily 50 "simple" problems, and 50 "harder" problems, according to their running time without analogy. (The problems are considered "simple" as they are solved without analogy within 15 to 25 seconds and "hard" as their running times fall in a higher range of 30-100 seconds.) Figure 8.11 (a) and (b) plot for each problem from the simple and hard problem sets respectively, the sum of the time for retrieval of the corresponding guiding cases and their replay time by analogy. The dotted curves with cross points corresponding to the runs without analogy are smooth because the problems are sorted according to their running time.

- A point (p, t) marked with a cross on the **dotted** curve of the graph of Figure 8.11 (a) and (b) shows that the **base-level** nonlinear problem solver spends t seconds to solve problem p. Examples for the graph in (a) are the points $(2, 16.26)$ and $(20, 19.29)$. Examples for the graph in (b) are the points $(4, 31.72)$ and $(47, 91.85)$.
- A point (p, t') marked with a star on the **solid** curve of the graphs of Figure 8.11 (a) and (b) shows that the **analogical** nonlinear problem solver takes t' seconds to retrieve the similar guiding cases from the case library and to replay them to solve problem p. Examples for the graph in (a) are the points $(2, 5.64)$ and $(20, 23.11)$. Examples for the graph in (b) are the points $(4, 7.77)$ and $(47, 26.96)$.

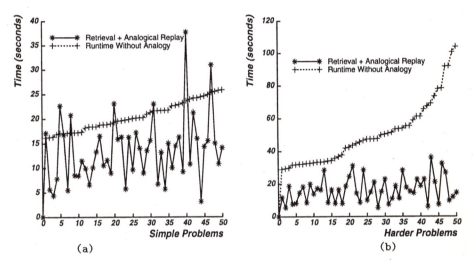

Figure 8.11: Retrieval plus replay time for 50 simple problems (a) and for 50 harder problems (b). The problems are sorted according to their running time without analogy.

Figure 8.11 (a) shows some occasional spikes above the curve of the running times without analogy. This is not surprising and shows that for some simple problems, it might not compensate to spend the effort of retrieving similar past cases and replaying them. Figure 8.11 (b) plots the equivalent results but now for the harder problems. The sum of the retrieval and replay times is now always less than the running time without analogy.

To report this comparison for the total set of the 458 problems solved both with and without analogy, we follow a slightly different way of graphing the relationship to avoid the irregular flavor of the unsorted curve. For each problem we take the difference between the running time without analogy and the sum of the retrieval and replay times. These differences are then sorted in increasing order. Figure 8.12 graphs this difference.

> • A point (p, δ) on the curve of the graph of Figure 8.12 shows that for problem
> p, there is a difference of δ seconds between its running time without analogy
> and the sum of the retrieval and replay time of its analogical problem solving
> episode. Examples are the points $(50, -5.37)$ and $(430, 112.31)$.

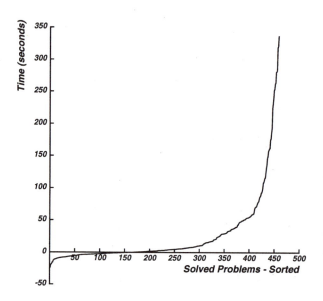

Figure 8.12: Difference between the running time without analogy and the sum of the retrieval and analogical running times for the problems solved both by base-level search and by analogy.

A negative difference corresponds to a problem for which the sum of the retrieval and replay times is larger than the running time without analogy. The problems with a negative differential are equivalent to the spikes above the dashed curve in Figure 8.11 (a). The few problems (16.5% of the total set of problems) with negative differences consist of the simpler ones for which the cost of searching for similar cases in memory and replay these, does not represent savings in the problem solving effort.

There is an interval for which the difference is close to null. These problems correspond to still simple to moderate complex problems for which it seems equivalent to search for a solution by unguided search or by analogy with similar past cases. Finally the curve abruptly takes off into a sharp positive interval. For the more complex problems the curve shows the difficulty that the base-level problem solver encounters as compared to the analogical reasoner. The plotted differences only report on the problems solved by both configurations. The next section extends the study of the cost of retrieving for all the 1000 problems along a different dimension.

8.2.7   Retrieval time against the size of the case library

We observed the effect of the size of the case library in the retrieval time. Figure 8.13 compares the overall replay and retrieval times. The problems are ordered in the exact order in which they were solved and stored into memory. As the case library grows incrementally, if a problem p_1 is solved after a problem p_2, then the size of the case library is larger when searching for similar cases for problem p_2. Figure 8.13 graphs the retrieval and the replay times for groups of 100 problems in the sequence in which they are solved.

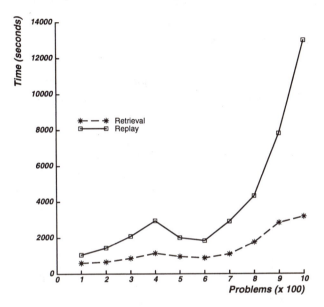

Figure 8.13: Problems ordered in the sequence in which they were run. The case library is growing along the x axis at the same time that more problems become solved. The graph represents the replay and retrieval times accumulated for chunks of 100 problems.

> • A point (p, t_r) on the **dashed** curve of the graph of Figure 8.13 shows that it takes t_r seconds to **retrieve** a set of similar cases for the p_{th} chunk of 100 problems. Examples are the points $(3, 859.74)$ and $(10, 3187.26)$.
> • A point (p, t_a) on the **solid** curve of the graph of Figure 8.13 shows that it takes t_a seconds to **replay** the retrieved set of similar cases for the p_{th} chunk of 100 problems. Examples are the points $(3, 2092.70)$ and $(10, 13006.69)$.

The curves are not monotonic. In particular, the decrease on the fifth group of 100 problems corresponds to the fact that the sequence of problems proposed to the system has two phases of monotonic increasing complexity (number of goals) with a restart to a simple complexity approximately after the first 400 problems. The two curves rise towards the end of the graph, not because of the increase in the library size, but because we increased the complexity of the last sets of problems in terms of the number of goals (up to 20). This led to longer solutions with longer reconstruction times and more retrieval effort to cover the new goals with similar past cases.

The conclusion from Figure 8.13 is that the retrieval time suffers no significant increase with the size of the case library. The data structures used to store the case indexes are to a large degree responsible for this behavior (see Chapter 6). With this memory organization, we reduced (or avoided) the potential utility problem [Minton, 1988a, Doorenbos and Veloso, 1993].

8.2.8   Search nodes explored

Finally Figure 8.14 compares the number of nodes explored from the search space in both configurations. The difference between the number of nodes searched without analogy and with analogy is computed, sorted in increasing order, and graphed for each of the solved problems.

---

* A point (p, δ) on the curve of the graph of Figure 8.14 shows that the base-level problem solver explored δ more search nodes than the analogical problem solver when solving the problem p. Examples are the points $(50, -3)$ and $(458, 820)$.

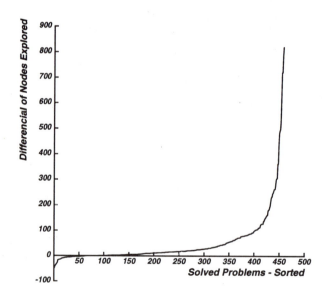

Figure 8.14: Difference between the number of nodes explored by base-level search and by analogy for all the problems.

There are some few problems for which the derivational reconstruction explores a larger number of nodes than the base-level search. Those situations are due to a favorable base-level search, or to the sparsity of better guiding cases in memory at the time, or to the exploratory strategy used to merge the similar cases at replay time. In general the results show that the guiding cases used by the derivational replay provide a reduction in the search space explored for a large majority of the problems – for approximately 78% of the solved problems, and 90% of all the problems.

8.3 Summary

This chapter presented empirical results comparing the performance of the analogical reasoner, PRODIGY/ANALOGY, with the base-level problem solver NoLimit.

The extensive results obtained from a logistics transportation domain showed that:

- The analogical reasoner increased the solvability horizon of the base-level problem solver considerably. Within a CPU running time bound of 350 seconds, the complete set of 1000 problems was solved by PRODIGY/ANALOGY, while only 458 of these problems are solved by NoLimit (see Figures 8.6 and 8.7).

- The cumulative running times for the analogical replay of the problems represent a speed-up of up 3.6 over the base-level problem solver, if only the problems solved both without and with analogy are considered. The speed-up increases to 5.3 if the problems not solved are also accounted for with the CPU time limit given to the base problem solver (see Figures 8.8 and 8.9).

- The solutions obtained by analogy are of equal or shorter length than the corresponding ones found by NoLimit for 82.75% problems (see Figure 8.10).

- When the retrieval time is added to the analogical replay time, PRODIGY-/ANALOGY still performs more efficiently compared to NoLimit for 293 problems out of the 458 problems solved by both configurations. The other 165 problems correspond to simpler problems for which NoLimit finds a solution to a problem in a shorter time than PRODIGY/ANALOGY retrieves analogs for and replays them (see Figures 8.11 and 8.12).

- Finally the retrieval time suffers no significant increase with the size of case library (see Figure 8.13).

The experiments were set up with the primary focus of comparing the analogical problem solver against the base-level problem solver for large and complex problems. The results largely demonstrate the scalable properties of the algorithms designed and implemented.

An interesting next phase of empirical studies would be to investigate on the sensitivity of the analogical reasoner itself along other dimensions, such as the dynamic reorganization of the case library, variable retrieval times, variable thresholds for the partial match, and recursive retrieval of cases for any extra planning needed.

Chapter 9

Related Work

We discuss related work on the generation, storage, retrieval, and reuse of acquired knowledge in analogical/case-based reasoning frameworks.

9.1 Generation and contents of cases

Most of the case-based reasoning (CBR) systems start initially with a case library that is provided by the external user. PRODIGY/ANALOGY generates its own case library of problem solving episodes generated from the problem solver's reasoning from a domain theory which usually provides knowledge to solve efficiently only simple problems. PRODIGY/ANALOGY incorporates the new replayed cases into its case library.

The contents of a case vary quite considerably ranging from an enumeration of steps to a variety of different levels of causal relationships between the steps. PRIAR [Kambhampati and Hendler, 1992] reuses plans in a nonlinear hierarchical planner. Following the derivational analogy philosophy, PRIAR generates plans by recording the *validation structure* of a plan, which represents the dependencies among the plan steps, namely the links between preconditions and effects of the plan steps. The subgoaling structure that PRODIGY/ANALOGY annotates at the case nodes corresponds to PRIAR's validation structure.

APU [Bhansali and Harandi, 1993] also stores at each case the subgoaling links among the plan steps. Bhansali's domain of UNIX programming involves plans which consist mostly of independent subplans for which it is expensive to search for the applicable schemas. Therefore APU also stores the set of alternative schemas that could be used in addition to the particular one that succeeded in the stored episode. In the new partially matched situation, APU gets information from the past case on alternative schemas to try instead of having to search for them once again.

Blumenthal implemented a replaying system, REMAID [Blumenthal, 1990] that creates human computer interfaces. The design problem consists in ordering a set of goals that specify the problem to be solved. REMAID annotates at the cases the goal orderings heuristics that successfully determined the correct goal ordering. It annotates also the specific rule that achieved each goal. The information stored is similar to the one stored in APU though REMAID emphasizes the goal orderings while APU focuses on the different rules that may achieve the goals.

PRODIGY/ANALOGY stores the available alternatives both at the goal ordering level and at the operator level, similarly to APU and REMAID. PRODIGY/ANALOGY records further the problem solving alternatives that failed and the reasons for the failure. PRODIGY/ANALOGY makes use of the failure record at replay time to reject the alternatives for which the justifications of failure still hold in the new context.

CHEF [Hammond, 1986] records exclusively the failures encountered. In fact CHEF centers its retrieval and adaptation reasoning around the failures. When a case is adapted but fails at a simulated execution phase, CHEF detects the violation of an expectation, recognizes the reason for failure, and uses it to index the new case.

KRITIK [Goel, 1991] stores at the cases the functional-structure dependencies among the different subparts of the design artifact. This qualitative information, as Goel calls it, is used at the adaptation phase to identify the parts that need to be modified and propose modifications. This is an interesting idea well suitable for design domains. PRODIGY/ANALOGY does not store automatically qualitative information eventually known at a higher level of abstraction than the one available directly at problem solving time. However the justification language developed for PRODIGY/ANALOGY leaves margin to user defined justifications that may be checked at replay time. These can capture an arbitrary qualitative level of dependency among the solution steps. It is an interesting future research direction to explore more in depth the user intervention in providing justifications, their utility, and automating the learning process from the user input.

9.2   Storage and retrieval of cases

Case-based reasoning and analogical reasoning are in the abstract the same but have very different computational emphases. The former focuses on developing appropriate memory structures and the bulk of the work concentrates in retrieving from memory the right similar situation to the problem under consideration. The latter uses complex traces with justifications for decisions and permits more flexible modification and reconstruction. In a nutshell, the main emphasis of derivational analogy is in experience-driven problem solving, whereas case-based reasoning emphasizes retrieval and practically direct application.

The episodic contents of the cases drive the indexing in a network of links. Schank proposed MOPs [Schank, 1982] as indexing structures for combining generalized and episodic knowledge. IPP [Lebowitz, 1980] and CYRUS [Kolodner, 1980] pioneered the use of these memory structures followed by several others CBR systems. The definition of the "right" indices to use is the essence of the majority of the CBR effort. PRODIGY/ANALOGY uses two predefined categories of indexing, namely the conjunctive goals and the initial state configuration. PRODIGY/ANALOGY automatically identifies the relevant features of the initial state to be used as indices by determining the weakest preconditions of the goal conjuncts according to the particular solution found.

An initial attempt to *retrieve* similar possible matching past cases was experimented in the early problem solving research by Newell, Shaw, and Simon in the Logic Theorist (LT) [Newell *et al.*, 1963]. LT was written in 1956 and its goal was to explore the use of heuristics in problem solving. LT's particular domain task was proving theorems in the propositional calculus from a set of axioms. LT has three operators, namely detachment, forward chaining, and backward chaining, that it can apply in chain to the theorem to be proven in order to transform it recursively into the base axioms. LT's method involved matching all the combinations of axioms to see which operator is suitable. In order to prune out some of these combinations from being candidates to the matching process, LT used a similarity metric that tested equality of some absolute features, like the number of distinct variables of the new theorem and the axioms. It is interesting that this similarity metric did not produce any gains, and in fact, when used, even made LT miss proofs because it sometimes rejected the correct analogs. The question of what features should be considered in a similarity metric is therefore raised as early as LT. LT is a case study that shows that a simple syntactic or superficial similarity metric may not lead to any particular good results. In this work we re-experienced this same problem and attempted to address it in particular by developing the foot-printing algorithm to find the goal-relevant features of the initial state. But it is still the case that the features in this foot-printed set are not uniformly relevant. In this work we also made an initial study of the dynamic reorganization of memory. This relative relevance of the foot-printed features can be incrementally understood by interpreting the utility found by the replay process of the guidance suggested.

After this comparison with the pioneering LT, we discuss now other more recent systems.

In ANAPRON [Golding, 1991] cases are stored as negative exemplars of rules and retrieved directly when a rule is proposed. ANAPRON explores several different similarity metrics. The retrieval strategy is also based on thresholds for an adequate match level. ANAPRON learns these thresholds. In PER [Kedar-Cabelli, 1985] Kedar studies the analogical concept learning problem where candidate analogs are retrieved based on the purpose of the analogy to be performed. Both PRIAR and APU retrieve candidate similar analogs by evaluating the parts of the stored plan or program that are still useful in the new context. The retrieval is done by searching the stored cases linearly. PRIAR's retrieval strategy considers the preconditions and effects of the operators represented in the stored validation structure. APU's retrieval strategy similarly considers the abstract structure of the solution to be replayed. Both systems try to follow Gentner's structure-mapping approach [Gentner, 1987] to evaluate the match between problems by comparing solution derivations rather than the features that define the problems. However as this integral process is very expensive, PRIAR still uses the initial state features in addition to the validation structure, while APU compares generalized and abstract program structures.

The retrieval strategy in PRODIGY/ANALOGY uses the features of the initial state and the goal statement. It automates the process of maximizing the understanding of the structure of the plan by foot-printing the initial state and finding the sets of interacting goals. These are the indices compared with the new problem solving specifications. There is no way to compare the solved past problems and the new still unsolved problem more structurally exactly because the new problem was not solved yet and is specified only in terms of of its initial state and goal statement. APU's approach of using the abstract structure to guide the retrieval process is very interesting and it is in consonance with our proposed future working direction in integrating analogy and abstraction in PRODIGY.

9.3   Utilization of learned knowledge

There are two extreme approaches to utilize acquired experience, namely the learned knowledge is used when it matches **totally** or **partially** the new decision context.

"Eager" learning strategies, like explanation-based learning techniques [Mitchell *et al.*, 1986, Minton, 1988b, Etzioni, 1993] acquire provably correct and generalized knowledge for local decision making (as discussed in chapter 1. This local control knowledge is applied only when the new situation matches completely the supporting necessary conditions of the control rules. In particular these methods may involve both a large construction effort [Pérez and Etzioni, 1992] and a large matching cost [Tambe and Rosenbloom, 1989]. When this is tolerable, the method is very beneficial in leading the problem solver to close to, if not so, optimal performance.

Several research efforts try to alleviate either or both the construction and the matching costs [Tambe and Rosenbloom, 1989]. In his thesis, Tadepalli [Tadepalli, 1989] developed a *lazy* explanation-based learning in which partial explanations are produced alleviating therefore the learning effort of proving generalized control knowledge. [Duval, 1991] also presents an explanation-based learning method in which the deductive step is replaced by an abduction reasoning step that produces knowledge that is validated by experience. More recently Bhatnagar [Bhatnagar, 1992] builds incomplete proofs of failures and learns potentially over-general control rules that are refined incrementally by experience.

The approaches for learning knowledge improving problem solving performance have been therefore relaxing their deductive learning eagerness along several dimensions, including the correctness, the generalization, and the reuse of the learned (accumulated) knowledge. PRODIGY/ANALOGY explores a lazy learning technique in which no provably correct generalization is attempted from one problem solving episode and only a partial match is required in order to apply the learned knowledge.

Chunking in SOAR also accumulates episodic global knowledge. The selection of applicable chunks is based however in choosing the ones whose conditions match totally the active context. The chunking algorithm in SOAR is able to learn interactions among different problem spaces. A chunk may therefore capture parts of the derivational trace of the problem solving episode, in particular the problem spaces structures, similarly to the subgoaling links. These episodic chunks however cannot be reused flexibly, i.e., by reusing and adapting its contents.

We compare in more detail now the reuse or replay strategy of PRODIGY-/ANALOGY with other replaying systems. Andrew Golding's thesis [Golding, 1991], implemented in the ANAPRON system, combines a rule-based system and a case-based reasoner and applies it to the task of name pronunciation. The problem solving task is based on proposing rules for individual parts of a word, then searching for cases that override the rules proposed, and deciding whether to follow the rule or the analogy. As opposed to PRODIGY/ANALOGY cases are used for just one-step decisions. A single case may override several rules, but at each individual time that a case is retrieved, it is used just to override a unique rule. The decision of using a case in ANAPRON does not interact with the previous choices made, i.e,. ANAPRON does not backtrack. The decision is based on elaborated similarity metrics that decide on what is the case that can be used at each individual step of the problem solving task. Allen and Langley [Allen and Langley, 1990] also replay successfully one step past cases as opposed to a complete sequence of problem solving decisions as in PRODIGY/ANALOGY.

Other systems integrate case-based reasoning with dedicated special-purpose rule-based systems. MEDIATOR [Simpson, 1985] , PERSUADER [Sycara, 1987], and CASEY [Koton, 1988] apply case-based reasoning to problem solving trying to use previous cases first and then use simple rules if they cannot adapt the old cases to the current problem. On the other hand, JUDGE [Bain, 1986], and HYPO [Ashley and Rissland, 1987] try first simple first principles encoded as rules, then if these fail they try their case library. CHEF [Hammond, 1986] applies case-based reasoning to planning meals. It generates explanations from failures detected while trying to adapt the case retrieved. GREBE [Branting, 1991] in particular integrates rules and precedents (cases) in the classification of assigning a case to a specific category and explaining why the assignment is set. Cases and rules are used in conjunction and impartially to support and explain the classification process.

BOGART [Mostow, 1989] is an example where the replay process is not automated. It is interesting however as one of the first systems to implement parts of the derivational analogy strategy of storing and reusing dependencies links among steps. BOGART is able to reuse problem solving experience from previous steps of the same problem solving episode. This within-problem reuse is however not automated as in the internal analogy framework [Hickman and Larkin, 1990]. Internal analogy [Hickman *et al.*, 1990] focuses in studying the analogical transfer of experience within single problem solving episodes. Transformational analogy [Carbonell, 1983] replays past solutions by systematically modifying a retrieved plan as a function of the differences recognized between the past and the current new problem.

POPART, REDESIGN, and ARGO apply explanation techniques to try to adapt an old design or program to meet new specifications [Mostow, 1989]. JULIA [Hinrichs and Kolodner, 1991] designs menus for meals. It also relaxes the guaranteed correctness of the analogs to propose plausible solutions. The adaptation does not involve replanning. It is more like a relaxation process for constraint satisfaction problems when over-constrained situations are encountered. The adaptation uses multiple alternative cases and is able to combine subparts of them. [Redmond, 1990] presents a CBR system where cases are stored in pieces, *snippets*. These pieces are of small granularity, i.e., one-goal-operator steps, as in [Allen and Langley, 1990]. Snippets are used as a whole but problem solving is viewed as a combination task of several snippets of other cases. This is similar to the approach used in this work although there is no restriction in the granularity of the subparts of the cases reusable by PRODIGY/ANALOGY. In addition, PRODIGY/ANALOGY determines automatically the independent subparts of a case.

9.4   Summary

We compared our work with several other research efforts. The comparison is not certainly exhaustive. Instead it tries to focus on the more pertinent particular aspects of the analogical reasoning process. Our work overall develops a flexible integration of a complete derivational analogy reasoner, into a general purpose problem solving and learning architecture. The work opened new perspectives to the reconstruction approach, e.g., allowing automatic generation of annotations to the solution trace by building an introspection capability into the problem solver, and using learning abstraction techniques to create adequate memory indices.

A final word of comparison between PRODIGY/ANALOGY and other replaying systems in general: this work is unique in having automated the complete analogical cycle, namely the generation (annotation), storage, retrieval, and replay of episodic knowledge. It is also unique in its domain-independent approach and is demonstrated in particular in a case library of several orders of magnitude greater than most of the other CBR systems, in terms of the size of the case library and the granularity of the individual cases. ANAPRON is another example of an integrated rule-based and case-based system that was scaled up for the task of name pronunciation. ANAPRON uses a case library with 5000 cases, i.e., examples of pronunciation of names. These cases were provided externally, and each case illustrates at most the application of 8 operators. The more than 1000 planning problems solved by PRODIGY/ANALOGY correspond to more than 8000 one-goal problems, the case library is built incremental and automatically, and cases grow up to sequences of more than 200 annotated decision steps.

Chapter 10

Conclusion

The results reported in this monograph addressed the problem of integrating analogical reasoning into general purpose problem solving. The main goal of the work was to investigate the feasibility of analogical reasoning as a machine learning strategy to improve the performance of general problem solving.

Reasoning by analogy consists of the flexible reuse of previously solved problems, i.e., cases, to guide the search for solutions to similar new problems. The issues addressed in the book to apply this reasoning strategy include: the generation of the cases for reuse, the organization of the case library, the retrieval of adequate past cases similar to the new problem, and the replay of these previous problem solving episodes. The book presented algorithms that fully automate these four phases of the analogical reasoning process in an integrated design with a general purpose nonlinear planner.

The global implemented system was tested in a variety of domains including a complex logistics transportation domain with a case library of more than 1000 cases. The results obtained demonstrated the scalable properties of the algorithms designed and implemented. The analogical problem solver increased the solvability horizon and reduced the search effort of the base level problem solver.

Summary

Base-level planner We developed a nonlinear problem solver, NoLimit that reasons about totally ordered plans and is able to interleave goals at different search levels. NoLimit is complete and therefore it extends largely the spectrum of problems that it can solve compared to a linear planner.

Case generation We automate the process of generating cases to incrementally build a case library. The generation is done by retaining the lines of reasoning underlying an episodic problem solving experience. The problem solver introspects into its internal decision cycle to determine the reasons for its choices. These justifications consist of the links between choices capturing the subgoaling structure, records of explored failed alternatives, and pointers to applied control guidance. A case, i.e., a stored problem solving episode, consists of the solution trace augmented with these annotations.

Case storage The storage algorithm identifies the appropriate indices for the cases and organizes the case library. The foot-printing algorithm determines the set of features of the initial state that are relevant to achieving the goal statement for the particular solution found. In addition the cases are multiply indexed by the sets of interacting goal conjuncts from the user-given goal statement. We developed an algorithm to recognize these goal interactions by partially ordering the totally ordered case steps. The connected components of the resulting partially ordered solution correspond to the independent case fragments that can be independently reused.

Case retrieval The retrieval procedure implemented uses a similarity metric to rank the partially matched candidate analogs which considers the foot-printed initial state and the goal interactions of the past cases. The matching is done incrementally to allow stopping retrieval if some "reasonable" partial match is found, as opposed to searching for the "best" match.

Case replay The replay mechanism involves a complete reinterpretation of the justifications structures from the past guiding cases in the new problem solving context. When the transformed justifications are no longer valid, the replay procedure either replans for the new situation or may recursively request additional guidance from the case library. The replay mechanism can integrate guidance from multiple past similar cases.

Scale up PRODIGY/ANALOGY is tested in several domains and in particular in a complex logistics transportation domain with a case library of 1000 cases. Extensive empirical results along different dimensions demonstrate the scalable properties of the algorithms designed and implemented.

Future research directions

This works opens several future research directions in particular as follow ups to the designed and implemented analogical reasoner.

The extension of the framework of PRODIGY/ANALOGY to more realistic domains requires the design of more powerful tools for planning. A direction of future work is to develop robust probabilistic planning approaches to account for the uncertainty characteristics of the real world. A second challenging direction is to explore the use of the episodic cases automatically generated by the analogical reasoner to bridging classical planning search and reactive planning methods.

This work did not have as an immediate goal to compare the different learning strategies within PRODIGY. However an immediate research direction is to investigate the integration of these different learning strategies within PRODIGY. This will entail further work of incorporating other learning methods into the non-linear planner framework. In fact, while the analogical reasoner is implemented within the nonlinear problem solver of the architecture, for chronological reasons, the previous learning modules are implemented within the linear planner.[1] Once this re-design and re-implementation is accomplished, it is possible to compare our multiple complex learning techniques and their synergistic interaction.

Previous work in the linear planner of PRODIGY uses explanation-based learning techniques, (PRODIGY/EBL), [Minton, 1988b] to extract from a problem solving trace the explanation chain responsible for a success or failure and to compile search control rules therefrom. While performing the goal regression on the derivational trace to determine the foot-print of the initial state, the analogical reasoner performs a lazy explanation of the solution encountered. Lazy because it goes up the successful path following the subgoaling chain without attempting to prove any generalization of the immediate success or recorded failures. However, although simple, it turns out to be quite useful to take into account this lazy explanation.

The joint EBL-analogical reasoner could decide the situations where it is worth spending effort using either of the following learning strategies: statically analyzing the domain theory, or interpreting a trace of a solved problem to generalize control rules therefrom, or to store the problem solving episode as a case for eventual future retrieval and replay. Analogy would benefit from the integration as some simple cases and simple problem solving situations would be translated into general control rules. On the other hand, EBL would benefit in incomplete domain theories, where the proofs for generalized explanations cannot be pursued. Additionally, in the nonlinear problem solving context, the number of alternatives explored is very large and very complex goal interactions may be explored. The joint EBL-analogical reasoner could switch from an eager costly attempt to explain a difficult trace to a lazy attitude of storing it as a case, as a function of some threshold of the cost of the two approaches.

PRODIGY/ANALOGY is also robust to changes in problem solving situations, as opposed to the rigid EBL or STATIC which require an exact match to re-apply their learned knowledge. Another future research direction is to combine PRODIGY/ANALOGY with a dynamically changing domain definition, by extending its current ability to flexibly handling changes in problem solving situations.

The axiomatized domain knowledge in PRODIGY is used to learn abstraction layers in the ALPINE [Knoblock, 1994]. A key issue in the process of solving problems by analogy is the identification of the *details* and the *relevant* features of a particular problem solving situation. As new and past situations are not expected to match fully, knowing the relevance of the information available increases the ability for successful partial matching of different problems. The foot-printing algorithm determinates the features from the initial state that were used in a particular solution to a problem. ALPINE provides a mechanism that analyzes a particular domain, and generates abstraction levels that group together features in a hierarchical structure, the most crucial, interrelated ones at the top. An interesting direction of future work is to explore the use of the ab-

---

[1] We are now in the process of transferring DYNAMIC, i.e., EBL + STATIC [Pérez and Etzioni, 1992], into the nonlinear problem solver of PRODIGY 4.0 [Carbonell *et al.*, 1992].

straction levels generated by ALPINE in addition to the foot-printing algorithm, as a measure of relevance to rank partially matched candidate analogs.

The dynamic organization of memory currently does a simple abstraction by generalizing instances into their type classes. However, the use the abstraction levels will help the dynamic organization of the discrimination network. The more relevant features of the problem can unify with the new problem before the detailed ones, where "relevant" is both a function of past experience and the level in the abstraction hierarchy.

A second major benefit of the integration of analogy and abstraction is the generality of stored plans for later indexing. That is, a solution at an abstract level may be more likely to be an applicable candidate analog than one at the ground level – although it will require refinement by adding in details of the current problem. In general, it would be interesting to use abstract analogs when specific grounded ones are not present to guide search in derivational analogy.

Another interesting direction for future work is to follow Allen Newell's challenge for "historical learning." The idea is to not reset the system from its learned knowledge and increment the capabilities of a problem solver over time building upon its learning history. The analogical reasoner could increase its own problem solving abilities by combining the knowledge in its different domain-dependent case libraries, accumulated along its lifetime.

Bibliography

[Aho *et al.*, 1974] A. V. Aho, J. E. Hopcroft, and J. D. Ullman. *The Design and Analysis of Computer Algorithms*. Addison-Wesley, Reading, Massachusetts, 1974.

[Allen and Langley, 1990] John Allen and Pat Langley. Integrating memory and search in planning. In *Proceedings of the DARPA Workshop on Innovative Approaches to Planning, Scheduling, and Control*, pages 301–312, San Diego, CA, November 1990. Morgan Kaufmann.

[Allen *et al.*, 1992] John Allen, Pat Langley, and Stan Matwin. Knowledge and regularity in planning. In *Working notes of the AAAI Spring Symposium on Computational Considerations in Supporting Incremental Modification and Reuse*, pages 7–12, Stanford University, 1992.

[Anderson, 1983] John R. Anderson. *The Architecture of Cognition*. Harvard University Press, Cambridge, Mass, 1983.

[Ashley and Rissland, 1987] Kevin D. Ashley and Edwina L. Rissland. Compare and contrast: A test of expertise. In *Proceedings of AAAI-87*, pages 273–278, 1987.

[Bain, 1986] W. Bain. *Case-based reasoning: A computer model of subjective assessment*. PhD thesis, Yale University, 1986.

[Barletta and Mark, 1988] Ralph Barletta and William Mark. Explanation-based indexing of cases. In *Proceedings of the First Workshop on Case-Based Reasoning*, pages 50–60, Tampa, FL, May 1988. Morgan Kaufmann.

[Barrett *et al.*, 1991] Anthony Barrett, Steven Soderland, and Daniel Weld. The effect of step-order representations on planning. Technical Report 91-05-06, Department of Computer Science and Engineering, University of Washington, 1991.

[Bhansali and Harandi, 1993] Sanjay Bhansali and Mehdi T. Harandi. Synthesis of UNIX programs using derivational analogy. *Machine Learning*, 10, 1993.

[Bhansali, 1991] Sanjay Bhansali. *Domain-based program synthesis using planning and derivational analogy*. PhD thesis, Department of Computer Science, University of Illinois at Urbana-Champaign, 1991.

[Bhatnagar, 1992] Neeraj Bhatnagar. *On-line learning from search failures.* PhD thesis, Rutgers University, 1992.

[Blumenthal, 1990] Brad Blumenthal. *Replaying episodes of a metaphoric application interface designer.* PhD thesis, University of Texas, Artificial Intelligence Lab, Austin, December 1990.

[Blythe and Veloso, 1992] Jim Blythe and Manuela M. Veloso. An analysis of search techniques for a totally-ordered nonlinear planner. In *Proceedings of the First International Conference on AI Planning Systems*, pages 13–19, College Park, MD, June 1992.

[Branting, 1991] L. Karl Branting. *Integrating rules and precedents for classification and explanation:Automating legal analysis.* PhD thesis, University of Texas at Austin, 1991.

[Cain *et al.*, 1991] T. Cain, M. Pazzani, and G. Silverstein. Using domain knowledge to influence similarity judgments. In *Proceedings of the 1991 DARPA Workshop on Case-Based Reasoning*, pages 191–199. Morgan Kaufmann, May 1991.

[Carbonell and Gil, 1990] Jaime G. Carbonell and Yolanda Gil. Learning by experimentation: The operator refinement method. In R. S. Michalski and Y. Kodratoff, editors, *Machine Learning: An Artificial Intelligence Approach, Volume III*, pages 191–213. Morgan Kaufmann, Palo Alto, CA, 1990.

[Carbonell and Veloso, 1988] Jaime G. Carbonell and Manuela M. Veloso. Integrating derivational analogy into a general problem solving architecture. In *Proceedings of the First Workshop on Case-Based Reasoning*, pages 104–124, Tampa, FL, May 1988. Morgan Kaufmann.

[Carbonell *et al.*, 1990] Jaime G. Carbonell, Craig A. Knoblock, and Steven Minton. Prodigy: An integrated architecture for planning and learning. In K. VanLehn, editor, *Architectures for Intelligence*. Erlbaum, Hillsdale, NJ, 1990. Also Technical Report CMU-CS-89-189.

[Carbonell *et al.*, 1992] Jaime G. Carbonell, Jim Blythe, Oren Etzioni, Yolanda Gil, Robert Joseph, Dan Kahn, Craig Knoblock, Steven Minton, Alicia Pérez, Scott Reilly, Manuela Veloso, and Xuemei Wang. PRODIGY4.0: The manual and tutorial. Technical Report CMU-CS-92-150, Carnegie Mellon University, June 1992.

[Carbonell, 1983] Jaime G. Carbonell. Learning by analogy: Formulating and generalizing plans from past experience. In R. S. Michalski, J. G. Carbonell, and T. M. Mitchell, editors, *Machine Learning, An Artificial Intelligence Approach*, pages 137–162, Palo Alto, CA, 1983. Tioga Press.

[Carbonell, 1986] Jaime G. Carbonell. Derivational analogy: A theory of reconstructive problem solving and expertise acquisition. In R. S. Michalski,

J. G. Carbonell, and T. M. Mitchell, editors, *Machine Learning, An Artificial Intelligence Approach, Volume II*, pages 371–392. Morgan Kaufman, 1986.

[Chapman, 1987] David Chapman. Planning for conjunctive goals. *Artificial Intelligence*, 32:333–378, 1987.

[Cheng and Carbonell, 1986] Pat W. Cheng and Jaime G. Carbonell. The FERMI system: Inducing iterative rules from experience. In *Proceedings of AAAI-86*, pages 490–495, Philadelphia, PA, 1986.

[DeJong and Mooney, 1986]
Gerald F. DeJong and Raymond Mooney. Explanation-based learning: An alternative view. *Machine Learning*, 1(2):145–176, 1986.

[Doorenbos and Veloso, 1993] Robert B. Doorenbos and Manuela M. Veloso. Knowledge organization and the utility problem. In *Proceedings of the Third International Workshop on Knowledge Compilation and Speedup Learning*, pages 28–34, Amherst, MA, June 1993.

[Doorenbos et al., 1992] Robert Doorenbos, Milind Tambe, and Allen Newell. Learning 10,000 chunks: What's it like out there? In *Proceedings of the Tenth National Conference on Artificial Intelligence*, pages 830–836, 1992.

[Duval, 1991] Béatrice Duval. Abduction for explanation based learning. In *Proceedings of the European Working Session on Learning*, pages 348–360. Springer-Verlag, March 1991.

[Ernst and Newell, 1969] George W. Ernst and Allen Newell. *GPS: A Case Study in Generality and Problem Solving*. ACM Monograph Series. Academic Press, New York, NY, 1969.

[Etzioni, 1990] Oren Etzioni. *A Structural Theory of Explanation-Based Learning*. PhD thesis, School of Computer Science, Carnegie Mellon University, 1990. Available as technical report CMU-CS-90-185.

[Etzioni, 1993] Oren Etzioni. Acquiring search-control knowledge via static analysis. *Artificial Intelligence*, 62(2):255–301, 1993.

[Fikes and Nilsson, 1971] Richard E. Fikes and Nils J. Nilsson. Strips: A new approach to the application of theorem proving to problem solving. *Artificial Intelligence*, 2:189–208, 1971.

[Gentner, 1987] Dedre Gentner. The mechanisms of analogical learning. In S. Vosniadou and A. Ortony, editors, *Similarity and Analogical Reasoning*. Cambridge University Press, New York, NY, 1987.

[Goel, 1991] Ashok Goel. A model-based approach to case adaptation. In *Proceedings of the Thirteenth Annual Conference of the Cognitive Science Society*, pages 143–148, Hillsdale, NJ, 1991. Lawrence Erlbaum Associates, Inc.

[Golding, 1991] Andrew R. Golding. *Pronouncing names by a combination of rule-based and Case-based reasoning.* PhD thesis, Stanford University, 1991. Available as technical report STAN-CS-92-1403.

[Hammond, 1986] Kristian J. Hammond. *Case-based Planning: An Integrated Theory of Planning, Learning and Memory.* PhD thesis, Yale University, 1986.

[Hammond, 1989] Kristian J. Hammond. Opportunistic memory. In *Proceedings of the Eleventh International Joint Conference on Artificial Intelligence*, pages 504–510, San Mateo, CA, 1989. Morgan Kaufmann.

[Harandi and Bhansali, 1989] M. T. Harandi and S. Bhansali. Program derivation using analogy. In *Proceedings of the Eleventh International Joint Conference on Artificial Intelligence*, pages 389–394, Detroit, MI, 1989.

[Hickman and Larkin, 1990] Angela K. Hickman and Jill H. Larkin. Internal analogy: A model of transfer within problems. In *The 12th Annual Conference of The Cognitive Science Society*, pages 53–60, Hillsdale, NJ, 1990. Lawrence Erlbaum Associates.

[Hickman *et al.*, 1990] Angela K. Hickman, Peter Shell, and Jaime G. Carbonell. Internal analogy: Reducing search during problem solving. In C. Copetas, editor, *The Computer Science Research Review 1990.* The School of Computer Science, Carnegie Mellon University, 1990.

[Hinrichs and Kolodner, 1991] Thomas R. Hinrichs and Janet L. Kolodner. The roles of adaptation on case-based design. In *Proceedings of the Ninth National Conference on Artificial Intelligence*, pages 28–33. AAAI Press/The MIT Press, 1991.

[Joseph, 1989] Robert L. Joseph. Graphical knowledge acquisition. In *Proceedings of the 4th Knowledge Acquisition For Knowledge-Based Systems Workshop*, Banff, Canada, 1989.

[Kambhampati and Hendler, 1992] Subbarao Kambhampati and James A. Hendler. A validation based theory of plan modification and reuse. *Artificial Intelligence*, 55(2-3):193–258, 1992.

[Kambhampati, 1989] Subbarao Kambhampati. *Flexible Reuse and Modification in Hierarchical Planning: A Validation Structure Based Approach.* PhD thesis, Computer Vision Laboratory, Center for Automation Research, University of Maryland, College Park, MD, 1989.

[Kedar-Cabelli, 1985] S. Kedar-Cabelli. Purpose-directed analogy. In *Proceedings of the Seventh Annual Conference of the Cognitive Science Society*, pages 150–159, 1985.

[Knoblock, 1991] Craig A. Knoblock. *Automatically Generating Abstractions for Problem Solving.* PhD thesis, School of Computer Science, Carnegie Mellon University, Pittsburgh, PA, 1991. Available as technical report CMU-CS-91-120.

[Knoblock, 1994] Craig A. Knoblock. Automatically generating abstractions for planning. *Artificial Intelligence*, 68, 1994.

[Kolmogorov, 1965] A. N. Kolmogorov. Three approaches to the concept of the amount of information. In *Probl. Inf. Transm.*, volume 1/1. 1965.

[Kolodner, 1980] Janet L. Kolodner. *Retrieval and Organizational Strategies in Conceptual Memory: A Computer Model*. PhD thesis, Yale University, 1980.

[Kolodner, 1984] Janet L. Kolodner. *Retrieval and Organization Strategies in Conceptual Memory*. Lawrence Erlbaum Associates, Inc., Hillsdale, New Jersey, 1984.

[Korf, 1985] Richard E. Korf. Macro-operators: A weak method for learning. *Artificial Intelligence*, 26:35–77, 1985.

[Koton, 1988] Phyllis Koton. Reasoning about evidence in causal explanation. In *Proceedings of AAAI-88*, pages 256–261, 1988.

[Laird et al., 1986] John E. Laird, Paul S. Rosenbloom, and Allen Newell. Chunking in SOAR: The anatomy of a general learning mechanism. *Machine Learning*, 1:11–46, 1986.

[Lebowitz, 1980] Michael Lebowitz. *Generalization and Memory in an Integrated Understanding System*. PhD thesis, Yale University, 1980.

[Minton et al., 1989] Steven Minton, Craig A. Knoblock, Dan R. Kuokka, Yolanda Gil, Robert L. Joseph, and Jaime G. Carbonell. PRODIGY 2.0: The manual and tutorial. Technical Report CMU-CS-89-146, School of Computer Science, Carnegie Mellon University, 1989.

[Minton et al., 1991] Steven Minton, John Bresina, and Mark Drummond. Commitment strategies in planning: A comparative analysis. In *Proceedings of the Twelfth International Joint Conference on Artificial Intelligence*, pages 259–265, 1991.

[Minton, 1985] Steven Minton. Selectively generalizing plans for problem solving. In *Proceedings of AAAI-85*, pages 596–599, 1985.

[Minton, 1988a] Steven Minton. *Learning Effective Search Control Knowledge: An Explanation-Based Approach*. PhD thesis, Computer Science Department, Carnegie Mellon University, 1988. Available as technical report CMU-CS-88-133.

[Minton, 1988b] Steven Minton. *Learning Effective Search Control Knowledge: An Explanation-Based Approach*. Kluwer Academic Publishers, Boston, MA, 1988.

[Mitchell et al., 1983] Tom M. Mitchell, Paul E. Utgoff, and R. B. Banerji. Learning by experimentation: Acquiring and refining problem-solving heuristics. In *Machine Learning, An Artificial Intelligence Approach*, pages 163–190. Tioga Press, Palo Alto, CA, 1983.

[Mitchell et al., 1986] Tom M. Mitchell, Richard M. Keller, and Smadar T. Kedar-Cabelli. Explanation-based generalization: A unifying view. *Machine Learning*, 1:47–80, 1986.

[Mooney, 1988] Raymond J. Mooney. Generalizing the order of operators in macro-operators. In *Proceedings of the Fifth International Conference on Machine Learning*, pages 270–283, San Mateo, CA, 1988. Morgan Kaufmann.

[Mostow, 1989] Jack Mostow. Automated replay of design plans: Some issues in derivational analogy. *Artificial Intelligence*, 40(1-3), 1989.

[Neves, 1980] David M. Neves. *Learning algebraic procedures from examples.* PhD thesis, Department of Psychology, Carnegie Mellon University, 1980.

[Newell and Simon, 1956] Allen Newell and Herbert A. Simon. The logic theory machine. *IRE Transactions on Information Theory IT-2*, 3:61–79, 1956.

[Newell and Simon, 1972] Allen Newell and Herbert A. Simon. *Human Problem Solving.* Prentice-Hall, Englewood Cliffs, NJ, 1972.

[Newell et al., 1963] Allen Newell, J. C. Shaw, and Herbert A. Simon. Empirical explorations with the logic theory machine: A case study in heuristics. In E. Feigenbaum and J. Feldman, editors, *Computers and Thought*. McGraw-Hill, New York, NY, 1963.

[Newell, 1980] Allen Newell. Physical symbol systems. *Cognitive Science*, 4-2:135–184, 1980.

[Pazzani, 1990] M. Pazzani. *Creating a Memory of Causal Relationships: An integration of empirical and explanation-based learning methods.* Lawrence Erlbaum Associates, Hillsdale, NJ, 1990.

[Pérez and Carbonell, 1993] M. Alicia Pérez and Jaime G. Carbonell. Automated acquisition of control knowledge to improve the quality of plans. Technical Report CMU-CS-93-142, School of Computer Science, Carnegie Mellon University, April 1993.

[Pérez and Etzioni, 1992] M. Alicia Pérez and Oren Etzioni. DYNAMIC: A new role for training problems in EBL. In D. Sleeman and P. Edwards, editors, *Proceedings of the Ninth International Conference on Machine Learning*, pages 367–372. Morgan Kaufmann, San Mateo, CA, 1992.

[Polya, 1945] George Polya. *How to Solve It*. Princeton University Press, Princeton, NJ, 1945.

[Quinlan, 1990] J. Ross Quinlan. Learning logical definitions from relations. *Machine Learning*, 5:239–266, 1990.

[Redmond, 1990] Michael Redmond. Distributed cases for case-based reasoning; Facilitating the use of multiple cases. In *Proceedings of the Eighth National Conference on Artificial Intelligence*, pages 304–309, Cambridge, MA, 1990. AAAI Press/The MIT Press.

[Rich and Knight, 1991] Elaine Rich and Kevin Knight. *Artificial Intelligence*. McGraw-Hill, Inc., 1991. Second edition.

[Riesbeck and Schank, 1989] Christopher K. Riesbeck and Roger C. Schank. *Inside Case-Based Reasoning*. Lawrence Erlbaum Associates, Hillsdale, New Jersey, 1989.

[Rissland and Skalak, 1991] Edwina L. Rissland and David B. Skalak. CABARET: Rule interpretation in a hybrid architecture. *International Journal of Man-Machine Studies*, 34(6), 1991.

[Rosenbloom et al., 1990] Paul S. Rosenbloom, S. Lee, and Amy Unruh. Responding to impasses in memory-driven behavior: A framework for planning. In *Proceedings of the DARPA Workshop on Innovative Approaches to Planning, Scheduling, and Control*. Morgan Kaufmann, November 1990.

[Sacerdoti, 1975] Earl D. Sacerdoti. The nonlinear nature of plans. In *Proceedings of IJCAI-75*, pages 206–213, 1975.

[Schank, 1982] Roger C. Schank. *Dynamic Memory*. Cambridge University Press, 1982.

[Simpson, 1985] Robert L. Simpson. *A computer model of case-based reasoning in problem solving: An investigation in the domain of dispute mediation*. PhD thesis, School of Information and Computer Science, Georgia Institute of Technology, Atlanta, GA, 1985.

[Sussman, 1975] Gerald J. Sussman. *A Computer Model of Skill Acquisition*. American Elsevier, New York, 1975. Also available as technical report AI-TR-297, Artificial Intelligence Laboratory, MIT, 1975.

[Sycara, 1987] E. P. Sycara. *Resolving adversarial conflicts: An approach to integrating case-based and analytic methods*. PhD thesis, School of Information and Computer Science, Georgia Institute of Technology, Atlanta, GA, 1987.

[Tadepalli, 1989] Prasad Tadepalli. Lazy explanation-based learning: A solution to the intractable theory problem. In *Proceedings of the Eleventh International Joint Conference on Artificial Intelligence*, pages 694–700, San Mateo, CA, 1989. Morgan Kaufmann.

[Tambe and Rosenbloom, 1989] Milind Tambe and Paul Rosenbloom. Elimi-
nating expensive chunks by restricting expressiveness. In *Proceedings of the
Eleventh International Joint Conference on Artificial Intelligence*, pages 731–
737, San Mateo, CA, 1989. Morgan Kaufmann.

[Tate, 1977] Austin Tate. Generating project networks. In *Proceedings of the
Fifth International Joint Conference on Artificial Intelligence*, pages 888–900,
1977.

[Veloso and Carbonell, 1989] Manuela M. Veloso and Jaime G. Carbonell.
Learning analogies by analogy - The closed loop of memory organization and
problem solving. In *Proceedings of the Second Workshop on Case-Based Reasoning*, pages 153–158, Pensacola, FL, May 1989. Morgan Kaufmann.

[Veloso and Carbonell, 1993a] Manuela M. Veloso and Jaime G. Carbonell.
Derivational analogy in PRODIGY: Automating case acquisition, storage, and
utilization. *Machine Learning*, 10:249–278, 1993.

[Veloso and Carbonell, 1993b] Manuela M. Veloso and Jaime G. Carbonell. Towards scaling up machine learning: A case study with derivational analogy
in PRODIGY. In S. Minton, editor, *Machine Learning Methods for Planning*,
pages 233–272. Morgan Kaufmann, 1993.

[Veloso *et al.*, 1990] Manuela M. Veloso, M. Alicia Pérez, and Jaime G. Carbonell. Nonlinear planning with parallel resource allocation. In *Proceedings
of the DARPA Workshop on Innovative Approaches to Planning, Scheduling,
and Control*, pages 207–212, San Diego, CA, November 1990. Morgan Kaufmann.

[Veloso, 1989] Manuela M. Veloso. Nonlinear problem solving using intelligent
casual-commitment. Technical Report CMU-CS-89-210, School of Computer
Science, Carnegie Mellon University, 1989.

[Veloso, 1992] Manuela M. Veloso. *Learning by Analogical Reasoning in General
Problem Solving*. PhD thesis, School of Computer Science, Carnegie Mellon
University, Pittsburgh, PA, August 1992. Available as technical report CMU-
CS-92-174.

[Waldinger, 1981] R. Waldinger. Achieving several goals simultaneously. In N. J.
Nilsson and B. Webber, editors, *Readings in Artificial Intelligence*, pages 250–
271. Morgan Kaufman, Los Altos, CA, 1981.

[Wang, 1992] Xuemei Wang. Constraint-based efficient matching in PRODIGY.
Technical Report CMU-CS-92-128, School of Computer Science, Carnegie
Mellon University, April 1992.

[Waterman, 1970] D. Waterman. Generalization learning techniques for automating the learning of heuristics. *Artificial Intelligence*, 1:121–170, 1970.

[Wilkins, 1989] David E. Wilkins. Can AI planners solve practical problems? Technical Note 468R, SRI International, 1989.

[Yang and Fisher, 1992] Hua Yang and Douglas Fisher. Similarity-based retrieval and partial reuse of macro-operators. Technical Report CS-92-13, Department of Computer Science, Vanderbilt University, 1992.

[Zelle and Mooney, 1993] J. Zelle and R. Mooney. Combining FOIL and EBG to speed-up logic programs. In *Proceedings of the Thirteenth International Joint Conference on Artificial Intelligence*, 1993.

Springer-Verlag
and the Environment

We at Springer-Verlag firmly believe that an international science publisher has a special obligation to the environment, and our corporate policies consistently reflect this conviction.

We also expect our business partners – paper mills, printers, packaging manufacturers, etc. – to commit themselves to using environmentally friendly materials and production processes.

The paper in this book is made from low- or no-chlorine pulp and is acid free, in conformance with international standards for paper permanency.

Lecture Notes in Artificial Intelligence (LNAI)

Vol. 681: H. Wansing, The Logic of Information Structures. IX, 163 pages. 1993.

Vol. 689: J. Komorowski, Z. W. Raś (Eds.), Methodologies for Intelligent Systems. Proceedings, 1993. XI, 653 pages. 1993.

Vol. 695: E. P. Klement, W. Slany (Eds.), Fuzzy Logic in Artificial Intelligence. Proceedings, 1993. VIII, 192 pages. 1993.

Vol. 698: A. Voronkov (Ed.), Logic Programming and Automated Reasoning. Proceedings, 1993. XIII, 386 pages. 1993.

Vol. 699: G. W. Mineau, B. Moulin, J. F. Sowa (Eds.), Conceptual Graphs for Knowledge Representation. Proceedings, 1993. IX, 451 pages. 1993.

Vol. 723: N. Aussenac, G. Boy, B. Gaines, M. Linster, J.-G. Ganascia, Y. Kodratoff (Eds.), Knowledge Acquisition for Knowledge-Based Systems. Proceedings, 1993. XIII, 446 pages. 1993.

Vol. 727: M. Filgueiras, L. Damas (Eds.), Progress in Artificial Intelligence. Proceedings, 1993. X, 362 pages. 1993.

Vol. 728: P. Torasso (Ed.), Advances in Artificial Intelligence. Proceedings, 1993. XI, 336 pages. 1993.

Vol. 743: S. Doshita, K. Furukawa, K. P. Jantke, T. Nishida (Eds.), Algorithmic Learning Theory. Proceedings, 1992. X, 260 pages. 1993.

Vol. 744: K. P. Jantke, T. Yokomori, S. Kobayashi, E. Tomita (Eds.), Algorithmic Learning Theory. Proceedings, 1993. XI, 423 pages. 1993.

Vol. 745: V. Roberto (Ed.), Intelligent Perceptual Systems. VIII, 378 pages. 1993.

Vol. 746: A. S. Tanguiane, Artificial Perception and Music Recognition. XV, 210 pages. 1993.

Vol. 754: H. D. Pfeiffer, T. E. Nagle (Eds.), Conceptual Structures: Theory and Implementation. Proceedings, 1992. IX, 327 pages. 1993.

Vol. 764: G. Wagner, Vivid Logic. XII, 148 pages. 1994.

Vol. 766: P. R. Van Loocke, The Dynamics of Concepts. XI, 340 pages. 1994.

Vol. 770: P. Haddawy, Representing Plans Under Uncertainty. X, 129 pages. 1994.

Vol. 784: F. Bergadano, L. De Raedt (Eds.), Machine Learning: ECML-94. Proceedings, 1994. XI, 439 pages. 1994.

Vol. 795: W. A. Hunt, Jr., FM8501: A Verified Microprocessor. XIII, 333 pages. 1994.

Vol. 798: R. Dyckhoff (Ed.), Extensions of Logic Programming. Proceedings, 1993. VIII, 360 pages. 1994.

Vol. 799: M. P. Singh, Multiagent Systems: Intentions, Know-How, and Communications. XXIII, 168 pages. 1994.

Vol. 804: D. Hernández, Qualitative Representation of Spatial Knowledge. IX, 202 pages. 1994.

Vol. 808: M. Masuch, L. Pólos (Eds.), Knowledge Representation and Reasoning Under Uncertainty. VII, 237 pages. 1994.

Vol. 810: G. Lakemeyer, B. Nebel (Eds.), Foundations of Knowledge Representation and Reasoning. VIII, 355 pages. 1994.

Vol. 814: A. Bundy (Ed.), Automated Deduction — CADE-12. Proceedings, 1994. XVI, 848 pages. 1994.

Vol. 822: F. Pfenning (Ed.), Logic Programming and Automated Reasoning. Proceedings, 1994. X, 345 pages. 1994.

Vol. 827: D. M. Gabbay, H. J. Ohlbach (Eds.), Temporal Logic. Proceedings, 1994. XI, 546 pages. 1994.

Vol. 830: C. Castelfranchi, E. Werner (Eds.), Artificial Social Systems. Proceedings, 1992. XVIII, 337 pages. 1994.

Vol. 833: D. Driankov, P. W. Eklund, A. Ralescu (Eds.), Fuzzy Logic and Fuzzy Control. Proceedings, 1991. XII, 157 pages. 1994.

Vol. 835: W. M. Tepfenhart, J. P. Dick, J. F. Sowa (Eds.), Conceptual Structures: Current Practices. Proceedings, 1994. VIII, 331 pages. 1994.

Vol. 837: S. Wess, K.-D. Althoff, M. M. Richter (Eds.), Topics in Case-Based Reasoning. Proceedings, 1993. IX, 471 pages. 1994.

Vol. 838: C. MacNish, D. Pearce, L. M. Pereira (Eds.), Logics in Artificial Intelligence. Proceedings, 1994. IX, 413 pages. 1994.

Vol. 847: A. Ralescu (Ed.) Fuzzy Logic in Artificial Intelligence. Proceedings, 1993. VII, 128 pages. 1994.

Vol: 861: B. Nebel, L. Dreschler-Fischer (Eds.), KI-94: Advances in Artificial Intelligence. Proceedings, 1994. IX, 401 pages. 1994.

Vol. 862: R. C. Carrasco, J. Oncina (Eds.), Grammatical Inference and Applications. Proceedings, 1994. VIII, 290 pages. 1994.

Vol 867: L. Steels, G. Schreiber, W. Van de Velde (Eds.), A Future for Knowledge Acquisition. Proceedings, 1994. XII, 414 pages. 1994.

Vol. 869: Z. W. Raś, M. Zemankova (Eds.), Methodologies for Intelligent Systems. Proceedings, 1994. X, 613 pages. 1994.

Vol. 872: S Arikawa, K. P. Jantke (Eds.), Algorithmic Learning Theory. Proceedings, 1994. XIV, 575 pages. 1994.

Vol. 878: T. Ishida, Parallel, Distributed and Multiagent Production Systems. XVII, 166 pages. 1994.

Vol. 886: M. M. Veloso, Planning and Learning by Analogical Reasoning. XIII, 181 pages. 1994.

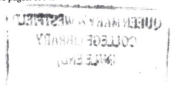
QUEEN MARY & WESTFIELD
COLLEGE LIBRARY
(MILE END)

Lecture Notes in Computer Science

Vol. 852: K. Echtle, D. Hammer, D. Powell (Eds.), Dependable Computing – EDCC-1. Proceedings, 1994. XVII, 618 pages. 1994.

Vol. 853: L. Snyder, K. Bolding (Eds.), Parallel Computer Routing and Communication. Proceedings, 1994. IX, 317 pages. 1994.

Vol. 854: B. Buchberger, J. Volkert (Eds.), Parallel Processing: CONPAR 94 – VAPP VI. Proceedings, 1994. XVI, 893 pages. 1994.

Vol. 855: J. van Leeuwen (Ed.), Algorithms – ESA '94. Proceedings, 1994. X, 510 pages.1994.

Vol. 856: D. Karagiannis (Ed.), Database and Expert Systems Applications. Proceedings, 1994. XVII, 807 pages. 1994.

Vol. 857: G. Tel, P. Vitányi (Eds.), Distributed Algorithms. Proceedings, 1994. X, 370 pages. 1994.

Vol. 858: E. Bertino, S. Urban (Eds.), Object-Oriented Methodologies and Systems. Proceedings, 1994. X, 386 pages. 1994.

Vol. 859: T. F. Melham, J. Camilleri (Eds.), Higher Order Logic Theorem Proving and Its Applications. Proceedings, 1994. IX, 470 pages. 1994.

Vol. 860: W. L. Zagler, G. Busby, R. R. Wagner (Eds.), Computers for Handicapped Persons. Proceedings, 1994. XX, 625 pages. 1994.

Vol: 861: B. Nebel, L. Dreschler-Fischer (Eds.), KI-94: Advances in Artificial Intelligence. Proceedings, 1994. IX, 401 pages. 1994. (Subseries LNAI).

Vol. 862: R. C. Carrasco, J. Oncina (Eds.), Grammatical Inference and Applications. Proceedings, 1994. VIII, 290 pages. 1994. (Subseries LNAI).

Vol. 863: H. Langmaack, W.-P. de Roever, J. Vytopil (Eds.), Formal Techniques in Real-Time and Fault-Tolerant Systems. Proceedings, 1994. XIV, 787 pages. 1994.

Vol. 864: B. Le Charlier (Ed.), Static Analysis. Proceedings, 1994. XII, 465 pages. 1994.

Vol. 865: T. C. Fogarty (Ed.), Evolutionary Computing. Proceedings, 1994. XII, 332 pages. 1994.

Vol. 866: Y. Davidor, H.-P. Schwefel, R. Männer (Eds.), Parallel Problem Solving from Nature - PPSN III. Proceedings, 1994. XV, 642 pages. 1994.

Vol 867: L. Steels, G. Schreiber, W. Van de Velde (Eds.), A Future for Knowledge Acquisition. Proceedings, 1994. XII, 414 pages. 1994. (Subseries LNAI).

Vol. 868: R. Steinmetz (Ed.), Advanced Teleservices and High-Speed Communication Architectures. Proceedings, 1994. IX, 451 pages. 1994.

Vol. 869: Z. W. Raś, M. Zemankova (Eds.), Methodologies for Intelligent Systems. Proceedings, 1994. X, 613 pages. 1994. (Subseries LNAI).

Vol. 870: J. S. Greenfield, Distributed Programming Paradigms with Cryptography Applications. XI, 182 pages. 1994.

Vol. 871: J. P. Lee, G. G. Grinstein (Eds.), Database Issues for Data Visualization. Proceedings, 1993. XIV, 229 pages. 1994.

Vol. 872: S Arikawa, K. P. Jantke (Eds.), Algorithmic Learning Theory. Proceedings, 1994. XIV, 575 pages. 1994. (Subseries LNAI).

Vol. 873: M. Naftalin, T. Denvir, M. Bertran (Eds.), FME '94: Industrial Benefit of Formal Methods. Proceedings, 1994. XI, 723 pages. 1994.

Vol. 874: A. Borning (Ed.), Principles and Practice of Constraint Programming. Proceedings, 1994. IX, 361 pages. 1994.

Vol. 875: D. Gollmann (Ed.), Computer Security – ESORICS 94. Proceedings, 1994. XI, 469 pages. 1994.

Vol. 876: B. Blumenthal, J. Gornostaev, C. Unger (Eds.), Human-Computer Interaction. Proceedings, 1994. IX, 239 pages. 1994.

Vol. 877: L. M. Adleman, M.-D. Huang (Eds.), Algorithmic Number Theory. Proceedings, 1994. IX, 323 pages. 1994.

Vol. 878: T. Ishida, Parallel, Distributed and Multiagent Production Systems. XVII, 166 pages. 1994. (Subseries LNAI).

Vol. 879: J. Dongarra, J. Waśniewski (Eds.), Parallel Scientific Computing. Proceedings, 1994. XI, 566 pages. 1994.

Vol. 880: P. S. Thiagarajan (Ed.), Foundations of Software Technology and Theoretical Computer Science. Proceedings, 1994. XI, 451 pages. 1994.

Vol. 881: P. Loucopoulos (Ed.), Entity-Relationship Approach – ER'94. Proceedings, 1994. XIII, 579 pages. 1994.

Vol. 882: D. Hutchison, A. Danthine, H. Leopold, G. Coulson (Eds.), Multimedia Transport and Teleservices. Proceedings, 1994. XI, 380 pages. 1994.

Vol. 883: L. Fribourg, F. Turini (Eds.), Logic Program Synthesis and Transformation – Meta-Programming in Logic. Proceedings, 1994. IX, 451 pages. 1994.

Vol. 884: J. Nievergelt, T. Roos, H.-J. Schek, P. Widmayer (Eds.), IGIS '94: Geographic Information Systems. Proceedings, 1994. VIII, 292 pages. 19944.

Vol. 885: R. C. Veltkamp, Closed Objects Boundaries from Scattered Points. VIII, 144 pages. 1994.

Vol. 886: M. M. Veloso, Planning and Learning by Analogical Reasoning. XIII, 181 pages. 1994. (Subseries LNAI).

Vol. 887: M. Toussaint (Ed.), Ada in Europe. Proceedings, 1994. XII, 521 pages. 1994.

QUEEN MARY & WESTFIELD
COLLEGE LIBRARY
(MILE END)